The World in Words

Based on over a decade of original archival research, this book shows how Urdu travel writing gave voice to a global imagination that reflected the ambition and aspiration of Indians and Pakistanis as they negotiated their place in the changing world of the nineteenth and twentieth centuries. In this interdisciplinary study, author Daniel Majchrowicz traces the social and literary history of the Urdu travelogue from 1840 to 1990 in six chronological chapters. Each chapter asks how travel writers used the genre to give meaning to the shifting social and political realities of their colonial and postcolonial worlds. The book particularly highlights the role of women writers in the production of a global imagination in Urdu with an emphasis on travel writing on Asia and Africa.

Daniel Majchrowicz is Assistant Professor of South Asian Literature and Culture and Director of the South Asia Research Forum at Northwestern University. He is a co-author of *Three Centuries of Travel Writing by Muslim Women* (2022).

The World in Words

Travel Writing and the Global Imagination
in Muslim South Asia

Daniel Majchrowicz

CAMBRIDGE
UNIVERSITY PRESS

CAMBRIDGE
UNIVERSITY PRESS

University Printing House, Cambridge CB2 8BS, United Kingdom

One Liberty Plaza, 20th Floor, New York, NY 10006, USA

477 Williamstown Road, Port Melbourne, vic 3207, Australia

314 to 321, 3ʳᵈ Floor, Plot No.3, Splendor Forum, Jasola District Centre, New Delhi 110025, India

103 Penang Road, #05–06/07, Visioncrest Commercial, Singapore 238467

Cambridge University Press is part of the University of Cambridge.

It furthers the University's mission by disseminating knowledge in the pursuit of education, learning and research at the highest international levels of excellence.

www.cambridge.org
Information on this title: www.cambridge.org/9781009340755

First published 2023

Printed in India by Avantika Printers Pvt. Ltd.

A catalogue record for this publication is available from the British Library

ISBN 978-1-009-34075-5 Hardback

Cambridge University Press has no responsibility for the persistence or accuracy of URLs for external or third-party internet websites referred to in this publication, and does not guarantee that any content on such websites is, or will remain, accurate or appropriate.

سیر کر دنیا کی غافل زندگانی پھر کہاں

زندگی گر کچھ رہی تو یہ جوانی پھر کہاں

सैर कर दुनिया की ग़ाफ़िल ज़िंदगानी फिर कहाँ

ज़िंदगी गर कुछ रही तो यह जवानी फिर कहाँ

Sair kar dunya ki ghafil zindagani phir kahañ

Zindagi gar kuchh rahi to yeh javani phir kahañ

Travel the world, O fool! you only have so much life to live,

And even if your life is long, when will you be young again?

—Khwaja Mir Dard (1721–1785)

Contents

Figures

Acknowledgments

This book is a travelogue, a narrative of my own peregrinations in search of a history. It is a map that details the countries and cities I traveled to for research, to give a talk, or simply to find a warm beach to write on. Nearly every page in this book reminds me of where I was when I wrote it. One passage bears me to a library in Lahore, where I conducted archival research, and another to Indonesia, where I spent the plague years of 2020 and 2021 editing and revising. As I flick through these pages, the Philippines, Colombia, India, Switzerland, Tanzania, Trinidad, and Turkey appear before me. I see in these pages too the many people who kept me safe, kept me fed, and saved me time and again from being lost in intellectual dead ends or from dying of thirst in deserts of academic despondency. I thank them all; I would never have reached my destination alone. They are more than I can name, for the journey to completing this book lasted well over a decade. Still, I will try.

I began this journey when I was still an undergraduate student at the University of Texas at Austin. There, while completing a degree in Spanish literature, I stumbled into learning Urdu and taking classes on South Asian history and literature. Akbar Hyder helped nurture my interest in this field, ultimately inspiring me to do a Master's and then a PhD. He has provided unflinching support and guidance ever since, and I am deeply grateful to him for it. While still at Texas, Kathryn Hansen, Rupert Snell, Gail Minault, Carla Petievich, Martha Selby, Cynthia Talbot, and Kamran Asdar Ali gave me further support and guidance; I am profoundly indebted to them all. My fellow graduate students at Texas have become both colleagues and lifelong friends, among them Ameem Lutfi, Adeem Suhail, Ammar Jan, Natasha Raheja, Nathan Tabor, Gwendolyn Kirk, Nishtha Mehta, Sarah Hakeem, Suzanne Schultz, Mubashir Rizvi,

Isabel Huacuja-Alonso, Peter Knapczyk and, a longhorn by association, Ghazal Asif. I am also thankful for the friendship of other members of the UT-*biradari* whom I met in the following years, among them Sabeena Sheikh, Yahya Khan, Eric Beverly, and Roanne Kantor. Roanne, who has always been willing to read a draft or help me explore an idea, has left her mark throughout this book. Sarah Waheed and Santosh Shankar gave critical early guidance and inspired me to keep thinking, learning, and writing.

I found my second intellectual home at Harvard University, where I completed my PhD. I will always be thankful to Ali Asani for giving me the guidance and support necessary to explore my interests and put them into writing; it was he who read and commented on the first feeble drafts of this book. I was also supported tirelessly by Richard Delacy, Amy Bard, Smita Lahiri, and Karen Thornber. Arafat Razzaque, Mircea Raianu, Farrah Jarral, Abbas Jaffer, Shan Khan, Namita Dharia, Sadaf Jaffer, Daniel Sheffield, Salwa Nur, Nicolas Roth, Tarik Ali, Johan Matthew, Mou Bannerjee, Dinyar Patel, Zahra Kanji, Ailya Vajid, Katherine Merriman, Andrew McDowell, Elise Burton, Alexandra Chen, and Prathama Nabi were all key to my survival. Julia Stephens was a critical interlocutor and, frankly, an inspiration. Michael Grossman spent years patiently teaching me to catalogue books from South Asia at Widener Library. This apprenticeship expanded my understanding of Urdu print and helped to lay a foundation for this book's engagement with the travelogue's material past. I discovered many shared academic interests—travel writing above all—with Sunil Sharma, at Boston University, who has given me key support and advice at every step. My scholarship would be much the poorer without his insight. It was he who invited me to join him and Siobhan Lambert-Hurley, of Sheffield University, to co-edit what would become my first book, *Three Centuries of Travel Writing by Muslim Women* (Indiana University Press, 2022). Siobhan herself has been a patient mentor, co-editor, and co-author who has left a deep mark on my work. She also introduced me to others mentors, including Sylvia Vatuk and Moneeza Shamsie, who have themselves helped shape the final form of this book.

In 2013–14, I had the exquisite luck to hold a one year position as *assistant-doctorant* at the University of Lausanne (UNIL). This was a formative period for me, one that gave me ample time, resources, and alpine air to think through this book. Switzerland is a land of riches, particularly when it comes to scholarship on South Asia. I benefited immensely from my long conversations and exchanges with my colleagues at UNIL, including Fanny Guex, Philippe Bornet, Nadia Cattoni, Noémie Veredon, Maya Burger, Ingo Strauch, Nicola Pozza, and, most recently, Melina Gravier. I owe a special debt to Blain Auer for his patience and advice, always subtly delivered. More than a few pages of this book remind me of ideas hashed out with him during near-daily discussions of Urdu and Persian literature over a *café* and, at least for me, a *tarte aux fraises*.

From Lausanne I traveled to Evanston, Illinois, where I joined Northwestern's Department of Asian Languages and Cultures. I have been incredibly lucky to spend the last several years working with Northwestern's vibrant and inclusive faculty. Laura Brueck's support has been immense; I have learned from her about practically every aspect of academic life. Rajeev Kinra has likewise provided constant, irreplicable support. My intellectual life at Northwestern has been enriched by its ever-expanding group of scholars working on South Asia, including Ashish Koul, Brannon Ingram, Sarah Jacobi, Yuthika Sharma, Rami Nair, David Boyk, Timsal Masud, and Mark McClish. I have also learned from so many colleagues in ALC and around the university, particularly Thomas Gaubatz, Paola Zamperini, Patrick Noonan, Corey Byrnes, Mi-Ryong Shim, Annabel We, Dahye Kim, Jules Law, and Amy Stanley. Jean Deven has kept me organized and on track, fielding all my oddball questions and offering foster care to my chronically neglected office plants. Lastly, I thank my students, whose enthusiasm and curiosity keep my own afire. Sharmain Siddiqui, Hassan Sayed, Narmeen Noorullah, Hajra Malik, Hamnah Malik, and Yashwardhan Bairathi all read portions of this book or helped me conduct research for it. May everyone be blessed with students like them.

Beyond the university, I have been supported by an army of people who have provided me with ideas, books, food, water, and shelter. They say "Lahore Lahore ey," but Lahore would not be for me what it is without the kindness of the Chughtai family: Akhtar Sohail, Rukhsana Sohail, Omar bhai, Maryam, Ali, Shareena, Reem, and Faisal. It would be impossible to recount all they have done for me. They made Pakistan a second home. Ali Aftab Saeed and Saad Sultan offered connections, suggestions, and much-needed companionship. In Karachi, Rija and Rimha Ahmad have always made the city feel like home; Ameem Lufti brought it alive. Still in Karachi, this book was also enriched by the support of the late Asif Aslam Farrukhi, while Zehra Masud shared her archive of family narratives with me.

I have been similarly blessed in India. In Hyderabad, the Pulizalas have always been the most gracious and understanding hosts. The Cheemas in Patiala taught me Punjabi and advanced *bhains*-milking techniques. In Delhi, the Mehta family willingly hosted me year after year, even when they themselves were not at home. The late Ashok Tomar was mission critical, perpetually ensuring I had a double peg in my hand after a grueling day at the archives. Mukta Tomar keeps the whiskey flowing today. During my British Library days, Sarah Passmore provided friendship and a roof. From my stint in Tajikistan, I can only say "naghz, rahmat" to Kevin Schwartz for his friendship and support since our Dushanbe days. In Washington DC, I thank Amena Saiyed, her mother, and her aunts for trusting me to work with their family history to introduce and help publish the translation of Muhammadi Begum's diary, *A Long Way from Hyderabad* (Primus Publications, 2021). Najeeb Jung and Mirza Jahandar have tirelessly and enthusiastically helped me to research their ancestor, Begum Sarbuland, who also features in this book.

This journey has not always seen smooth sailing, but others have always leapt to help me steady the ship. In March 2020, a long-planned book workshop was blown off course due to the Covid-19 pandemic. Instead of being an in-person event, the workshop became virtual, inaugurating what would become two years of video conferencing. This book was radically transformed by the feedback I received during that virtual workshop, from Francesca Orsini, Barbara Metcalf, Laura Brueck, and Rajeev Kinra. In the months afterward, Tara Denkel helped fashion this book's inchoate ideas into solid form. In the later stages of writing, I received critical editorial assistance from Hannah Archambault and Sarah Selvidge, both of whom dotted my i's, crossed my *kaf*s, and pushed me to think more incisively and write more expressively.

I offer my immense gratitude to David Boyk and Andrew McDowell. They have provided near-constant guidance and insight for almost fifteen years. Each has read every word in this book multiple times. They have talked through every idea and fact-checked every claim; if the reader finds any errors here, it is surely because I foolishly disregarded their advice. I am also grateful for the mentorship, guidance, conversations, friendship, and scholarship of the many friends and mentors upon whose shoulders this book stands, including C.M. Naim, Frances Pritchett, Akbar Hyder, Francesca Orsini, Asiya Alam, Andrew Amstutz, Haris Qadeer, Timsal Masud, Sean Pue, Jennifer Dubrow, Akbar Zaidi, Pasha Khan, J. Barton Scott, Sahil Warsi, Arthur Dudney, Razak Khan, Margrit Prenau, Megan Robb, Ryan Perkins, Zahra Sabri, and Usman Hamid. Dr. Abdurrashid gave me countless tips, and has continued to send relevant material my way for over a decade. Rifaqat Ali Shahid, Zubair Jameel, Muhammad Zubair, Irfan Khan, Ata Khurshid, Mazhar Muin Khan, and Abdullah Khalid helped me find rare sources. Ziaullah Khokhar in Gujranwala and the trustees of the Masood Jhandir Library in Mailsi allowed me to view and photograph their stores of treasures. I must also broadly recognize the work of librarians and archivists all across South Asia who have fought to preserve and make available the materials that I access here. For their patience in teaching me Urdu, I thank Aftab Ahmad, Zeba Parveen, and Ahtesham Khan. For teaching me the *abjad*, the Tayyeb family. And for reviewing this book manuscript, the three anonymous readers whose feedback undoubtedly made it much better than it had been.

A journey like this does not come cheap. The earliest research and writing was supported by funding from the American Institute for Pakistan Studies, a Fulbright–Nehru Fellowship, a Mrs. Giles Whiting Dissertation Completion Fellowship, a Florence Tan-Moeson Library of Congress Asian Division Research Fellowship, and a Momina Cheema Memorial Fellowship for Research in Pakistan. Before even that, I benefited from Foreign Language and Area Studies Fellowships and other language-focused scholarships that allowed me to study Urdu, Persian, Punjabi, and Hindi. In the second phase of writing, critical funding came from Northwestern

University and the Department of Asian Languages and Cultures. A yearlong fellowship from the Alice Kaplan Center for the Humanities gave me the time and space I needed to write and revise.

The ideas in this book were honed over several years of presenting papers and participating in conferences. In Austin, Akbar Hyder gave me multiple opportunities to learn from the faculty and students there. In Boston, Sunil Sharma, Roberta Micallef, and James Uden have all invited me to join in the conversations and publications that emerged from Boston University's annual workshop on travel writing. In Kuala Lumpur, I benefited from conversations with Rian Thum, Mehreen Jamal, Seema Golestaneh, and Olly Ackermann. The Hakluyt Society Symposium introduced me to Riyaz Chenganakkattil. I explored my work in comparative perspective via a lively post-talk conversation at Gadjah Mada University in Yogyakarta. A generous invitation to speak at the Conference on Early Modern Literatures in North India renewed my acquaintance with Tyler Williams and introduced me to Manpreet Kaur. I received helpful feedback at presentations at the University of Buffalo, the University of Chicago, and at the Oriental Institute in Prague. I am likewise thankful for opportunities to speak in Lahore, Delhi, Karachi, and Washington DC. I thank Brill for allowing me to reuse material from my article, "Fingernails Torn from Flesh: Intiẓār Ḥusain, Rām Laʻl, and Travel Writing across the India–Pakistan Border," published in the *Journal of Urdu Studies*. I also thank Indiana University Press for allowing me to reproduce portions of my translation from Qaisari Begum's "Book of Life," as published in *Three Centuries of Travel Writing by Muslim Women*. I thank everyone at Cambridge University Press for helping to make this book a reality.

Lastly, I thank my family for keeping life lively and for always excusing my constant disappearances. My parents, my siblings, my nieces and nephews, and particularly Anusha, have always been supportive, and it is thanks to them that I have always had somewhere to call home, and now have somewhere to return to as the travelogue that is this book comes to an end.

Note on Translation and Transliteration

This book uses a consistent transliteration scheme for all South Asian languages, including Urdu, Hindi, Persian, Arabic, Punjabi, Gujarati, and Marathi, according to their spelling in the Perso-Arabic script and pronunciation in the South Asian context. This scheme is a simplified version of that advocated by the *Journal of Urdu Studies*. To facilitate readability for non-specialists, I have generally eschewed the use of diacritics and removed the silent final -*h* from words such as *safarnama*. The *izafa* is written -*i*, and the Arabic definite article as *al-*. Foreign terms are generally only italicized on their first occurrence in each chapter. Proper nouns are given according to their English spelling where relevant. All translations are my own unless otherwise noted.

Introduction

It was in Rampur, a small town a few hours northeast of Delhi, that I first heard tell of a local library with thousands of books, but only three walls. Of course, I went to investigate immediately. I introduced myself to the head librarian of this curious institution and explained that I was writing a book on nineteenth- and twentieth-century Urdu travelogues, or *safarnama*s, and their place in South Asian social and literary history. Could I review the library's collections? I asked gingerly. The librarian quickly assured me that I was free to use whatever material I wanted, but only so long as I managed to find anything usable. "The library's still functioning," he said, "but the back wall came down in a rainstorm. A lot of books were destroyed." The travelogue section had been one of the storm's casualties.

Stepping into the main reception area of the Saulat Public Library, I saw a few men seated at tables, sipping tea and reading the newspaper. Behind them, sunlight streamed in from a cavernous opening at the far side of the room. It was true. The wall really had collapsed.[1] All of the books that had been damaged by the cave-in—including most of the library's travelogues—had been piled together in an adjoining room that lacked both ventilation and electricity. The shelves were in fantastic disarray, with hundreds of books piled about at random. Some were waterlogged, while others were brittle and ravaged by termites. A good number, though, were still intact. For a week, we picked our way through the heaps, ultimately retrieving dozens of colonial-era travelogues in Urdu and Persian. I made digital copies of them all and returned home to New Delhi to inspect our findings.

Flipping through the files, the first thing to strike me about the travelogues in Saulat's collection was how many of them were local productions. Though their subject matter spanned the globe, the books themselves came from authors or presses located in or near Rampur. Their cover pages trumpeted their author's destinations ("Mujtaba Khan's voyage ... to Egypt, Jerusalem, and the Levant..."), with the place of publication ("Printed in Rampur") in a smaller font below (Figure I.1). Further inspection revealed that these books were not just products of

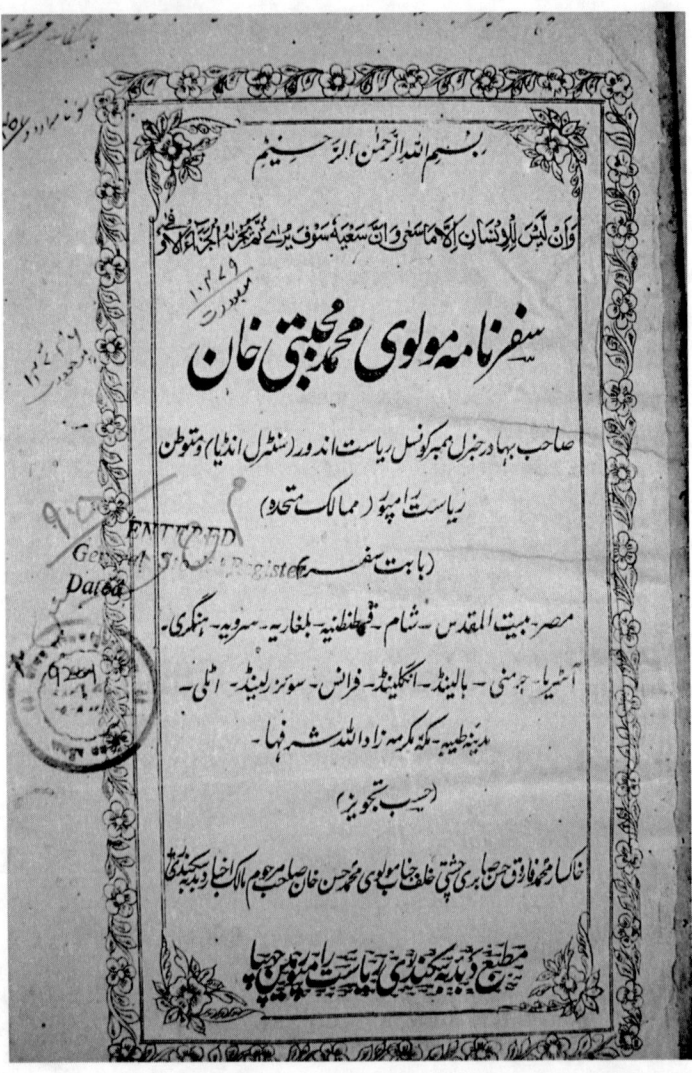

Figure I.1 Maulvi Muhammad Mujtaba Khan's travelogue

Source: Author.

a privileged elite either. Saulat's travelogue collection includes writing by everyone from kings to draftsmen. Collectively, the cover pages of these locally produced but globally sourced travel accounts brought another picture of Rampur into view, one that belied its seeming provinciality. Instead, they suggested that this small town was in fact closely tied, physically and intellectually, to the wider world. Through the Urdu travelogue, authors like Mujtaba Khan were able to imagine the world and represent it to their readers in Rampur and the surrounding areas using their own local lenses. Just as I had already noticed in libraries in cities and towns all across the subcontinent, in Rampur the travelogue allowed local Urdu writers to imagine the world in words, and to place that imagination before their readers.

The imaginative power of this literature is exemplified by one Doctor 'Ali Sabzvari, whose travelogue introduces Chapter 4. A turn-of-the-century dentist living in the small town of Arrah in Bihar, Dr Sabzvari had a passion for travel and a penchant for writing. Bearing scintillating titles like *Khaufnak Dunya: Jazira-i Borniyo meñ Safar aur Jangaloñ meñ Shikar* (Terrifying world: a voyage to the island of Borneo and hunting expeditions in the jungle, [1908] 1935), the exploits he described in his travelogues once enthralled Urdu readers. Naiyer Masud (1936–2017), one of Urdu's greatest short-story writers, reminisced that *Khaufnak Dunya* had been among his favorite childhood reads: "I fell in love with this book. I would read it again and again, and every time I read it, I would discover a new kind of pleasure."[2] In other words, the travel writing of an obscure dentist in Bihar helped shape how a young boy in Lucknow imagined Africa and Southeast Asia. In Urdu, travel writing was a ubiquitous medium for this kind of textual encounter with the world.[3]

This book takes up Urdu travel writing between 1840 and 1990 to show how accounts like Sabzvari's conjured an aspirational global imagination. It argues that the travelogue did more than simply describe the world as it was. It offered a means for writers to imagine, to aspire, and to share their views and visions with readers and listeners back home. And it gave people like Masud new ways to imagine the world and consider its possibilities.[4] The Urdu travelogue, this book will show, is not just a literary genre or a source for definitive facts about the past; it is also a continuous historical record of how Urdu speakers engaged with the world. This book studies that record to understand the history of its readers' and writers' global aspirations. Proceeding largely chronologically, it emphasizes the socio-historical, intellectual, and geopolitical contexts in which the Urdu travelogue was produced, while attending closely to questions of literariness, intertextuality, materiality, and circulation.

This study begins from the mid-nineteenth century, when political and technological changes were introducing more and more Indians to an evolving world now ordered by steamship routes, railways, and an increasingly interconnected global economy. These changes made India into a central node in a transport network that circled the world.[5] Increased mobility coincided with the arrival of cheap print, rising literacy, and the recognition of Urdu as an official language in much of Britain's Indian empire. New presses mushroomed everywhere, offering a nascent reading public an ever-expanding range of books, newspapers, journals, and pamphlets.[6] As Indians fanned out across the globe, the Urdu travelogue emerged to tell their stories and propagate their global imaginations. By the late nineteenth century, printed descriptions of Penang and Mombasa in Urdu were pedestrian. Basra and Aden were household names, and Tokyo and Havana no longer seemed quite so far off. Read in isolation, these travelogues, typically by obscure authors like Dr Sabzvari, can only tell us so much. Read collectively, however, they reveal how mobility, print, and literature combined to shape South Asia's global pasts and to inform how South Asians see the world today.[7]

This book is located between the fields of history and literature. It is a social history of aspiration and ideas, but one built on the premise that the travelogue tells us the most about the past when we treat it not as a mine for information, but as a culturally grounded and temporally located literary genre with its own rules and logics. Part I shows how, between 1840 and 1880, the Urdu travelogue emerged as a hybrid of colonial and local textual traditions as it was adopted and developed by explorers (Chapter 1), indigenous rulers (Chapter 2), and schoolhouse pedagogues (Chapter 3). Part II examines the period from 1880 to 1990, when the genre moved into the mainstream. In this period, rising literacy encouraged authors to vary their style and content to match the aesthetics and aspirations of an increasingly diverse readership. These changes are traced through a focus on three major themes: pleasure (Chapter 4), pilgrimage (Chapter 5), and the 1947 Partition (Chapter 6). Together, the six chapters show how the travelogue functioned as a space for travel authors to cultivate and disseminate their own visions of the world.

By theorizing the travelogue as a literature of aspiration and global engagement, this book opens up a neglected social history while introducing new voices and perspectives on critical questions about class, language, gender, race, and power in colonial and postcolonial South Asia. Of course, with many thousands of travel accounts available for study, one study cannot do justice to the full richness of the genre's global imagination. In this book, I have limited myself primarily to writing on Asia and Africa, particularly at the expense of travel writing on Europe, which has so far received the lion's share of scholarly attention to the genre. In addition to moving beyond Europe, this book also makes a concerted effort to correct a similar academic overemphasis on male travel writers. Instead, this book introduces a wide range of travel writing in Urdu by women, nearly all of it previously unknown and unstudied.[8] By clearly demonstrating women's full engagement in the production of Urdu's global imagination, this emphasis adds to the belated but growing recognition of women's contributions to literary and intellectual life in colonial South Asia. It also affirms one of this book's central arguments: that even the most marginalized writers could contribute meaningfully to the cultivation of Urdu's global imagination.

To appreciate how this global imagination was cultivated requires acknowledging Urdu's specific social dynamics over the last two centuries. Urdu is among the most widely spoken languages in South Asia. In its written form, it has historically appeared primarily in an adapted form of the Perso-Arabic script.[9] The language and its literary tradition are best described as being Islamicate—a term that Marshall Hodgson famously coined to refer "not directly to the religion, Islam, itself but to the social and cultural complex historically associated with Islam and the Muslims, both among Muslims themselves and even when found among non-Muslims."[10] The Islamicate, crucially, is shared by Muslims and non-Muslims alike, in the same way that non-Christians can unselfconsciously share in European Enlightenment and intellectual practices that are derived from or associated with Christianity. Geographically, Urdu's "heartland," if it can be said to have one, has historically been located in the Gangetic plain from Delhi to Bihar. Yet the story is not so simple, for Urdu has been—and largely remains—a widely used language well beyond this "heartland." It has long existed in parts of southern India, where Urdu literature was patronized from at least the sixteenth century. It has also flourished as a language of commerce and literature in central and southern India, as well as in Bengal, Gujarat, Sindh, and, particularly, Kashmir and Punjab.[11]

Long a popular language of oral poetry, in the nineteenth century Urdu took on a more formal role when it replaced Persian as the language of law and the public sphere across northern and central India, even in regions like the Punjab where Urdu was spoken fluently only by a small minority. During this period, the use of Urdu was not limited to a single religious or ethnic group; members of all groups enjoyed largely shared access to this Islamicate language. Knowledge of it was widely considered a mark of education and sophistication. In researching for this book, I regularly encountered colonial-era Hindu and Jain pilgrimage accounts written in Urdu, such as the text that introduces Chapter 1; the language's Islamicate identity in no way prevented these non-Muslim authors from expressing their own religious identities. This cosmopolitanism survived well into the twentieth century, though it was soon contested. From the late nineteenth century, a growing movement to promote Hindi (which used a grammar identical to Urdu, but written in the Devanagari script and preferring a Sanskritic vocabulary) as the true language of Hindus and of the Indian public sphere contributed to the increasing sense that Urdu was not just an Islamicate language, but a Muslim one.[12] Though in popular perception this has now become the dominant view of Urdu, in fact, Urdu's transition from an "Islamicate" to an "Islamic" language is far from complete and it remains, in many ways, a transregional and trans-communal language. Streaks of this abiding cosmopolitanism can be seen through to the final chapter of this book, which engages with Urdu travel writing of the 1980s. Today Urdu remains a popular language in both India and Pakistan among Muslims and non-Muslims alike, and a common link language between people from across South Asia, and beyond.[13]

This long history and vast geography make Urdu an ideal medium for the study of the South Asian travelogue and its global imagination. Geographically speaking, Urdu is unique among the region's vernaculars for its particularly broad reach.[14] Until the transregional rise of Hindi in late colonial India, Urdu was the only vernacular linguistic tradition to gain currency across the subcontinent.[15] Urdu is also revealing because of its historical ecumenicism and wide social reach, particularly in earlier decades and centuries. The wide range of authors cited throughout this book give testament to this diversity. They also emphasize that writing in Urdu, and participating in the Urdu public sphere, was a conscious choice. Urdu's travel authors were often not "native speakers." Nor were they monolingual. Rather, the writers and readers studied in this book chose Urdu—in other words, a particular language, script, vocabulary, and rhetorical style—from a range of linguistic options.[16] Chapter 3, for instance, discusses the travel account of a colonial administrator named Aminchand. Aminchand chose to write his travelogue in Urdu, though his private correspondence reveals that he also had equal facility with both Persian and English and that he actually considered himself to be a native speaker of Punjabi. Myriad examples like this serve to underline that Urdu's history of travel writing reflects a consciously created and diverse intellectual and literary tradition.

That said, Urdu is by no means the only South Asian language with a vibrant travel writing tradition. Every major South Asian vernacular produced travelogues, and many of this book's arguments apply to these traditions too. Literary traditions in South Asia frequently spring from shared sources, and are often in dialog with one another. Urdu influenced travel writing in other languages, and was likewise influenced by them. What is more, colonialism's pervasive reach meant that every region and language in India was affected by shared stimuli in the form of colonial policies and broad social transformations. Thus, while this book focuses on Urdu, it simultaneously provides a model for the study of the genre more broadly in South Asia, and even in other British colonies.[17] To draw out these parallels,

I regularly include references to travel writing from other linguistic traditions, South Asian and otherwise.

Urdu's Global Imagination

By chance, one of the first books we salvaged from Saulat Library's storeroom was a flimsy paperback travelogue of Burma (present-day Myanmar) by one Mirza Kazim Barlas, a small-time trader in late-nineteenth-century Muradabad, a town near Rampur. Titled *Sair-i Darya ki Pahli Mauj: Sair-i Rangun* (The first wave of a tour of the sea: a tour of Rangoon, 1892), it was the first installment in a series of travelogues by Barlas that took readers around the rim of the Indian Ocean, from the Maldives to Sri Lanka, Burma, Malaysia, and Singapore.[18] In Barlas's day all this territory belonged to the British Empire, making it more easily accessible to the Crown's Indian subjects. Indeed, by the late nineteenth century, huge numbers of them had already crossed the Bay of Bengal, a region "at the heart of the global, imperial economy."[19] However, most Indians who made the crossing came from southern coastal communities, not from the Urdu-speaking north.[20]

Barlas hoped to change that. He lamented the apathy with which "Hindustanis," or north Indians, regarded the Indian Ocean rim.[21] In his account he suggested his readers imagine these lands not as distant and irrelevant, but as a resource-rich frontier ripe for Hindustani exploitation. If only they would alter how they saw the world, he insisted, they stood to make a lot of money. Through travel they might even, he hoped, rejuvenate their own "stagnant" society. To make this argument convincing, Barlas dangled before his readers the promise of financial reward, social respect, and even conjugal pleasure. In his travelogue on Sri Lanka, Lakshadweep, and the Maldives, he first wrote:

> There is immeasurable profit to be made by leaving Hindustan for the islands and settled regions that neighbor it for both skilled and unskilled laborers, as well as for men of commerce. These islands and regions have a great need for commercial traders, but few means to address that need, for the native people of these regions are almost completely savage in their customs and disposition.

Then he turned harsh:

> The myopic people of Hindustan proper refuse to relinquish their "love of the homeland." They would rather starve than be away from their loved ones. This is why they live in penury, a penury that grows by the day.... I am writing this book to lead my countrymen to the path of prosperity.... Yes, you will face discomfort when you leave home. There will be no more soft, tender chapatis prepared for you

by delicate hands. But inshallah, you will acquire that [wealth] which will help you acquire those soft chapatis, those delicate hands.[22]

Barlas's travelogues thus introduced the region's languages and cultures to Hindustani readers not out of cosmopolitan curiosity, but to inspire them to travel there, and to facilitate their business transactions. His travel narrative focused on the Indian Ocean's resources, commercial dealings, and potential for profit. He even compiled a phrasebook of practical business vocabulary in Sinhala, Tamil, and Malay.[23] With "just a little sense, and this book," he avowed, readers would find financial success.[24]

Barlas's exploitative aspiration complicates some dominant approaches to exchange in the Indian Ocean. Scholarship on Indian Ocean mobility often depicts indigenous trade and cultural exchange on terms that were far more accommodating and less coercive or hierarchical than the grossly uneven systems introduced by Europeans.[25] Scholars also emphasize how South Asians supported African anticolonial movements and rejected racializing policies and practices.[26] Barlas, though, had little interest in these ideals. He wrote with a presumption of cultural and intellectual superiority. Today's perception of the Global South as the antithesis of the North perhaps inspires a tendency to assume horizontal solidarities, but Barlas's text suggests otherwise. Barlas imagined an ascendant Hindustan that would build wealth through travel, and he described his project— and imagined his world—in terms reminiscent of imperialist European travel writing on India.[27]

Critically, though, not everyone saw things as Barlas did. His view was just one in a marketplace of imaginations. Through participation in Urdu's travel writing tradition—as writers, as readers, as commentators—ordinary people like Barlas contributed their own visions to a broad, open-ended, and accessible project of "making the global."[28] The concept of globalization has been critiqued for suggesting either that global engagements spread on their own or that they are dictated to passive recipients from centers of power (whether by "the West" or by urbane elites).[29] Instead, Michael Hathaway advocates for a "world-making" approach to the discursive shifts of global engagement. He argues that "identities are formed relationally through interaction," as individuals from across a range of groups engage with and negotiate the production and circulation of ideas and imaginations.[30] This model explains how marginal figures like Barlas could become participants in this "world-making process," by contributing to what I call Urdu's global imagination through travel writing. By global imagination I mean a decentralized, socially constructed, sometimes contradictory, set of ideas, images, and desires about the world, or specific places within the world, that are produced, negotiated, and circulated through the collaborative space of literature.

In her study of cosmopolitanism and the late-nineteenth-century Urdu novel, Jennifer Dubrow argues that "Urdu readers and writers imagined themselves as citizens of an Urdu-speaking, transregional, yet nonnational community that was global in outlook," and that literature offered a "global imaginative space" to construct a vision of the world.[31] This type of world-making process was fully operative in the travelogue, a genre typically premised on first-hand experience. To speak of Urdu's global imagination within the framework of "making the global" is to suggest that, through travel writing, every stakeholder with access to literature could contribute to discourses about the world while making space for themselves, their ideas, and their aspirations. Urdu's global imagination was not dictated solely by "great men," nor imposed on the populace by a colonial power. It was, rather, fashioned collectively from within the dialogic arena of Urdu literature.

In invoking the term "global imagination" here, I do not mean to suggest that individual Urdu readers and writers were necessarily consciously or constantly thinking "globally." Nor were they necessarily cosmopolitan actors who embraced and reveled in difference. Like Barlas, they might even see the world in distinctly un-cosmopolitan ways. The point, rather, is that Urdu travel literature encompassed the globe. Postcolonial scholarship has been critiqued for focusing on texts that "write back" to empire, neglecting other circulatory routes and pathways of exchange and interaction.[32] Rather than focus on "contact zones" between colonizer and colonized, speaking of a global imagination reflects the reality that Urdu literature engaged with the whole world, typically in ways that cannot be reduced to neat structures of asymmetrical power.[33] Dialogue between regions in South Asia was common, as was engagement with Asia and Africa. No single individual read about every part of the world, but readers had only to pick up the latest issue of their favorite monthly magazine to access new, first-person perspectives. Not everyone agreed what the world looked like or which parts of it really mattered. But, through the process of reading, writing, publishing, and reciting—even by jotting comments in the margins of library books—readers and writers negotiated collectively how to imagine it.

Postcolonial scholarship has similarly been critiqued for its emphasis on nationalism (whether Indian or Muslim nationalism), thus losing sight of "internal" heteroglossia within and between South Asian regional and social contexts.[34] A focus on Urdu's global imagination, though, emphasizes that while some travel writers did imagine the subcontinent's geography in ways that fit nationalist aspirations, this was only one way of thinking about community and belonging.[35] This book looks beyond nationalism to explore several others. Chapter 2, for instance, discusses how travel writing produced ideas of belonging based on kingship and aristocracy, while Chapter 5 describes how women travelers in Asia, Africa, and the Middle East imagined Muslimness as a primary marker of identity.[36]

Moving away from nationalist teleology and toward thinking globally reorients our view of the map of South Asia itself. Even within the subcontinent, Urdu travel writers encountered enormous variety. Moving through India's complex administrative and cultural spaces, they often spoke not of national unity but of insurmountable difference. They spoke of crossing borders, changing currencies, managing linguistic difficulties, digesting exotic foods, and negotiating shifting legal regimes. They wrote, in other words, as though they were describing travel abroad. And indeed, they were. A traveler on a short journey from Pune to Aurangabad crossed an international border between British India and the State of Hyderabad, to which Aurangabad belonged.[37] Meanwhile, some travels that seem clearly international were technically domestic: the legal structure of the British Raj meant that if that same traveler went from Pune to Aden, in Yemen, they never step foot on land outside the Bombay Presidency.[38] In short, what separates home from abroad, domestic from international, and what defines where exactly the local ends and the "global" begins, is opaque, negotiable.

Finally, speaking of a global imagination is meant to emphasize South Asia's enduring and multimodal global engagement. Today, South Asian travel is often imagined less as capricious, inquisitive wanderlust (a common characterization of Western travel in the mode of Elizabeth Gilbert, Anthony Bourdain, or Mark Twain), than as a purposeful movement from East to West, and from poverty toward wealth.[39] News reports frame South Asian mobility in terms of organized labor migration.[40] Yet South Asian mobility and migration take many forms, and have many destinations. As I reflect on these alternative mobilities—the ones that do not always appear in mainstream Western writing—I am reminded of a Bihari man I met while traveling in Phnom Penh in 2017 who was selling plastic whistles along the riverside. I did not buy a whistle, but he had that charming Bihari ability to make everything he said sound witty and philosophical, and so I invited him to join me for a beer. While we drank, he told me in Hindi (or was it Urdu?) about how he had wandered over to Cambodia from Thailand the previous year. He was unsure how long he would stay before heading home. I think, too, of the Kannadiga man I encountered in 2018 on the streets of Bangui, Central African Republic. We were both in the country simply to see more of the world. We conversed in a mix of Urdu and French, two lingua francas we had learned through our travels. He funded his travels by selling herbal oils and touting the benefits of a good *champi*, or head massage. His next destination, he told me, was Kinshasa.

These two travelers seem to me contemporary instantiations of the long history of travel that this book explores. Perhaps neither man has yet written a travelogue, but they certainly recall colonial-era travelers to Africa and Asia who did. Dr Sabzvari was one. Ramnath Biswas was another. A cosmopolitan figure from Sylhet, Biswas published a travelogue in Bengali about bicycling from Mombasa to Cape Town in the 1930s.[41] Historical and contemporary travelers like these give reason to think more expansively—more globally—about how men and women in landlocked towns like Rampur saw the world, how they presented it in nineteenth- and twentieth-century South Asian literatures, and how these imaginations circulated in print, lining the shelves of spaces like the Saulat Library. By focusing on Urdu's global imagination, this book aims to coherently juxtapose disparate views about the world and to deny hegemony to any one intellectual orientation— whether it be cosmopolitanism, universalism, or Muslim exceptionalism—and to show that Urdu travel literature in fact contained what Nile Green calls "multiple mental 'horizons.'"[42]

Analytical Approaches to Urdu Travel Writing

In the pages that follow, I consider travelogues to be narratives that relate, typically in the first person, journeys that the reader generally supposes to have taken place and to have been performed by the author.[43] That said, rather than follow my own contemporary American intuition in assessing if a given work is a travelogue, I have tried to examine each piece of writing from within its own literary, cultural, and social contexts. In making these determinations, I am guided by the clues left by writers, readers, and editors. Genre affiliation is signaled in many ways, including though the invocation of labels or indexical words like *safar* (travel), *yatra* (travel or pilgrimage), *safarnama* (travelogue), *sair* (tour), *siyahat* (journey), *vaqa'i'* (happenings), *tarikh* (a history or account of events), or *ahval* (a description of a place or events).[44] It is also signaled when an author compares their work to other travelogues.[45] Reviewers or newspaper editors offer more clues when they describe an account with these words, as do librarians or booksellers who categorize them as such in handlists or catalogs.

Even still, the travelogue is a difficult genre to define, and I have tried particularly to remain receptive to regional and temporal variations, and to how the travelogue's form and production is shaped by class, gender, and educational background. Elite, Urdu-speaking men, for instance, were typically educated in Arabic and Persian and might also be familiar with European writing practices. Their travelogues sometimes recall colonial gazetteers, or Persian-language reconnaissance reports, called *akhbar*, common in precolonial India.[46] It was likely with this literature in mind that the scholar Shibli Nu'mani (1857–1914) wrote in 1892 that "a travelogue should necessarily include a description of beautiful sights, how to make [living and travel] arrangements, the principles of the judiciary, the current state of trade, [and] diagrams of buildings."[47] He also stipulated that "one of the mandatory requirements of the travelogue is that the author discuss the contemporary form of language spoken in the country being described."[48] Many in Shibli's elite circles would have agreed with all this, but countless others happily read or wrote travelogues that did not contain any of these elements.

Approaches to travel writing vary even within a social class. Women typically practiced the genre differently from their male counterparts. A remarkable example of this is explored in Chapter 5, where two accounts, written by Hamidullah Khan Sarbuland Jang (1864–1930) and his wife, Begum Sarbuland (1876–1957), appear side by side. His account was exactingly scientific, systematically noting historical sites and geographical statistics. His wife's account of the same journey was personal and reflective. He compiled facts and figures, while she recorded daily minutiae and pondered cultural difference and the nature of womanhood. He wrote his book for publication, while she circulated her account privately, in the form of a diary. The Sarbulands' twinned travelogues show how gender, as much as class or geography, shaped the content, theme, form, and materiality of travelogues.

Attending to these types of difference is key to understanding Urdu's global imagination. The case of women's travel writing particularly demonstrates how a rigid approach to the genre can obscure certain voices, implicitly limiting our understanding of how marginalized groups or lesser-known individuals contributed to the process of making the global. Most existing studies of South Asian travel writing focus on printed books. But, particularly before the 1960s, women's travel writing was rarely published in books, or even published at all. It was more typically circulated semi-privately in letters, family newspapers, women's journals, or poems. Some women were able to publish books thanks to the protection offered by their social status or by the liminality of widowhood, but most were unable or uninterested.[49] They instead adopted formats that were easily circulated among friends and family, or that could be quickly written out on a single sheet of paper and mailed in to a magazine for publication. Unfortunately, the forms most available to women are seldom recognized by scholars of travel writing today.

Instead, existing studies tend to focus on works using styles, forms, and materialities familiar to those educated in English, mostly from a small cluster of prominent, elite writers. The effect of this tendency is so powerful that even senior scholars are led to the erroneous conclusion that Indian travel writers were "mostly upper-middle class and male."[50] If travel writing was a site where

Urdu's global imagination was elaborated, then focusing on an elite, male coterie necessarily means privileging the worldview of a select few while neglecting the experiences, imaginations, and ambitions of everyone else. Scholars of African travel writing have already begun to address the failure to recognize popular or indigenous traditions of telling travel, particularly writing by non-elites in localized forms like poetry.[51] They exhort historians and literary scholars to avoid transposing "assumptions about genre derived from western literary cultures to African literary cultures," and to "recognize the many forms that travel and writing about travel have taken."[52] This book follows their cue.

Accordingly, I have cast a wide net to better access the full range of Urdu travel writers. However, this does not mean including everything. I exclude accounts that are marked as fiction by authors or their readers. Nor do I include poems that muse on travel but that are not grounded in specific locales or travel experiences. Nevertheless, some of the accounts discussed in this book may challenge contemporary, English-speaking readers' expectations. You may be left wondering: Is this *really* a travelogue? That tension, though, points to the literary differences between Urdu and English and to the constantly shifting nature of literary genres. It clues us in to the different ways genre functioned, how different actors understood and produced it, and how the travelogue cultivated a global imagination using conventions and points of reference that are not our own.

Genre, Form, Hybridity

Off the cuff, we might say that the travelogue is a genre of literature that tells us stories about travel that we generally presume to be true. This statement says something about the genre's content, but nothing about its literary structure. In this regard, the travelogue is somewhat unique. "Genre," after all, often refers to form as much as content. Most literary genres are associated with some particular form. Novels and scholarly monographs almost always appear in lengthy prose broken into chapters and paragraphs. Epics tend to appear in verse (scholarly monographs, thankfully, do not) The travelogue, though, does not have any prescribed form. Instead, it participates in a variety of formal genres of literature. Travel in Urdu can be told as an epic poem, as a scholarly investigation, or as a long prose narrative. In fact, the Urdu travelogue often even participates in multiple genres simultaneously. A single account often switches among multiple genres. The absence of formal restrictions gives authors broad freedom to compose their accounts as they wish, at least in theory.

If genres "actively form the experience of each work of literature," then shifting among genres lets travel authors enhance that experience through hybridity.[53]

Speaking of Western travel writing, Jonathan Raban has remarked on the travelogue's hyper-hybridity, calling it "a notoriously raffish open house where different genres are likely to end up in the same bed."[54] Raffish or not, Aedín Ní Loingsigh argues that attending to this mixing of genres and forms is critical to decolonizing travel writing. Even when offered European models, she finds, African travel writers consciously played with form and genre to reflect their own ideas about travel and representation.[55] To read travel writing meaningfully, then, it is not enough to simply identify "travelogues" and then study them without reference to their situatedness within a specific literary space or form. Hybridity and the interplay of genres are central to their experientiality and, thus, their ability to evoke emotion and make meaning. This is particularly true for Urdu literature, where genres are often closely tied to specific literary forms, and even to specific emotions.[56] The safarnama, though, is not. It exists in a variety of poetic forms (*marsiya, masnavi, ruba'i, azad nazm*, etc.) and in prose as history (*tarikh*), ethical literature (*akhlaq* or *nasihatnama*), guidebook (*rah-numa*), essay (*insha*), diary (*roznamcha*), epistle (*khatt o khutut*), and *hajjnama* (hajj account), among many others. These accounts are to be read not just according to the conventions of a single genre (the travelogue) but also according to their hybridized genres. Thus, travel accounts that participate in the genre of the *dastan*, or epic romance, trigger fascination more than credulity. Travelogues written as explorers' logbooks project verisimilitude and solemnity. Authors' ability to create meaning and evoke emotion is shaped by how they manipulate this hybridity and formal fluidity. Hybridity also points to the ways that the travelogue, while newly popular in nineteenth-century India, drew on existing literary traditions, rather than being derived wholesale from Persian or English models, or created out of whole cloth.

The poet Sayyid Maqbul Husain "Zarif" Lakhnavi (1870–1937) offers an example. Zarif was a Shi'a Muslim from Lucknow, a city famed for its elegiac verse narratives that relate the massacre of the Prophet Muhammad's family in Karbala, Iraq, in 680 CE.[57] These pathos-laden poems, called marsiyas, are typically written in the *musaddas* form, which was nearly synonymous with sorrow and tragedy.[58] Iraq was the *mise en scène* of the marsiya, and so, after traveling to Iraq himself, Zarif employed the musaddas form for his travelogue, *Siyahat-i Zarif* (Zarif's journey, 1905). One section of his travel poem describes the violence of the British medical quarantine, as female pilgrims were forced out into a chaotic public space to face the trials of examination. As they went, the garments symbolizing their purdah and respectability were torn:

> One said, "Well there! My burqa's gotten stuck!
>   Oh, no! It was new, now it's torn in three places."

"Sir, help me, my scarf's slid down!"
    "Well then! My hem's gotten tangled, my veil's now slipped off."
What's this calamity overcoming everyone on board!
    What a tremendous mistake it was, coming on this ship![59]

Women's suffering constitutes an important theme in the marsiya. Zarif's passage is somewhat lighthearted, but here too the women's laments capture the chaos of the scene. In the preceding stanza, Zarif had evoked the men's struggle to maintain their families' honor amid these travails. It is easy to imagine the panic onboard as so many people, perhaps first-time sea travelers, negotiated governmental controls. Meanwhile, the authority of the male guardians was challenged by a forced inspection. In the chaos, there was no attention to purdah, as the ship literally tore the women's veils. Zarif gave meaning to his travel poem by linking it to the pathos-inspiring marsiya through its form, rhyme scheme, and theme. This hybridity allowed Zarif to point to issues of grave social injustice meted by a callous, superior force. In Zarif's day, the medical inspection was the bane of Indian sea travelers, and this episode offered a very real critique of state technologies of control as Zarif waded into an ongoing debate over how best to integrate women within modern transport.[60] The use of marsiya conventions heightened the emotive power of his critique.

Not all travelogues were written as poems, of course, but most accounts include at least some poetry. It is a common practice in Urdu travelogues to narrate motion in prose and emotion in verse. Shifting between forms in this way helps the author to access genre codes that are tied to specific sentiments, ideas, and reader responses.[61] The invocation of these codes through verse constitutes a critical site of meaning-making. Embedded emotional shifts were particularly important in contexts where proper mastery over emotion was a virtue. As Margrit Pernau notes of nineteenth-century Persian and Urdu literature, "Whenever harsh emotions threatened to overtake the narrative, they were transfigured by quoting the appropriate verse."[62] This movement is seen in Shibli Nu'mani's canonical *Safarnama-i Rum o Misr o Sham* (Travelogue of Turkey, Egypt, and the Levant, 1892). A ponderous text by an august academic, this prose account was punctuated with charts and numbered lists. Yet Shibli occasionally switched modes, composing verse poems in Persian to memorialize emotional moments like his arrival in Istanbul or the commemoration of Eid.[63] These verses captured the moment in a way prose could not. Shibli himself suggested readers would find particular "enjoyment and pleasure" in them, and his readers seem to have agreed.[64] One contemporary reviewer wrote that "the pleasure of [the] prose is doubled" by the poetry.[65] Shibli's generic hybridity delighted this reader and invested him emotionally in Shibli's narrative. Hybridity and the mutability of form were thus fundamental to the success of the account.

Genre hybridity had aesthetic consequences too. In 1853, one Brij Bhukanlal of Agra was asked to translate into Urdu an account of South Africa written by a British author living in Calcutta.[66] In the process, he found himself caught between fidelity and readability. A direct prose translation would not realize the text's potential for Urdu readers, he felt, and would even render it unpalatable. He thus decided to improve the original through the addition of verse, ultimately privileging emotiveness over strict fidelity.[67] Though he hoped to faithfully reproduce the book's content, his aesthetic sense compelled him to make the text meaningful to Urdu readers by employing a hybridity absent in the original.

Early Scholarly Approaches to Urdu Travel Writing

Scholars once primarily considered travel writing a source for factual information about the past. More recently, though, and particularly in the wake of Edward Said's work on discourse and Orientalism, it has come to be studied for what it can teach us about the circulation of ideas. Since the 1990s, travel writing in South Asia has been invoked to understand India's encounter with the West,[68] Indian nationalism and the colonial experience,[69] pan-Islamism,[70] pan-Asianism,[71] religious experience,[72] and precolonial identity.[73] The greatest density of work, though, has focused on how Indians "wrote back" to colonialism. This body of literature argues that Indian travelers increasingly saw themselves as colonized subjects, and ultimately constructed a sense of Indianness that contrasted with a European Other. It explores how anti-colonialism and nationalism led some travel writers to imagine the true essences of India and Europe as entirely at odds. Reflecting in the 1930s on several decades of travel, Begum Sarbuland wrote,

> Unfortunately for India, Western culture is spreading here, and the women of India are charging forward recklessly toward the freedoms of the West. What stood out to me most strongly after completing my travels abroad was that the very same blind freedom that was destroying India had already plundered the tranquility and true repose of the West. This blind freedom and their foreign culture have made their lives appear outwardly to be very attractive and pleasant indeed, but their internal life is not so pleasant at all; rather, it seems to be devoid of any spiritual contentment.[74]

During the heyday of postcolonial studies, these types of questions surrounding identity and belonging loomed large.

A related line of scholarship probed the travel writing of reformist Muslim intellectuals beginning with Sir Sayyid Ahmad Khan (1817–98), who believed Indian Muslims could rejuvenate their society by incorporating European intellectual and scientific accomplishments. Sayyid Ahmad saw travel writing as an ideal vehicle for promulgating a new global imagination that presented Europe as a source of reform for Indian Muslims. He dedicated his life to the adaptation of European modernity for Muslim India and founded the Mohammedan Anglo-Oriental College (known today as Aligarh Muslim University) to prepare Indian youth for the contemporary world. Consonant with his mission, the Aligarh movement produced several well-known travelogues.[75] Sayyid Ahmad himself published a series of articles on his travels in the Middle East and Europe.[76] However, the heavy scholarly focus on his travel writing risks overemphasizing his influence on the genre. Though widely known today, Sir Sayyid's travelogue of Europe was lost for nearly a century before being rescued from the back issues of two long-defunct magazines.

Nevertheless, Sayyid Ahmad did popularize the genre among his followers, some of whom wrote accounts of their own educational travels to Europe. Begum Sarbuland's father-in-law, Sami'ullah Khan (1834–1908), published an account that Sir Sayyid praised as a useful guide to instruct young men on ideal European practices.[77] In time, Aligarh's faculty and alumni expanded their interest beyond Europe. The most successful Aligarh-affiliated travel author was Shibli Nu'mani, whose popular account introduced Ottoman modernity to Urdu readers as a non-European model for India's Muslims. In the 1920s, Syed Ross Masood, Sayyid Ahmad's grandson, spoke and wrote about his observations on education and society in Japan as a model for India.[78] Through his travel writing, Masood conjured a global imagination in which Asia would rise up to challenge the hegemony of the West. All these works have now been the subject of sustained academic study.

Academic interest in Urdu travel writing also burgeoned in the 1990s and 2000s thanks to the emergence of a robust consensus over the importance of studying not just colonial records, which are largely in English, but also writing in vernacular South Asian languages. Numerous scholars, working in languages from Tamil to Bengali, have shown how vernacular literature encodes distinct discourses and epistemes, and that they command the power to create social imaginaries within their own literary genres. Working on the precolonial period, Sheldon Pollock argues that the emergence of vernacular literatures was not inevitable, but that they were created through "the conscious decisions of writers to reshape the boundaries of their cultural universe."[79] Medieval Kannada writers drew on cosmopolitan Sanskrit forms in their own vernacular to "[make] the global local," in much the same way that the travel authors discussed in this book fashioned an

Urdu travel writing tradition partly from Persian and English forms. Nearer to us on the temporal spectrum, Farina Mir argues that colonial-era literary formations in Punjabi tended to exist at a remove from the province's communal politics. Though English and Urdu were both common languages in the Punjab, Punjabi itself encoded ideas of belonging that remained distinct from both these hegemonic forms. Study of the expression of emotion in the vernacular has likewise shown not only that vernacular languages convey emotional responses unavailable in English, but also that the expression of emotion was highly context- and language-specific.[80] Another set of studies shows how movements in vernacular languages sought to remake colonial-era institutions. Charu Gupta identifies Hindi print as a means to look beyond the "hegemonic function of colonial rule" for indigenous voices, while Anandita Ghosh argues that the Bengali language allowed indigenous groups "to consolidate power, along multiple axes of class, gender, and community."[81] This book book builds on this scholarly consensus that understanding the social and literary history of South Asia requires a sustained engagement with vernacular writing, read and studied in the original.

Sourcing the History of Urdu Travel Writing

Doing so is not always easy, though. Urdu travelogues can be hard to access. They largely lie outside the ordered and accessible colonial archive. Many were published in poorly preserved newspapers and magazines. Given the ephemeral nature of these media and the present state of preservation in South Asia—Saulat Library is indicative—researching the Urdu travelogue at scale requires a wide reach and unconventional methods. I began archival work for this book by visiting major archives and libraries in India, Pakistan, the United States, and the United Kingdom.[82] I reviewed Urdu and Persian materials carefully, but always checked holdings in other languages as well. Drawing from online catalogues, printed registers, and handwritten book lists, I searched for travel writing in book form and also, to the greatest extent possible, reviewed magazine and newspaper collections for travel accounts. Then, I moved on to smaller and less conventional archives. This shift in focus brought many more accounts to light. As I learned in Rampur, sometimes the richest troves of travel accounts lie hidden in neighborhood libraries and small-town collections.[83] These sites were crucial to my research methodology. While much of my work focused on Pakistan and northern India, I also researched in central and southern India, though to a lesser extent.

   As part of my research process, I became a regular at secondhand book sales, snooping around for travelogues that might not have made it into more formal institutions like libraries. While more haphazard than conventional archival research, these forays were often just as fruitful, introducing me to forgotten local materials that revealed just how widespread travel writing really was. They also laid bare the politics of circulation. Bazaars tend to hold works that libraries and archives do not, a broad category of literature that particularly includes travel writing by women and non-Muslim authors. I bought dozens of issues of otherwise lost mid-century Urdu women's magazines in the back room of a "used book bank" in Rawalpindi. They contained upwards of a hundred travel accounts by women from the 1940s and '50s. To my knowledge, none of this writing is today available in formal archives, nor anywhere else.[84]

During the roughly ten years I spent researching this book, the realities and materialities of research shifted significantly. When I began, many institutions, like the British Library, forbade photographing material, meaning that I had to work quickly within a limited timeframe. Increasingly, though, libraries in both South Asia and abroad began to liberalize, allowing me to take photographs of books and to study them in detail at home—and crucially, return to consult them again as necessary even years later. Though several institutions continue to forbid photography—or, more concerningly from a preservation standpoint, to insist on photocopy—I have been able to build a large digital library of travelogues alongside a physical collection of more recent works purchased at bookstores or donated to me by sympathetic scholars. In the later stages of my work, my material access to Urdu literature expanded with the growth and sophistication of digital libraries on an institutional scale. These resources include Rekhta.org, the (now defunct) Digital Library of India, and the British Library Endangered Archives program. These projects introduce a new consideration into conversations about materiality and preservation, and particularly for grappling with the implications of dislocating sources from their physical settings.[85]

Despite these many avenues for research, recovering the full range of travelers' voices remains an impossibility—I regularly encounter historical citations to travelogues that are no longer extant. Grappling with the disappearance of literature is just as important as acknowledging those sources that are still available to us. Wherever possible, this book points not just to works that I have been able to study, but also to those (like Barlas's lost phrasebook of Sinhala, Tamil, and Malay) that no longer exist. I must point, too, to the limits of the archives I used, and what they obscure, for, ultimately, each of these research sites have their own shortcomings. Archives are fraught spaces. They are "'post-imperial landscapes' meant to 'conceal as much as they reveal.'"[86] Scholars in South Asia have long debated how best to acknowledge the limitations of the formal archive and to recover the experiences of marginalized groups.[87] These concerns have resulted in a reconsideration of what constitutes an archival source.[88] For travel writing, this means looking beyond print materials, to handwritten letters, privately held diaries, poetic recitations, transcripts of speeches, and so on (these material formats are discussed in Chapter 1). And yet, although "the archive" has been thoroughly problematized, in their writing scholars still seldom account for where and how they found their sources, as though texts are not materially located somewhere, preserved by someone. To "rematerialize" the archive and keep the past and present lives of these works in view, I acknowledge the spaces in which I found my texts, their material condition, their format, and how I found them.[89] By introducing into this book my own travel, and my own interactions with these materials, I hope to draw attention to the ways my arguments have been shaped by this alternative archive, and by my investigative itinerary.

Quantifying Travel Writing

This book offers quantitative statistics on the production history of Urdu and Persian travel writing in South Asia. This data comes from my digital database of all the South Asian travelogues *in book form* I encountered in Urdu and Persian. At present, the database contains approximately 2,700 unique entries dated between 1824 and 2000. This data provides important insights, but comes with some caveats. The biggest is that the actual production of travelogues was much greater than these figures suggest. Most travel writing was published in magazines, journals, and newspapers, not in books. But few early periodicals were preserved, and full runs are rarely available. To make my data meaningful, I control for the mode of publication by excluding these more ephemeral sources. Books have comparatively more staying power. They are more durable, and leave a clearer archival trace in the form of entries in library catalogues, sales lists, and book reviews. Even if a book is read to tatters, its existence remains attested in historical catalogs. This makes printed books more easily enumerated, providing not just a clearer picture of how many travel books were published, and when, but also where authors traveled and where they published. As outlined in the previous section, I compiled my data on published books by visiting public and private libraries, book fairs, and bazaars; by working with rare book vendors; and by consulting online databases and other published indexes, sales lists, and handlists. Some of these lists were created in the nineteenth century and reference works that no longer exist.[90] This data provides a robust picture of publication and travel trends, and it is on this that the estimates provided in this book are based. To emphasize, my quantitative data—but not my evidence or arguments—are limited to books, and exclude accounts published in journals, magazines, and newspapers.

Macroanalysis of this kind has many limitations, but it also sheds critical light on the genre's reach, as well as on our own biases. Scholars may focus on one kind of travel writing, for example, pushing others into obscurity, but broad access to raw data can serve as a partial corrective. For instance, existing scholarship on South Asian travel writing emphasizes travel to Britain, implicitly suggesting that the colonial metropole was the "center" of South Asia's global geopolitical imaginary. Statistical analysis, however, reveals that for Urdu travel writers, Europe was always provincialized, just one region among many.[91] Urdu speakers wrote far more about South Asia and the Middle East (Figure I.2). For Urdu travel writing, the world

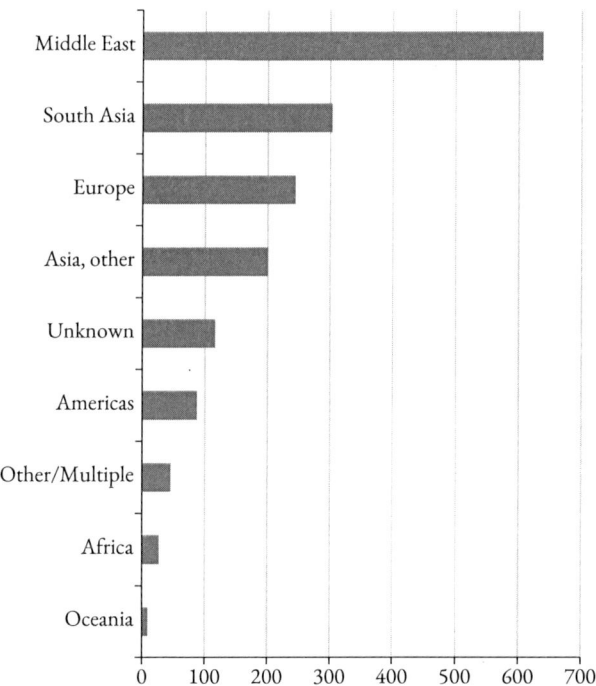

Figure I.2   Twentieth-century book-length travel accounts in Urdu by destination

Source: Author's personal database, 2021.

Notes: This and other charts include approximately 2,700 works dated between 1824 and 2000. The data was collected using online databases, indexes and handlists, and citations, and through visits to archives in the United States and United Kingdom. In India and Pakistan, I visited archives, public and private libraries, rare book sellers, and book bazaars. Research was conducted across all of Pakistan; in India, research sites were in Punjab, Delhi, Himachal Pradesh, Rajasthan, Uttar Pradesh, Bihar, Maharashtra, and Telangana. For further details, see pp. 18–20.

was always bigger than Europe, and many of its most appealing possibilities lay closer to home.

A Note on Reception

Gauging how literature was read and understood in colonial South Asia is difficult. In this book, I avoid speculative claims but, where possible, I document reception by citing readers or reviewers who commented on individual works. I also cite authorial claims regarding reception. For instance, Qaisari Begum (1888–1976) wrote in 1936 that her daughter Muhammadi Begum's (1911–90) epistolary travelogues were extremely popular among women subscribers to the magazine *'Ismat*:

> Muhammadi Begum mailed me many fascinating letters about England which I had published in *'Ismat* magazine with the intention of entertaining and informing my *'Ismati* sisters [i.e., fellow readers] simultaneously. All my sisters read the letters avidly. When a new letter was delayed in coming, the sisters grew impatient.[92]

I also employ citations and publishing records. Citations to earlier travel accounts give some indication of what works travel authors most appreciated.[93] Tracking how many copies of a given travelogue currently exist, and where they are located, hints at the extent and geographical range of an individual book. Publication history provides clues, too. If a travelogue that first appeared in a periodical was reprinted as a book, this may indicate popular demand. A book that was published multiple times, or translated into several languages, might also have been particularly successful. I emphasize, though, that these are speculative methods.

Outline of the Book

The book's chapters are arranged chronologically, reflecting the travelogue's role as a space for the articulation of an evolving global imagination. Many more travelogues were produced than can be addressed in a single study. Rather than attempt to be exhaustive, the following chapters draw on a selection of representative works that exemplify several of the genre's major themes. Every chapter is preceded by a translation of an excerpt from a travel account. These translations offer an entry into the argument to follow. They are also an argument in themselves. In including them here, I seek to add to a growing acknowledgement of the critical role that translation can and should play in the study of vernacular literature.[94] Their inclusion also recognizes the need to introduce woefully understudied historical voices from Indian vernacular history directly into the academic conversation.

This is to bring attention to their voices, but also to avoid acting as the sole and uncontested mediator of their writing. In this sense, the inclusion of direct translations of otherwise inaccessible travel writing is a political choice.[95] It is also an aesthetic choice, one shaped by this book's desire to grapple with the ways that South Asian travel writing was as much about pleasure as it was about ideological projects. Travel writing, in European as in South Asian languages, is often meant to be enjoyed. Pleasure, emotion, and the evocation of curiosity and surprise are some of its most fundamental ingredients. By presenting these extended excerpts before introducing my own analysis, I invite the reader to freely participate in this pleasure and to pause for a moment to access directly the emotive power of this literature.

Chapter 1 offers a brief history of the travelogue in South Asia, moving from precolonial antecedents to the social and technological changes that helped the genre flourish in colonial India. It then introduces the primary material forms in which the travelogue circulated and examines how it reached a diverse readership. The final portion of the chapter reflects on how the present politics of preservation shape our understanding of South Asians' historical mobility. Chapter 2 turns to princely travel writing. Indigenous native rulers, I argue, were among the first in India to use the genre as a form of aspiration. In the face of British colonial rule, Indian rulers were compelled to demonstrate their own continued legitimacy, sovereignty, and relevance. To this end, the princes became among India's earliest and most enthusiastic travel writers, even though their voyages put them at risk of being accused of financial excess.[96] Chapter 2 studies this princely practice through a reading of the two earliest such accounts in Urdu, written in the central Indian states of Indore and Jaora in 1851–52. These accounts exemplify how the travelogue could propose a vision of India in which regional princes had an enduring role at a time of rising colonial hegemony, but also how the courts fused Persian and Urdu literary genres with colonial literary practices to propagate new visions of the world.

If the princes were busy cultivating travel writing in their states, in British-ruled territory another type of global imagination was being proposed in colonial schools, where the British and their Indian employees heavily promoted travel writing. The pedagogical travelogues they produced were meant to revolutionize Indians' perception of the world and fashion them into ideal colonial citizens. Chapter 3 explores what I call the colonial "travel lesson." The travel lesson, taught in schools across the subcontinent, was premised on the idea that Indians knew and cared little about the world. Colonial pedagogy sought to address this supposed deficiency by instructing students in the benefits of travel and encouraging them to engage with the world through the framework of British colonial modernity. Students were given travelogues as textbooks, whether translated from English or commissioned from Indian writers. These travel textbooks emphasized British imperial power and civilizational hierarchies, but because it was Indians themselves doing the telling and the translating, the travel lesson reflected the ideas of Indians as much as those of the colonial education committees.

The genre further diversified in the final decades of the nineteenth century as efficient travel, cheap print, and rising literacy rates allowed it to flourish. Freed from the constraints of colonial patronage, travel writers diversified. Chapter 4 shows what happened as travel writing became a popular genre. This was an age of empires, and India was a central link in a network of steamships circling the globe. Men—and soon, women—moved out into the world, and then returned home to write about what they had seen. They adapted local genres and popular forms to reimagine the world according to their own aesthetics. This chapter explores the explosion of popular travel accounts between 1880 and 1930 with a focus on how writers invoked the idea of pleasure in Asia and Africa. This pleasure was tinted with the imagined possibilities of sexual excess, but also by the fantasy of colonialism, as authors imagined themselves as visitors to inferior peoples who could be exploited as well as taught, as previewed in the quotation from Barlas earlier. These books did not abandon the idea—familiar both from Persian and colonial literature—that travel was beneficial. However, they insisted that travel was a source of both pleasure and worldly success.

No region of the world outside of South Asia has received more attention from Urdu travel writers than the Middle East, the subject of Chapter 5. This affinity was not just a reflection of some sort of universal or timeless bond between Indian and Middle Eastern Muslims. People have always traveled between these regions, and there has always been intellectual exchange between them. Yet Urdu travel texts from the late nineteenth and early twentieth centuries reveal an explosion in new and temporally located forms of Indian Muslim aspiration that sought to create affective links between Indian and Middle Eastern Muslims.[97] As philosophers and politicians began think of India as a part of something they were beginning to call the "Muslim world," travelers produced their own imaginations, not only by theorizing the nature of pan-regional Islamic links, but also by making them tangible through first-person narrative. This turn was nearly simultaneous with the emergence of travel writing by women, who were at last able to step into the realm of print culture. An examination of their writing on the "Muslim world" reveals how this concept was shaped by the experiences of Indian Muslim women abroad, typically in gender-segregated spaces. Through a reading of eleven accounts written between 1900 and 1950, this chapter shows how the aspirational ideal of Islamic unity emerged in Urdu travel writing even as it was fractured by class- and race-based discrimination.

The book's final chapter turns to postcolonial South Asia and the literary legacy of the Partition of 1947, when India and Pakistan were divided into separate countries. This event led to the emergence of a subgenre I term the cross-border travel account. This writing marks not a going-out into the world, but rather a surreal homecoming. After 1947, every Indian was forced to join a new nation, either India or Pakistan. Some were able to select their new homeland, but others had little choice. Every citizen negotiated new relationships to their homes, and to these newly independent countries, as do their children and grandchildren today. Chapter 6 argues that travel writing was a primary site for negotiating the meaning of Partition in the decades after 1947. Cross-border travel writers do not just lament the past. More commonly, they imagine newer, better futures for these estranged nations, offering an individual hope in a time of political hopelessness. This chapter explores the alternative futures proposed in cross-border accounts written by spiritual leaders, journalists, and litterateurs. The chapter's analysis covers the period immediately after Partition, when the border was still porous and uncertain, through the 1970s and '80s, when any lingering hope for détente had disappeared.

Finally, the book's conclusion turns to the Urdu travelogue's ongoing role as a site of aspiration in contemporary South Asia. Travel writing continues to be exceptionally popular in Pakistan, where travelogues by famous travel writers like Mustansir Husain Tarar (b. 1939) remain bestsellers even decades after their first publication. In a region where travel is limited by visa regimes and prohibitive transport costs, the travelogue still allows Pakistanis to imagine the world in words.

Conclusion

Contemporary geopolitical imaginations offer few tools to understand the full historical range of Indian travelers and adventurers. The scholarly literature on mobility from Bihar, for instance, follows migrant laborers to Fiji, Trinidad, and Bombay, but leaves little room for a middle-class tourist like 'Ali Sabzvari in Borneo. While much of this book is about the colonial past, I regularly return to descriptions of present-day readers, living archives, and ongoing textual circulation to emphasize the depth, vibrancy, and diversity of Urdu's travel stories. Urdu literature remains a meaningful, world-defining force for its speakers. As I myself traveled across India and Pakistan, I encountered people reading this literature or working to preserve it. The story, or stories, of the Urdu travel account would be incomplete without acknowledging its continued relevance for everyday readers.

One of Urdu's travel stories belongs to Raja Bhavani Singh (b. 1869), the unassuming crown prince of Khilchipur State whose travel narrative opens Chapter 1. Prince or not, Bhavani Singh was heir to a kingdom with few resources, and his limited travel budget forced him to bargain ferociously when he set out for Badrinath in the high Himalayas in 1896. But whatever he lacked in fame and funding he made up for with ambition. Bhavani Singh was determined to expand his place in the world. For him, that meant learning to read Urdu, then the language of interstate communication. It meant traveling to new regions and observing how other states conducted their affairs. And, finally, it meant publishing a travelogue to cement his new status as a literate, well-traveled man, a ruler who had earned his own place. Bhavani Singh left the borders of his state, traveling internationally, in a sense, to see the world and be seen by it. He achieved the latter by publishing his travels, putting his advancement and worldliness on display. As he did so, he contributed to Urdu's ever-expanding global imagination. The following chapter introduces his efforts and traces out the genre he chose to write in as it emerged in nineteenth-century India.

Notes

1. C.M. Naim has documented the tragic plight of such institutions in South Asia. Naim, "Disappearing Treasures," 53. On the slow disintegration of Saulat Library itself, see Khan, "Falling Walls," 27. Saulat's decline can be attributed not only to the lack of support for libraries and archives in contemporary South Asia, but also to the Indian state's efforts to delegitimize Urdu in the country in the years after 1947.

2. Mas'ud, *Mazamin*, 175–76.

3. Not just in Urdu, but in other South Asian vernaculars too. Hindi travel writing, which flourished in the twentieth century, held a similar power to inspire. Charu Gupta notes that Swami Satyadev Parivrajak's travelogues "enthralled and inspired many young Hindu men to take to the road." Gupta, "Histories," 844. The great Hindi poet Harivansh Rai Bachchan was himself similarly inspired to travel. In his autobiography he reminisced that as a child "he had dreamt of traveling to the places described in Swami Satyadev Parivrajak's *Travels in America*." Gupta, "Histories," 839.

4. Remarkably, Masud left India only once, to visit Iran. Otherwise, this sophisticated and acclaimed writer satisfied his curiosity about the world purely through books.

5. Singha, *Coolie's Great War*, 2; Green, *Bombay Islam*, 2–3.

6. The Chapakhana digital project offers a visual representation of the rapid growth of presses across South Asia. Stark, "Chapakhana."

7. When discussing the period before 1947, I use the terms "South Asia" and "India" and their adjectival forms interchangeably. For the periods after 1947 and 1971, when India was partitioned into India and Pakistan (and, later, Bangladesh), I use "Pakistan," "Bangladesh," and "India" to refer to these individual nations, and "South Asia" to refer to all three collectively.

8. These women were all Muslim, because Urdu's historical ecumenicism was gender-segregated. Men of all communities wrote travelogues in Urdu, but non-Muslim women almost never did. On the demographic makeup of women travel writers in Urdu, see p. 165. These authors only appear in the second part of this book because low literacy rates and restricted access to print prevented nearly all women from participating in the genre publicly in the nineteenth century.

9. Historically because, in India, this association is now decreasing in practice as writing Urdu in the Devanagri script becomes increasingly common. See Ahmad, "Urdu in Devanagari," 260. Meanwhile, technological advances have further complicated the correlation of language with script by making it possible to convert text instantly between Nasta'liq and Devanagari online. Finally, the popular, ad hoc adoption of the Roman script to write Urdu and Hindi in texts, on TV, and in advertisements also complicates the use of script as a primary identifier of Urdu.

10. Hodgson, *Venture of Islam*, 1:59. For a recent application of the term in South Asia, see Fuerst, "Locating Religion." For a nuanced critique and partial endorsement of the Islamicate, see Ahmed, *What Is Islam?* 157–75.

11. Beyond South Asia proper, it has also been widely used in Afghanistan, the Middle East, and in parts of British-ruled eastern Africa.

12. Definitive sources on the history of this polarization include: King, *One Language*; Dalmia, *Nationalization of Hindu Traditions*. On the popularization of Hindi, see Orsini, *Print and Pleasure*; Orsini, *The Hindi Public Sphere*.

13. Among non-Muslims, Urdu's popularity is best seen in the pervasive popularity of Urdu poetry and in the continued use of Urdu in Indian cinema. This although, in India, spoken Urdu now often bears the name "Hindi," a speech variety that is grammatically identical to Urdu, as exemplified by the term "Hindi film music."

14. In this book, the term "vernacular" refers to South Asian languages that were widely spoken and understood, as opposed to "elite" languages, primarily English, Persian, and Sanskrit, in which only a small minority has ever been fluent.

15. The elite, cosmopolitan languages of English, Persian, and Sanskrit constitute obvious exceptions.

16. Some authors even chose to write in multiple languages, sometimes even describing the same trips in separate publications in distinct languages.

17. Moses Ochonu's *Emirs in London*, which appeared just as this book was going to press, examines travel and travel writing practices among the Hausa-speaking kings of British-controlled northern Nigeria. His argument bears remarkable similarities to many of the lines of enquiry explored here. There are also similarities here with Rebecca Jones's study of colonial-era Yoruba travel writing from Southern Nigeria. These similarities suggest a rich potential for the comparative study of travel writing between Nigeria and India (not to mention other British colonies). To emphasize this comparative potential, I point to these similarities throughout this book. Ochonu, *Emirs in London*; Jones, *Crossroads*.

18. I later found a copy of another of the books in this series for sale on a sidewalk in Delhi, and third at the University of Pennsylvania.

19. Amrith, *Crossing*, 2.

20. Most, but not all. There was already a history of travel, and travel writing, between northern India and Southeast Asia. This story is brilliantly told in Khazeni, *The City*.

21. On the historical valences of the term "Hindustani," see Naim, "Interrogating 'The East,'" 190–92.

22. Barlas, *Rangun*, 1–2. Discussions of "savage," "subhuman," or even "animalistic" Others are prevalent in South Asian travel writing, though not uncontested. In 1934, for instance, Muhammadi Begum wrote in her travel diary that "there is more in common between the Asian and African peoples than is accepted." Muhammadi Begum, "Diary," n.p. For a historical view of northern Indian attitudes towards south India and the potential for financial exploitation, see Archambault, "Geographies," 89.

23. Barlas, *Lisan*.

24. Barlas, *Lanka*, alif.

25. Relevant works include Ho, *Tarim*; Sheriff and Ho, *The Indian Ocean*; Green, *Bombay Islam*; Bose, *Hundred Horizons*; Alavi, *Muslim Cosmopolitanism*; Casale, *Exploration*. For an introduction to this view of the Indian Ocean and South Asian historiography, see Bose and Jalal, *Modern South Asia*, 10–22; Manjapra, "Introduction," 1–21. For a convincing critique of a "nostalgic" approach to Indian Ocean history, see Desai, *Commerce*, 20–54.

26. Slate, *Colored Cosmopolitanism*, 3.

27. Spurr, *Rhetoric*, 92–124. Barlas's arguments also recall colonial rhetoric on the need to reform the business practices of what Ritu Birla calls India's "vernacular capitalists." See Birla, *Stages*, 3.

28. Hathaway, *Environmental Winds*, 10.

29. Hathaway, *Environmental Winds*, 11–12.

30. Hathaway, *Environmental Winds*, 25.
31. Dubrow, *Cosmopolitan Dreams*, 7–8.
32. Jones, *Crossroads*, 10; Alavi, *Muslim Cosmopolitanism*, 12.
33. Pratt, *Imperial Eyes*, 7–8.
34. In South Asia, travel writing has overwhelmingly been studied through the lenses of nationalism and anti-colonialism, inadvertently naturalizing ideas of India that imagined it to be a single, undivided space (even if not yet realized). Important works include Chatterjee, "Discovering India"; Chatterjee and Hawes, *Europe Observed*; Burton, "Spectacle of Empire"; Goswami, *Producing India*. Beyond travel writing, though, historians have argued for rethinking what constituted a community, nation, or country in nineteenth- and twentieth-century India. This book builds on those insights. See Qasmi and Robb, *Muslim League*, 10–23; Naim, "Interrogating the East," 189–204; Deshpande, *Creative Pasts*, 94–150. For a sweeping consideration of the historical durability of the concept of "Hindustan," see Asif, *Hindustan*, 1–27.
35. On travel writing and nationalist aspiration, see Goswami, *Producing India*; Majeed, *Autobiography*; Chatterjee, "Discovering India." See also Chapter 3.
36. There are more possibilities than this book can address, but many are now being taken up by other scholars. Ryan Perkins, for instance, explores the emergence of the Indian "global city," arguing that 'Abd al-Halim Sharar's (1860–1926) serialized magazine travelogues in the 1890s and 1900s allowed "Lucknow to be imagined in relationship and contrast to global cities like London and Paris. Such new ways of framing Indian cities provided a growing Indian public with different ways of imagining their world." Perkins, "Global Indian City," 625.
37. Beverley, *Hyderabad*, 1–18.
38. Adminsitratively, Aden belonged to Bombay Presidency. Reese, *Imperial Muslims*, 13–14.
39. This vision is reflected particularly in Indian films, where travel to the West is a favorite theme. For instance, characters experience transformative visits to Spain in *Zindagi Na Milegi Dobara* (2011), the United States in *English Vinglish* (2012), and France in *Queen* (2013). Academic study of South Asian mobility has likewise largely examined travel to Europe. Despite this, several important studies push in the other direction to examine mobility between India and Asia, Africa, and the Americas. See Amrith, *Crossing*; Simpson, *Muslim Society*; Alavi, *Muslim Cosmopolitanism*; Nair, "Diaspora"; Mongia, *Migration*; Aiyar, *Indians in Kenya*; Kantor, *Global English*.
40. As this book argues, South Asian travelogues immediately dispel these simple characterizations. The complexity and diversity of contemporary South Asian travel is exemplified in V. Muzafer Ahamed's Malayalam-language travel

accounts. Dispatched from Riyadh and published between 2006 and 2012 in the Calicut-based weekly *Mathrubhumi Azhchappathippu*, Muzafer's narratives recount his travels throughout the Arabian Peninsula as a permanent resident of Saudi Arabia. Rather than simply describe "Arabian" life, he vividly portrays the deeply rooted Keralan communities that now permanently dot the desert. Through Ahamed's evocative writing, Arabia becomes an extension of Kerala itself. Ahamed, *Camels in the Sky*. For a sensitive study of labor travel between India and the Gulf, see Wright, *Between Dreams and Ghosts*.

41. Bisvas, *Andhakarer Afrika*.
42. Green, "Waves," 848.
43. This is a modification of Jan Borm's broad definition of the genre as "any narrative characterized by a non-fiction dominant that relates (almost always) in the first person a journey or journeys that the reader supposes to have taken place in reality while assuming or presupposing that author, narrator and principal character are but one or identical." Borm, "Defining Travel," 13.
44. Each of these terms is used to describe travel accounts, and each carries its own shades of meaning. Today, the term "safarnama" is by far the most common. Its dominance began in the 1880s and eventually emerged as a catch-all term for travel writing generally. Even still, most of these terms remain current. It is also noteworthy that before the 1870s, almost all the travel accounts to use the term "safarnama" in their title were colonial productions; independently written travelogues preferred the other terms noted here.
45. For example, Rathi, *Bagh*, 495.
46. See Pernau and Jaffery, *Information*, 1–8.
47. Nu'mani, *Safarnama*, 1–2.
48. Nu'mani, *Safarnama*, 192–93. In a humorous twist on this idea, roughly a century later the great travel writer Ibn-i Insha warned his audience that "if anyone tries to learn new information from my travel account, that will not be a good thing. And if anyone tries to turn this into a guide, they do so at their own risk and responsibility." Ibn-i Insha, *Avara-gard*, 5.
49. Majchrowicz, "Malika Begum's Mehfil," 866. For a study of a similar situation in Bengali, see Sarkar, *Words to Win*, 2–3.
50. Bhattacharji, "Indian Travel Writing," 130.
51. Ní Loingsigh, "African Travel Writing," 186.
52. Jones, *Crossroads*, 8; Ní Loingsigh, *Postcolonial Eyes*, 15–24.
53. Fowler, *Literature*, 38.
54. Raban, *For Love*, 253–54.
55. Ní Loingsigh, *Postcolonial Eyes*, 2, 14–20.
56. Pernau, *Emotions and Modernity*, 203.
57. Hyder, *Reliving Karbala*, 11.

58. Shackle and Majeed, *Hali's Musaddas*, 9.

59. Zarif Lakhnavi, *Intikhab*, 98.

60. Goswami, *Producing India*, 122–23. See also Mishra, *Pilgrimage*; Low, *Imperial Mecca*.

61. Williams, "Songs," 592–93.

62. Pernau, *Emotions and Modernity*, 38. On shifts in the how emotion was written in Urdu literature, see Pernau, "Morality," 38–51.

63. Shibli Nu'mani, *Turkey*, 20, 36–40, 100–04.

64. Shibli Nu'mani, *Turkey*, 36.

65. Cited in Shibli Nu'mani, *Turkey*, 267. Translation by Gregory Maxwell Bruce. Note, too, that these poems were mailed home and printed in Indian newspapers while Shibli was still abroad.

66. The original work was likely published in a Calcutta journal or newspaper.

67. Kinlock, *Vaqa'i'*, 3–4.

68. Works include: Burton, "Spectacle of Empire"; Fisher, *Counterflows*; Chatterjee and Hawes, *Europe Observed*; Fisher, *The First Indian Author*.

69. Chatterjee, "Discovering India"; Sen, *Travels to Europe*; Majeed, *Autobiography*.

70. Green, "Trans-Border Traffic"; Ziad, "Return of Gog."

71. Mukhopadhyay, "Writing Home"; Green, "Anti-Colonial Japanophilia."

72. Metcalf, "What Happened"; Asani, "Through the Lens"; Digby, "Bāyazīd Beg."

73. Alam and Subrahmanyam, *Indo-Persian Travels*; Sharma, *Mughal Arcadia*; Khazeni, *The City*.

74. Begum Sarbuland Jang, *Dunya*, 7.

75. Other religious reformist movements also actively cultivated travel writing, but only the writing of Aligarh's intellectual elite has garnered sustained study. Deoband, and later the Tablighi Jama'at, particularly cultivated the travelogue. On Deobandi travelogues, see Ingram, *Revival*, 160.

76. The articles were finally collected together as a book almost a century later. Khan, *Musafiran* (1961).

77. Khan, *Musafiran* (2012), 4. See also Khan, *Safarnama-i Maulvi*. This book was originally published in installments in the *Aligarh Institute Gazette* and again in *Tahzib al-Akhlaq*. It was also apparently published in English translation. No copy now exists. Khan, *Musafiran* (2012), 16. His son was Nawab Sarbuland Jang, the travel writer mentioned earlier.

78. Masood, *Impressions*; Masood, *Travels in Japan*. Like many aspects of the Aligarh movement, Masood's response to Japan is relatively well studied. See Chapter 4, and Lelyveld, "Jute Hain Japani"; Datla, *Secular Islam*, 59–62; Green, "Forgotten Futures," 617–21.

79. Pollock, "Cosmopolitan and Vernacular in History," 592. See also Mitchell, *Language*, 35–67.
80. Chatterjee, "Introduction," 19–21; Pernau, *Emotions and Modernity*, 38.
81. Gupta, *Sexuality*, 12; Ghosh, *Power*, 2.
82. The archives I visited are too numerous to list here, but major sites include: in the US, the Library of Congress, and libraries at Harvard University, University of Pennsylvania, the University of Texas, and the University of Wisconsin; in the UK, the British Library and Oxford University; in Pakistan, Punjab Public Library, ʻAbd al-Majid Khokhar Memorial Library, and Jhandir Library; in India, Raza Rampur Library, the Andhra Pradesh State Archives, Idara-i Adabiyat-i Urdu, Aligarh Muslim University, and Jamia Millia Islamia University. For detailed notes on many of my research sites in Delhi, see also Majchrowicz, "Twenty Libraries."
83. Here I followed the research methodology developed by Omar Khalidi. Khalidi, "Guide," 3–9.
84. This example also highlights how the archive shifts with political and social changes. While colonial-era women's magazines are difficult to recover (with various institutions today trying to reunite disparate issues), these materials suddenly become far more accessible from the 1960s, when the US took a strategic interest in South Asia and the Library of Congress began to amass materials like the women's magazine *Akhbar-i Khavatin*. On this archival shift, see Kirk, "Books," 539–41; Robb, "Gendered Nationalism," 286.
85. Rekhta, for instance, has digitized tens of thousands of books, but assiduously obscures the locations from which its books are sourced, putting new resources at the fingertips of scholars, but also hamstringing their ability to think materially about texts and circulation, and sidestepping questions about the many lives of a given text. The Endangered Archives program, in turn, raises questions about accessibility, preservation, and justice in a postcolonial world. The British Library contains perhaps the world's greatest collection of South Asian literary archives—all of it totally inaccessible to most South Asian scholars and readers who are prevented by visa and financial restrictions from visiting. The Endangered Archives program, though, asks how Western institutions can preserve material digitally without removing the original works from their physical locations. Finally, and more recently, the digitization project of the Chughtai Public Library leads the way in bringing Pakistani collections online and making them available on both sides of the border, and globally.
86. Reid and Paisley, "Introduction," 1.
87. For key moments in this debate, see Ghosh, *Sex and the Family*, 15–31; Arondekar, *For the Record*, 1–15. For a reflective take on shifting approaches to the archives, see Dirks, *Autobiography*, 27–49.
88. Burton, *Dwelling*, 5; Nerlekar and Orsini, "Postcolonial Archive," 212–18.

89. On rematerialization, see Burton, "Introduction," 9; Boyk, Amstutz, and Perkins, "Unpacking the Library," 446. On alternative archives, see Nerlekar and Orsini, "Postcolonial Archive," 3–4.

90. Francesca Orsini discusses the potentials and pitfalls of using such lists. Orsini, "Present Absence," 311–27.

91. Chakrabarty, *Europe*, 6–9. Margrit Pernau reaches the same conclusion in her study of early Persian and Urdu newspapers and their "mental map" of the world. Reviewing issues of the *Delhi Urdu Akhbar* in the 1840s and '50s, she finds that articles on the Middle East, Central Asia, and even China, greatly exceed the number of articles on Europe. Pernau, "The *Delhi Urdu Akhbar*," 123–25.

92. Qaisari Begum, *Kitab-i Zindagi*, 450.

93. Sulaiman Nadvi, for instance, once compiled a short list of the best *hajjnamas* (accounts of the hajj) of the year 1931. Nadvi, "Dibacha," 4. These types of references provide useful guidance.

94. Gupta et al., "Literary Sentiments," 814–16; Shankar, *Flesh and Fish Blood*, 103–42.

95. Inaccessible in two senses. Physically, because copies of these works are now often rare and hard to find; and conceptually, in that the displacement of sustained study of vernacular South Asian languages over the last seventy years has made reading even relatively recent nineteenth-century writing styles and print formats challenging to many non-specialist native speakers.

96. For a wider view of this double bind, see Asad, "Two European Images," 263.

97. On the history of itineraries between the Middle East and South Asia, see volume one of Farhan Nizami's forthcoming *Atlas Project*.

Part I

Account of a Journey to Sri Badri Narayan-ji Maharaj

as composed by His Highness Janab Rao Raja Bhavani Singh-ji
sahib bahadur, Ruler of Khilchipur State
Bidya Bhushan Press, Muradabad, 1900

Praise Lord Ganesh.

These are the circumstances of my third journey. I was twenty-two years old
when the courts [in Khilchipur] stopped conducting their business in Hindi.[1]
This resulted in a great turnover among the clerks and other functionaries.
The situation was such that any department that did not conduct its business in
Persian greatly displeased His Royal Highness.[2] His preference for Persian was so
strong, in fact, that Persian-reading *munshi*s and Muslim advisors were beginning
to gain access to the highest echelons of government service. By this time I was
overcome with worry, for ordinances from the state government, orders from the
courts, and documents from the [Central India] Agency, etc., were all in Persian.
To be sure, Hindi was still nominally sanctioned for use in the lowest offices, but
for how much longer? There was even an assistant literate in Persian there too.
Surely the day was not far off when Persian would be adopted everywhere, and
it would be no surprise if Hindi were shaken off completely. Forget Persian, if
you don't count Hindi, I was completely illiterate even in Urdu. It seemed that
I would soon endure great suffering and immense embarrassment as a result of
my ignorance of Persian. If I could not manage to learn Persian, it was crucial that
I should at the very least attempt to learn Urdu as best I could. Then, no matter
how deficient I might be, I would still be able to read documents sent by the
Agency and the courts of the various departments, and also be able to read letters
and maps. This was critical. The situation [in the region] was very delicate in those
days, and there were all manner of people about.

The only problem was, I was no longer a child. I could not be expected to tolerate so much hard work. Unwilling to commit, a year passed by.... One day [in 1891] I realized that it would be wise to subscribe to the *Avadh Akhbar*, an acclaimed newspaper from Lucknow that published worthwhile articles on community, national, political, and social issues, so that I could have it read aloud to me during moments of leisure. I shared this idea with Purohit Madan La'l-ji, who was a royal priest and my confidant and advisor. He also had a suitable knowledge of Persian. He happily agreed to my proposal, and for a time the newspaper was read out to me. The essays in this wondrous newspaper only fanned the flames of my desire to learn Persian. I told the priest [*purohit*] so and asked him if I might one day be able to read the newspaper for myself. He responded that this was no great matter, provided I apply myself completely for one year.... I readily consented to this, said *bismillah*, and began the very next day. Purohit-ji taught me with such affectionate devotion that within twenty-five days I learned the alphabet in its entirety. At this juncture, we began to read.

***

I finished the next three books [in my curriculum] within six months and then began to read the *Gulistan* of Sa'di. Dear God, did I have a very difficult time with this book! I didn't have even the slightest intellectual ability. Whenever I would open that book my very soul would shudder and a pall of darkness would descend over my heart. I would begin to stammer and murmur God knows what. When things came to this pass, my courage waned. My anxious heart counseled me, saying, "You can bear the mockery of others, but you cannot bear to read this." But still I pressed on and read three or four stories [*hikayat*].... At last, I apprised Purohit-ji of the situation, and he gave me this advice: "Do not let six months of labor go to waste. Do whatever it takes to finish two chapters of the *Gulistan*. You can't learn Urdu without knowing a little Persian.... Everything is difficult at first, but it eventually gets easier, and you will even come to enjoy it. What is more, [Lord] Narayana is all-powerful. He will not let your labors go unrewarded. If He looks upon you favorably, then Urdu is nothing, He will even grant you a mastery of Persian. His Pure Being gives favor to those in need. He smooths the path for all."

These heart-piercing words bolstered my courage anew. I told him, "Persian aside, if I am able to learn even functional Urdu, then this will be such a blessing for me that, and I declare this in front of you all now and with all my heart, if [God grants me this,] I solemnly vow that I will not profit from my newfound knowledge until I have taken the darshan of that Great Being, Parmeshvar Sri Badri Narayan-ji Maharaj with my own eyes...."[3]

[Eventually,] I completed the *Gulistan*. This was followed by more books... which I read over a period of five years. But now that the tree of my hopes had borne the fruit of success it was necessary to fulfill my vow. This meant I had a new worry: how was I to get permission from [my father,] His Highness Sri Huzur Durbar, to depart for this journey? God knows this problem robbed me of my sleep night after night until I was in quite a state. Eventually, my heart told me that there was no need to be so melancholy. "Just go and explain yourself to Sri Huzur Darbar, saying nothing more or less than the plain truth. Then make your request. Would it be any surprise if the God that granted you such success bestows this upon you as well?" Eventually I asked [the astrologer] Maharaj Brij Bhushan Das-ji to identify an auspicious moment to act. After great reflection and study, he calculated the most auspicious time [to approach my father].

***

"[Father,] if I were to ask for anything, what would it be? Just this, that I be given two or three months' leave to take the darshan of Sri Badri Narayan-ji Maharaj. In addition to this darshan, I would also like to make a touristic visit to all the sites on the route. I will do this and return quickly to kiss the feet of Sri Huzur Darbar.... I simply wish to relieve myself of my vow." When I completed my petition, the durbar fell silent, as though the entire assembly was in a trance. I mustered my courage and got down on my knees.... After deep reflection, he [the king] announced his decision: "Go, but return quickly. And send a letter every day confirming your well-being." I expressed my gratitude, and sat myself reverentially at Sri Darbar's feet with my head bowed low.[4]

Notes

1. It is unclear what language the author refers to here as "Hindi," but it is likely a localized form of the language, or else a dialect of Marathi. It does not refer to modern Hindi. The period in question dates to the year 1891. I thank Dalpat Rajpurohit for his insight on this question.
2. The author's father, Rao Bahadur Amar Singh-ji, later referred to as Sri Huzur Darbar.
3. Badrinath, a pilgrimage site in the Himalayas.
4. Singh, *Safarnama*, 3–14.

1

Bhavani Goes to Badrinath

I found Bhavani Singh's travelogue at Subhan's bookstall on a Sunday visit to the Daryaganj neighborhood of Delhi. Every Sunday, Daryaganj's shops close their shutters and surrender their sidewalks to independent booksellers. Most of the books in this roadside bazaar are in English: *The Lady's Desire*, *Commentaries on the Gujarat Sales Tax Act of 1968*, *The Miracle Berry Diet Cookbook*. A few sellers, though, have a niche, and Subhan's was old Urdu print. His titles were an odd mix. They were often written in obsolete jargon and dealt with obscure topics, including treatises on homeopathy, guides to administrative shorthand, and *takfir*-laden tracts on stale religious disputes. Subhan acquired his books cheaply, likely enlisting neighborhood scrap dealers (*kabari-vale*) to pull out promising material. Perhaps he also visited homes where an elderly relative had recently died. The younger generation rarely valued these books and might part with them cheaply.[1] Even Subhan's rarest books almost never sold for more than ten or twenty dollars.[2]

There are Sunday book bazaars all over South Asia. They are an incredible archival resource, but they are also fickle. You must visit them weekly, because stocks change constantly, and a book once sold may never reappear. Libraries and archives are more reliable and organized, but they are not natural, representative, nor comprehensive.[3] Libraries include books according to their own missions. Collectors only buy items they value. The bazaar's offerings, though, are not dominated by any consistent ideology, logic, or morality. Here religious manuals for proper prostration are piled below *kok shastra* and *suhag rat* guides to sex positions and family planning. This randomness makes the Sunday bazaar a paradise for discovering regional works and lowbrow publications.[4] It is an unstable, uncatalogued archive for everything libraries could not, or would not, accept. And so it was that no matter what city I was in, I would visit the Sunday book bazaar to poke around. The official archives are closed on Sundays, anyhow.

One day at Subhan's, I spotted a dogeared volume titled *Safarnama Shri Badri Narayan-ji Maharaj Ka* (Account of a journey to Sri Badri Narayan Maharaj, 1900). Its author was Rao Raja Bhavani Singh (b. 1869), the raja of Khilchipur, an obscure state in central India. I was intrigued. I had never even heard of Khilchipur, much less its ruler's travelogue. Stranger still was a bookplate bearing the image of Moolam Thirunal (r. 1885–1924), Maharaja of Travancore, in distant southern India. Had His Highness's book once belonged to His other Highness, perhaps in his famous state library? And if so, how did it travel from Muradabad, where it was published, to the tip of India before resurfacing on a sidewalk in Delhi? The book's physical appearance spoke volumes about the mobility, fragility, and resilience of Urdu print. Its contents, meanwhile, reflected the historical popularity and social ecumenicism of the Urdu travelogue. This was a Marathi-speaking Hindu prince from central India who learned Urdu, made a pilgrimage to the Himalayas, and then published a book about it in Urdu in the expectation that it would find readers.

These points make Bhavani Singh well suited to introduce the social and literary history of the Urdu travelogue. This chapter explains how a mass-produced, vernacular-language travelogue like his could come to exist. Just a half-century earlier the travelogue had been a marginal genre in India. Additionally, few Indians were even literate, and many who were often preferred Persian to Urdu. And yet, by the end of the nineteenth century, Bhavani Singh's decision to write an account of his pilgrimage in Urdu was unremarkable. This chapter's account of the early history of the genre and its material pasts will inform the remainder of this book, which takes up the relationship between travel writing and Urdu's global imagination directly. To facilitate this tour, the following section offers an overview of Bhavani Singh's account, which will serve as a reference point to the shifts in travel writing and attitudes toward travel in South Asia between the sixteenth and twentieth centuries. It is followed by a history of the Urdu travelogue, a survey of the major technological and ideological changes that facilitated its efflorescence, and, finally, by an introduction to its writers, and to the genre's material forms. But first, we join Bhavani Singh on his trip to Badrinath.

A Royal Tour of Badrinath

Classical Urdu romances often begin with a crisis that compels a young prince or hero to undertake a quest to a distant land. Prince Bhavani Singh's travel account similarly began with a crisis that ultimately compelled him to undertake a quest of his own: the realization that kingship would require literacy in Persian and Urdu, both prominent mediums of state and society in his day. The colonial administration in central India functioned in these languages, and Khilchipur was adopting them too. Meanwhile, the newspapers and journals he wished to read to remain informed about the world were likewise in Urdu. While "Hindi" may have been enough to get by in Khilchipur, making a mark for himself in central India would require Bhavani Singh to do more, for, even in the late nineteenth century, "no one who had not mastered the Persian classics, both in poetry and in prose, could claim to be truly cultivated."[5] Alas, at twenty-two, Bhavani Singh was beyond the age of diligent study. Nevertheless, he began to learn Urdu, vowing not to put his hard-earned knowledge to use until he had made a pilgrimage to Badrinath, one of Hinduism's holiest sites (Figure 1.1). Five years later, he succeeded. He was fluent in Urdu, and it was time to fulfill his vow. The prince gathered his servants, his servants gathered the prince's belongings, and together they set off to Badrinath.

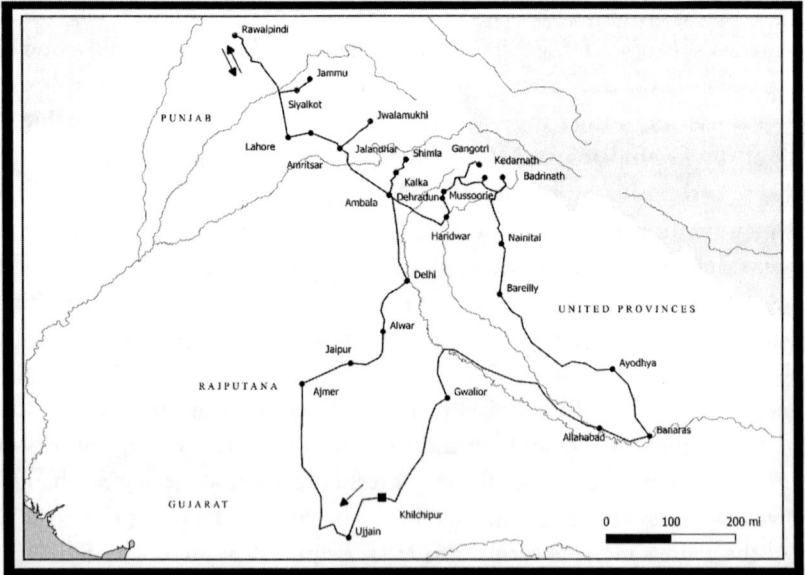

Figure 1.1 Bhavani Singh's travels in northern India

Source: Author.

Traveling at first in an open horse-cart, the party constantly lost its way on the dusty paths around Khilchipur. Bhavani Singh eventually reached Ujjain, where he boarded a train to Jaipur, and soon after, to Delhi. He visited the Red Fort and several temples, performed ablutions, and sent letters home. From there, he took the train through Punjab and into the Himalayan foothills, visiting temples along the way. These regions were filled with Europeans and Indian rulers whom he observed with fascination. In Haridwar he spent a few days preparing supplies and reading about Badrinath. From here the journey would be slower, for Bhavani Singh would have to either walk or be carried through the upper Himalayas. The first stop was Dehradun, where an innkeeper gave him a guidebook:

> I told him about my plans to make a pilgrimage to Sri Badri Narayan, upon which the owner of the house called for a book. He gave it to me, saying that his grandfather had gone to Sri Badri Narayan once. "He wrote a detailed guide to the area and all the places near it. Please keep it," he said. "It will be useful for you."[6]

Bhavani Singh may have used the guide, but did not say so. He felt no need for citations: he was simply recording his own personal journey, focusing less on the sights and more on his own experiences, from personal interactions to everyday nuisances. At Kedarnath, he stopped at a pilgrims' rest house (*dharamshala*), where he met a group of travelers from near Khilchipur, an indication that travel was then so common that one might encounter one's neighbors in the high Himalayas. Bhavani Singh was excited to meet the group, but also preoccupied by a stubborn case of diarrhea (bowel movements, both routine and exceptional, are a staple of Urdu travelogues). Incontinent but undeterred, he traveled on to Badrinath, where he spent several days performing rites. His prose gushes with emotion here and, for once, we do not see him bickering over fees with porters and priests.

Having fulfilled his vow, it was time to go home. As Bhavani Singh descended the mountain, he claimed that the locals appeared increasingly "human" the closer he got to the plains, a reminder that the Urdu travelogue, like its colonial counterpart, invoked ethnographic typologies and hierarchies, even within the subcontinent. Finally, he arrived in Nainital, a colonial hill station he knew from his reading:

> Pandit Ratan Nath [Sarshar], the author of *Sair-i Kuhsar* [A tour of the mountains, 1890], wrote about this mountain, Nainital, in his book. For a long time I had wanted to see Nainital, but I had always assumed that his description was a flight of poetic fancy. But now I saw that, in truth, everything the pandit wrote was absolutely true.[7]

Perhaps he saw something of himself in *Sair-i Kuhsar*, the humorous tale of a decadent young nawab who leaves home and travels to the mountains. The book was originally published in installments in the *Avadh Akhbar*, the very newspaper that inspired Bhavani Singh to learn Urdu.[8] This fictional travel narrative made Nainital an irresistible stop for Bhavani Singh, demonstrating how Urdu literature could inspire journeys, shape itineraries, and fire the imagination.

Bhavani Singh's road home from Nainital was circuitous, but the trains made it easy. He first went to Ayodhya, a pilgrimage site he knew from an earlier visit, and Banaras. After boarding the wrong train, he ended up in Gwalior but eventually got back on track. The final homeward leg required travel by camel. When he reached the borders of Khilchipur, a crucial transformation occurred as his party emerged from the liminal space offered by travel:

> We stopped under a pipal tree near a well. I called for sweets and roasted chickpeas, and while we ate, I said to my companions, "For all the time that we have been on this trip, I have not once forbidden you from eating, drinking, laughing, playing, or engaging in any type of impertinence [in my presence]. Now, though, we are once again in our own country and I expect you to act with decorum, as before. The behavior I indulged on the journey will no longer be tolerated."[9]

The speech signaled a return to protocol. As they rode into town, Singh's subjects lined the streets, singing. His father came out to meet him, and at an auspicious moment, they returned to the fort together. He distributed gifts and Ganges water, and the account concluded.[10] His vow fulfilled and his quest complete, he was now fit to rule. By the time his book went to press, he had already replaced his father as head of state.

Travel and Travel Writing in Precolonial South Asia

Bhavani Singh's account was typical of its era, but it differed radically from precolonial antecedents in two regards: first, that he felt travel to be unambiguously positive; and second, that his account focused entirely on his own sense of self. His account resembled a bildungsroman in which he struggled through his studies, fulfiled his vow, and returned home to rule. He rarely described sights or wonders, but rather focused on what he did, thought, saw, and felt. Before the nineteenth century, Indian travelers, when they wrote at all, rarely wrote in this way.

In colonial sources, Indians were usually depicted as sedentary residents of a timeless land.[11] India was not a country of travelers, but "travelees."[12] Colonial writers insisted that Indians had "the strongest possible prejudice against travelling."[13] In reality, South Asians were highly mobile. Kings, for example, regularly shifted their headquarters to maintain control of their territories.[14] To sustain their legitimacy, rulers "adopted the practice of darśan [viewings] and regularly toured their domains, making themselves visible and accessible to their subjects."[15] The name of the Urdu language itself encodes courtly mobility: it is derived from a reference to the Mughal emperor's "exalted camp," the "Urdu-i muʻalla."[16] Subjects were mobile, too. Nobles, princes, artists, and poets roamed in search of employment, patronage, or political support.[17] Pilgrims journeyed to temples, shrines, and holy sites, often by land and sometimes by sea.[18] Soldiers traversed thousands of miles on foot, while merchants traded across the subcontinent, and sailors ventured to the far reaches of the Indian Ocean.[19] Indians have been itinerant for so long, in such great numbers, that the vocabulary, scripts, and religious practices they brought with them to Southeast Asia persist there to this day.[20]

Although Indians were constantly on the move, the details of their movements were rarely given much attention in writing. Travel writing is effectively nonexistent in Sanskrit, and scarce in precolonial vernacular languages like Bengali, Tamil, and Braj Bhasha.[21] Of course, travel itself was always an organizing principle in Indic literature. Sanskrit and Prakrit narratives are filled with travel and geographic description, as in Kalidasa's *Meghaduta* or the journeys of Rama and Sita in the *Ramayana*.[22] Persian and Hindavi romances and Sufi narratives were likewise replete with accounts of enchanted journeys.[23] Nevertheless, before the late eighteenth century accounts of journeys by living individuals were rare.[24]

Some scholars argue that the travelogue was a quintessential genre of Islamic literatures and that, consequently, travel writing in Urdu should be traced to Arabic literature and the founding of the Islamic sciences between the seventh and fourteenth centuries.[25] There is no doubt that the Urdu travelogue inherited much from the Persian *safarnama*, which was in turn impacted by Arabic travel genres like the *rihla*. At the same time, these links should be treated with care. A facile linking of Ibn Battuta's *Rihla* to Bhavani Singh's *Safarnama* risks conflating distinct societies and literatures and ignoring the many intellectual and social changes they underwent. Muslims did not compose travel writing in all times or places. Nor did they draw from the same travel writing traditions directly.[26] Urdu literature was certainly influenced by centuries of Islamic thought and writing, but as Barbara Metcalf concludes, "despite the splendid travelogues written in Arabic in the centuries after the ʻAbbasids [after 1258], there does not seem to be a continuous genre of travel writing in Muslim societies generally."[27]

In India, the genre flickered to life in Persian during the sixteenth century, seven hundred years after the arrival of Islam. It only truly gained any prominence in the late eighteenth century, but still played only a minimal role in intellectual life.[28] A comprehensive survey of existing studies, catalogs, and manuscript collections suggests that, on average, one travel account was written per decade between the years 1500 and 1750, with the rate of composition gradually increasing over time.[29] Compared to Bhavani Singh, precolonial travel literature was ambivalent about the value and desirability of travel. Its two schools of thought were represented by the phrases "travel is hell" (*safar surat-i saqar*) and "travel is a means to success" (*safar vasila-i zafar*). Persian literature is filled with debates between the two positions. The paradigmatic example is Husain Kashifi's fifteenth-century *Anvar-i Suhaili* (The lights of Canopus), a collection of stories originally translated from the Sanskrit *Panchatantra*. Kashifi's version was standard reading for centuries. Even Bhavani Singh read it. One of the book's early stories recounts the fictive King Dabashim's longing for travel. One day at court, he announced his intention to visit Ceylon and asked his advisors to debate the idea. They were divided.[30] One advisor related the parable of a pair of pigeons. Bazinda ("playful") wanted to see the world, but the more cautious Navazinda ("caring") warned:

> You have not borne the toils of travel, nor seen the struggle of being far from home, nor has your soul yet heard the phrase "being far from home is anguish." Travel is a tree that gives no fruit except that of separation, and being away from home is a cloud which gives naught but the rain of abjection.[31]

Bazinda countered that travel bestows glory and soothes the intrepid soul. He argued that God called humans to travel, and that wise men say that "travel is the means to victory." Bazinda ignored Navazinda's advice and took flight. Compelling evidence was mustered on both sides, leaving readers to judge for themselves.

The corpus of early modern Persian travel accounts in India can be divided into two categories: intelligence reports and narrative accounts. The former emerged from Mughal informational networks wherein travelers and spies recorded informational accounts with precise geographical details. The results tended to be targeted towards specific goals, rather than toward contributing to a general body of information.[32] Reports of this type might include, as in one account of Tibet, "distances, the position of routeways, rivers and sources of fresh water ... details of local products and, in particular, gold-panning farms."[33] Informational accounts went by several names, including news (*akhbar*), events (*vaqa'i'*), conditions (*halat*), as well as history (*tarikh*). Mughal intelligence networks were later absorbed into the British colonial system, which relied on them to maintain and expand colonial rule until well into the nineteenth century.[34] Using these networks, the British sent explorer-spies called *munshi*s into the territories northwest of Delhi that were beyond their grip. The munshis were expected to write reports on their return, typically in Persian.[35] These eighteenth- and nineteenth-century accounts offered one early model for Urdu travel writers.

The second category, narrative accounts, included a wide range of travelogues written for other than strategic or informational purposes. Some writers recorded events they witnessed (festivals, battles, and so on), while others focused on strange sights or curious incidents.[36] Unlike Bhavani Singh, precolonial writers tended not to focus on the journey itself, nor to share their emotions.[37] In many premodern and early modern cultures, journeys "were prominently utilitarian or generally undertaken out of necessity. Wayfarers were mostly concerned with the destination rather than the road, for movements through space were essentially contingent to the accomplishment of other goals."[38] Princess Jahanara's (1614–81) travel accounts thus discussed her spiritual pursuits almost exclusively. Her entire journey to Kashmir was summarized in two lines: "During this time of auspicious beginning and end, my great father [Shah Jahan] set out for Kashmir, the peerless and charming place that does not need any praise or description. I reached Kashmir with him on 31 March 1640 of the same year."[39] 'Abd al-Karim's (d. 1784) *Bayan al-Vaqi'* (A narrative of events, 1750) related how he joined the Persian emperor Nadir Shah's army after the sack of Delhi in 1739. He did discuss his journeys, but not his thoughts or reactions. There is still no narrative arc based on a sense of self:

> From Baghdad we passed through the village of Nekjeh to the city of Sermen Rai, commonly called Samerah. Here we visited the shrines of Imam Ali Naqi and Imam Haffan 'Askari, who are both buried in their own houses, which are most magnificent buildings. The *khadims* [managers] and all the attendants at these two shrines are very rapacious."[40]

We find almost no mention of 'Abd al-Karim's daily life or his personal experiences beyond general statements (the khadims are rapacious). What did it mean for 'Abd al-Karim to visit these sacred sites, to perform the hajj? What did the rapacious khadims do? Did he ever have diarrhea? He does not say.

This narrative distance was a convention of the age and a reflection of 'Abd al-Karim's authorial self, one very different from that of Bhavani Singh. Compare 'Abd al-Karim's taciturnity with Bhavani Singh's emotive description of a snowy morning in the Himalayas:

> My companions had never seen such a thing before, and they were astonished at the sight. They made such a commotion that I was awoken from my sleep. They all came running to me, speaking words of wonder, "Come outside! Come look at this!

Just see what has happened." I went to the door of the house to look. Ahead of me was a vast and undulating sea of silvery mercury. Nothing but pure whiteness, spread across the ground up to the trees and along the mountains. By this time, the sun had come out and the snow was beginning to melt. I went out to the side of the house and headed towards an area where there was a covering that protected it from the accumulation of snow. I went there to relieve myself.[41]

Bhavani Singh's focus on his own emotions and experiences on the road reflected a broader shift toward modern conceptions of the self around the world.[42]

Studies of travel writing from a range of cultural contexts point to similar shifts from the idea of travel as a "necessity ... as a suffering, even a penance," towards a celebration of it as a "means to pleasure," self-growth, and social advancement.[43] In Japan, from the eighteenth century travel became "a conscious sociocultural act, undertaken not out of practical necessity but from the simple desire to break with the ordinary.... No longer the inert, flat line between two points of interest, it became an active stage on which meanings could be 'discovered, created, and communicated.'"[44] For modern travelers, "reaching the final destination became subordinate to the greater goal of being in motion."[45] The same logic explains why Bhavani Singh's "travelogue of Badrinath" only dedicated a few pages to Badrinath itself. As in Japan, in India, too, by the end of the eighteenth century travel gradually shed its ambiguous status, a shift that coincided with the growth of travel writing. At least seventeen new travel accounts appeared in Persian between 1750 and 1800.[46] English-language accounts too began to appear, some of which drew a direct connection between British mobility and prosperity.[47] Travel writing in colonial India would come to look very different from Mughal-era accounts. These changes, though, were not the result of a sudden, "complete epistemic shift" occasioned by the arrival of colonialism.[48] Travelers continued to move along old routes, just as they always had, but increasingly they began to think about, and represent, that movement in new ways.[49]

Travel Writing in the Colonial Era

Three major changes in the nineteenth century brought the travelogue to prominence in India and normalized a positive literary attitude toward travel. First, new technologies like trains and steamships made travel increasingly feasible.[50] Second, new print technologies facilitated textual production. Meanwhile, colonial policy shifts liberalized press ownership, allowing almost anyone with the money to become a publisher. Efforts to reduce the cost of ink and paper brought down the expense of printing (and books) drastically. Finally, colonialism engendered broad changes to social and intellectual life. There was a genuine fascination with the changes taking place in the world. It might seem that most Indians would have been introduced to the wider world through the lens of colonial discourse—learning about Africa through English texts or translations, for instance—but, in fact, it was ultimately Indians themselves who primarily dictated the terms of their engagement. Colonial sources offered one possible view of the world. Indians made their own too.

One of the major conceptual shifts in this period facilitating the production of new, indigenous global imaginations was the unambiguous celebration of travel. Through the 1860s, Urdu travel authors wrote elaborate prefaces justifying their decision to travel, seemingly with the intent of convincing skeptical readers of its value. By Bhavani Singh's time, though, this aspect of travel writing had either disappeared or been formalized. Authors took it for granted that readers recognized travel's benefits. They did not lament leaving home, but rather thanked God for the opportunity to do so. Travel was now often associated with moral and social improvement.[51] Title pages and introductions proclaimed that travel was "the means to victory." Authors suggested that "the wise traveler and the discerning voyager gain experience from their travels and become clever and intelligent. The wise of the age then count them among the possessors of experience and value their words."[52] No longer an onerous obligation, travel became the source of "countless blessings" increasingly accessible to ordinary people, both as travelers and readers.[53]

Novel Travel Technologies

In part, travel was easier to celebrate in the nineteenth and twentieth centuries because it was safer, cheaper, and more efficient than ever before. Precolonial modes of transport—horses, bullock carts, elephants, palanquins, walking—limited speed and comfort. Though some routes boasted well-maintained roads with inns at regular intervals, many others were uneven or unsafe.[54] Seafarers risked cholera and Portuguese pirates.[55] Efforts to integrate the Indian interior into colonial communication and transportation networks began in the 1820s, offering enough comfort and predictability to enable increased movement and the possibility of leisure travel.[56] Not coincidentally, this occurred around the same time that mass tourism began to develop in Britain.

Rail, which spread rapidly in India from the 1850s, was critical. The British initially assumed trains would only be used to move commodities, because Indians, due to their "prejudice, timidity, and stationary character," would not travel.[57] This colonial view was of course completely wrong. Indians flocked to the trains for their cheap fares, safety, and speed. A comparison of two travel accounts puts this change into perspective. Traveling through northern India in 1851, Maharaja Tukoji Rao Holkar's journey slightly predated the inauguration of train travel. Traveling by horse and camel, he and his party moved slowly and often camped outdoors. At the worst moments, they were despondent:

> One amongst us said, "If I make it out of this place, I will never mention travel again." What had happened to the maharaja? He'd left his palaces and begun to travel. Now he's stuck in the wilderness and shivering uncontrollably from the cold. Travel really is the very image of hell after all. Staying in your own home is the best course of action. Nothing is gained from going abroad.
> Immobility is the height of respectability
>   The raindrop becomes a pearl when enveloped in mother-of-pearl.[58]

Forty years later, Bhavani Singh had a much easier time. He traveled in one day distances that took Holkar a week. Rather than spend the journey being jostled on a horse or searching for fresh water, he passed his time in transit writing letters:

> We stopped for a while at Fatehabad station. Here I was visited by Chandmal Sahukar, and I spoke with him until the train left again. While I was sitting in the train I wrote out a letter to Thakur Sahib of Runija.... Meanwhile, we arrived at the station in Runija. I gave one of the Brahmin water-bearers on the station a tip and told him to take my letter to the Thakur.[59]

New technologies meant that travel was no longer so fearsome, nor so difficult. And yet, train travel had its downsides. At times Bhavani Singh found it unbearable and corrupt:

> We arrived in Kalka that evening. We rested up, and early the next morning ate and boarded the train for Haridwar at four a.m. Allah, save us! The festival was on at Haridwar, which meant the train was absolutely packed. The railway employees took full advantage of this situation. The passengers who gave them a little something were able to board; whoever did not pay was pushed back and prevented from entering: "The train has no space, you travel some other time." The passenger would stand there yelling, "But my brother's on board, my wife is on board!" But who was going to listen?[60]

Bhartendu Harishchandra (1850–85), the "father" of the Hindi travelogue, wrote scathing satires of the ills of train travel in the 1870s.[61]

Conditions were no better in women's compartments, as Begum Hasrat Mohani (1885–1937) attested in 1936:

> The train from Amritsar was so packed that we only managed to get the luggage and the men into a carriage with the greatest difficulty. As for me, I went with [my grandson] Rizwan and [helper] Khushrang to the women's carriage. This carriage was small and all the women in it were Punjabi. They put up a determined boycott to protest our arrival. One claimed she was resting and couldn't move; another ranged her children out around her to guard her territory. We barely managed to get a few fingers' worth of space.[62]

Despite its challenges, however, the railways allowed Bhavani Singh, Harishchandra, and Begum Hasrat Mohani to reach their destinations quickly and safely.

Nevertheless, travel did remain unpopular in some quarters, particularly where it was discouraged by social norms or religious strictures. Some upper-caste Hindus feared train travel would bring them into contact with lower castes, endangering their purity.[63] Others believed crossing the "black water"—traveling beyond the borders of India—would result in a loss of caste or religion.[64] Given the centrality of the hajj to their faith, upper-class Muslims did not share the same concerns, but they had their own doubts, particularly concerning access to halal food.[65] Travelers proposed various solutions, including self-catering or temporarily changing their school of Islamic law to sidestep inconvenient restrictions.[66]

Upper-class women of all religions faced greater social restrictions. To address them, social reformers advocated special travel arrangements for "respectable" women.[67] These included exclusive waiting rooms or train carriages, and even special covered rickshaws to carry them directly from their vehicle to their train car without breaching purdah.[68] Nevertheless, criticism of women travelers abounded. In a derisive magazine article about women travelers titled *Bila Zarurat Safar* (Unnecessary travel, 1955), 'Abida Mu'in carped:

> Women will drag a herd of children with them onto the train, and back off it again. You ask them where they're going, and they tell you their aunt's brother's son is getting married. Or their uncle invited them over. Some distant relative trumps up some invitation and begum sahiba gathers up a dozen children, gunny sacks, boxes, and bedding and sets off! I tell you, these women either suffer from unbearably excessive amount of familial love, or they enjoy pain and suffering.[69]

Social stigma like this often prevented women from traveling or compelled them to find a male relative (*mahram*) to accompany them. Naturally, some women ignored these restrictions. Others articulated novel justifications for unaccompanied travel, including producing ingenious theological solutions, as in this exchange at sea in 1934 witnessed by Fatima Begum (1890–1958):

One of the maulanas said at the gathering [on the ship] that it was impermissible for a woman to perform the hajj without a mahram, and also a sin. Suddenly, a middle-aged woman who had performed the hajj several times stood up and asked him, "Would the hajj of such a woman be accepted [by God]?" [He] replied that whoever completes the hajj with pure intentions will not be denied by God. The woman then retorted, "But you had said [earlier] that the hajj washes away all sins, such that one becomes as pure as they day they emerged as an innocent baby from their mother's womb. If we complete the hajj, the sin [of traveling without a mahram] will be forgiven." The maulvi had no answer. [70]

In sum, while improved technology and the social and political changes of the nineteenth century made travel easier than before, access was not equally possible for everyone, and social and religious conventions continued to limit who could travel, and how.

Print and the Adoption of Urdu

The nineteenth century also saw increased literacy and access to printed materials, including newspapers and books. South Asia was curiously late to adopt print technology, which had been in use for millennia in East Asia, and for centuries in Europe. In India it only became common in the nineteenth century. [71] Early print used moveable type, which was expensive and aesthetically unsatisfying. The manuscript, which was familiar, accessible, and visually appealing, thus remained India's preferred mode of production. Ultimately, it was lithographic technologies—which could reproduce calligraphy and decorations—that made print appealing and accessible. [72] Lithography spread rapidly after arriving in India in 1823. [73] Soon thereafter, laws regarding the ownership of printing presses were liberalized, giving entrepreneurial Indians the ability to print material themselves with relatively few restrictions. By the late 1830s, Indian-owned presses had sprung up across northern India. [74] Despite this, a full-fledged Urdu publishing industry only truly took shape after the 1850s. [75] Initially, most travelogues were published from a handful of cities around the United Provinces, but production soon expanded elsewhere, particularly to Punjab (see Figure 1.2). The spread of print became so pervasive that "commercial mass printing altered power configurations within the cognitive and literary domain. Knowledge was no longer the preserve of small elites but expanded into the public realm." [76]

1820–99		1900–47		1947–99	
City	Count	City	Count	City	Count
Lucknow	29	Lahore	90	Lahore	535
Agra	11	Hyderabad	62	Karachi	304
Delhi	9	Delhi	51	Delhi	101
Kanpur	9	Lucknow	26	Hyderabad	46
Lahore	8	Agra	11	Lucknow	39
Muradabad	7	Aligarh	11	Multan	38
Meerut	6	Meerut	8	Islamabad	37
Hyderabad	5	Bijnaur	8	Rawalpindi	34
Patna	3	Muradabad	7	Faisalabad	21
Aligarh	3	Madras	6	Peshawar	19
Multan	2	Amritsar	5	Patna	13
Barabanki	2	Calcutta	5	Aligarh	11
Sialkot	2	Allahabad	4	Calcutta	11
Rampur	2	Rampur	4	Gujranwala	10

Figure 1.2   Number of Urdu travel titles by city of publication

Source: Author's personal database, 2021. For further details, see pp. 18–20.

Notes: The figures here give the number Urdu travelogues published as books in major cities. The data shows a rapid expansion westward, as the United Provinces were eclipsed by presses in Pakistan and particularly in Punjab after 1947. In the period 1900–47 only one of the top fourteen cities was in today's Pakistan; after 1947, more than half were.

These transformations occurred as Urdu was itself becoming popular as a written language. While Urdu had roots dating back centuries, it was primarily a language of everyday conversation and poetry and oral literature. It was rarely used for scholarly or official purposes; that's what Persian was for. Literary historians struggle to locate Urdu prose before the nineteenth century.[77] Barring a few exceptions, Urdu prose first appeared in translations of the Qur'an and in religious treatises, largely written by Muslim reformists in the early 1800s.[78] Meanwhile, the colonial administration and reform-inclined elites were transforming Urdu into a language of governance and modern learning—the very reason Bhavani Singh was so embarrassed by his lack of fluency.[79] From the 1830s, Urdu replaced Persian as the colonial administrative language in much of British northern India, including in regions like Punjab where it was not widely spoken.[80] Colonial education policies meant that "by the mid-1840s ... Urdu had become the principal vernacular medium for the publication of 'useful' knowledge, and Delhi and Agra, with their large Muslim and Urdu-speaking populations, had become important locations of textbook translation, publication, and distribution."[81] This project was supported by many Indian intellectuals, who assisted in the transfer of knowledge via translation. By 1870, India's literary and intellectual sphere had radically changed. Vernacular discourse moved to the fore (Figure 1.3).

Ironically, the same forces that displaced Arabic and Persian also brought classical travelogues in these languages to prominence. Growing fascination with the genre meant that older works could now be brought out in print comercially. From the 1880s, publishers began to print travel writing by South Asians like Jahaniyan Jahangasht (1308–84) and non–South Asian travelers like the Persian Nasir-i Khusrau (1004–88) or the Moroccan Ibn Battuta (b. 1304), creating in the process a historical canon of travel writing.[82] Previously, classical Arabic and Persian travel accounts had had limited circulation in India. These accounts were rarely cited by early Urdu travel authors. Yet, once this new historical canon transitioned to print, references to it became ubiquitous. It began to appear in syllabi and Urdu travelers, for the first time, began to compare themselves to Ibn Battuta.[83] As this classical canon became better known, the Urdu travelogue was reimagined by some as an Islamic genre, reinforcing the notion that a love of travel had always been an Islamic value.[84]

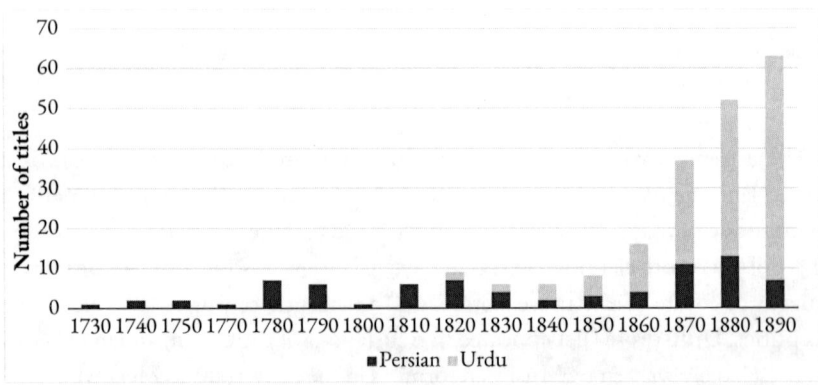

Figure 1.3 Eighteenth- and nineteenth-century Urdu and Persian travel accounts in books and manuscripts

Source: Author's personal database, 2021. For further details, see pp. 18–20.

Colonial Influence on Early Urdu Travel Writing

Travel writing was popular in nineteenth-century Europe, and as the East India Company pivoted towards a "civilizing" (rather than just a mercantile) mission, it sought to promote the genre in India too. Travel writing thus gained wider visibility as accounts written in or translated into Urdu were included in colonial school syllabi (see Figure 1.4). Even beyond school texts, though, many of the earliest Urdu travelogues bear the unmistakable stamp of colonial influence thanks to the close collaboration between Indian travel writers and their British friends and mentors.

Given the perceived association between Islam and the genre, it might seem radical to claim that the safarnama was popularized in the colonial period. And yet, one of Urdu's most erudite scholars supported this view.[85] Writing in Persian in the 1880s, Shibli Nu'mani argued that Indians had entirely neglected the genre:

> Even since ancient times, the intellectuals and scholars of Europe have engaged themselves in the composition of volumes of travels and chronicles, and above all in writing travel accounts (*safarnama-ha*) ... and when, in Arabia, the Islamic Empire was ascendant and Muslims held the reins of power, they also did not neglect the opportunity to perform this work. They too adorned travel accounts on the world around them.... But the truly astonishing thing is that in the lands of Hind [India], this precious resource made absolutely no impression. Even if any of them had the good fortune to travel, they would not record anything of their personal experiences so that others could share in it, or learn from it.[86]

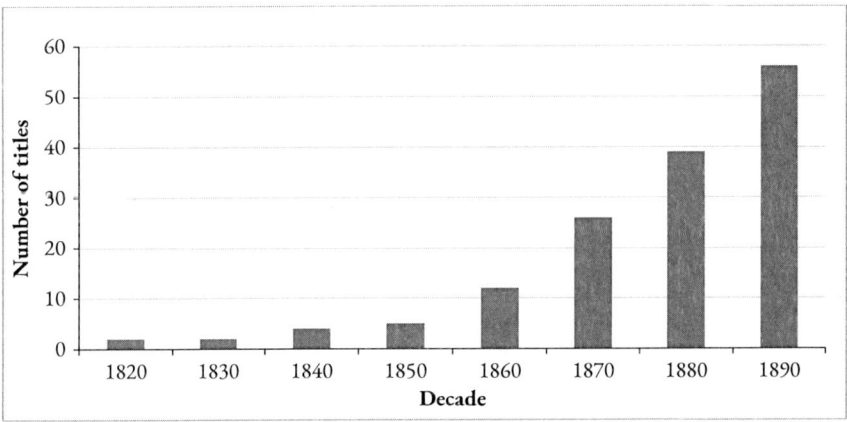

Figure 1.4 Nineteenth-century book-length travel accounts in Urdu by decade

Source: Author's personal database, 2021. For further details, see pp. 18–20.

This was an exaggeration. Shibli overstated European and Arab commitment to travel writing and willfully ignored Indian travel writing. Yet he did so in service of the broader truth that the travelogue was marginal to India's literary and intellectual worlds. This appears less radical when the travelogue is compared to other genres that emerged—or reemerged—in the colonial period, which Francesca Orsini describes as era of "genres reproduced and genres introduced." Similar shifts were taking place everywhere in Urdu literature.[87] Partha Chatterjee details this process with regard to vernacular historiography: "Forms and styles made familiar by colonial modernity began to enter the domain of the vernaculars, setting new standards and giving new content to the idea of the 'modern.'"[88] The Urdu travelogue was thus a largely novel genre that sprang from multiple sources, Indic, Islamic, and European.

Although the British actively promoted travel writing, their preferred models did not entirely replace older styles, nor prevent new ones from emerging. They offered examples (by subsidizing Urdu translations of English travelogues, for example), but in practice Urdu authors developed the genre based on their own aesthetics and preferences in conversation with British translations and precolonial antecedents. The earliest Urdu authors had many potential models before them. They took their inspiration from different strands of Urdu, Persian, Sanskrit, and English literature, borrowing from nearly every literary form available to compose travel accounts that were familiar and appealing. In this way, a colonial project to promote the travelogue, the quintessential genre of European imperialism, was localized.[89]

By the 1900s, no one could seriously suggest, as Shibli had two decades earlier, that Indians were uninterested in writing about travel. Travel writing had increased throughout the nineteenth century, surging in popularity in the first years of the twentieth. Production slowed during times of upheaval, such as during the World Wars and the Partition of India in 1947, but it always rebounded.[90] It grew further after independence. It remained popular through the 1970s in both India and Pakistan before undergoing a metamorphosis in the following decade, when it became fashionable among the literati, particularly in Pakistan. It was in the 1980s that Urdu scholars began to acknowledge the genre as a unique and important branch of literature. Today offerings remain diverse and sell briskly, with more being produced per year than ever before.[91] Vernacular guidebooks for foreign countries, though, are no longer popular in South Asia. The elite now prefer to use English-language guides, while the non-elite face harsh visa restrictions preventing leisure travel. For these immobilized readers, it is the stories that sell, not the practical advice.

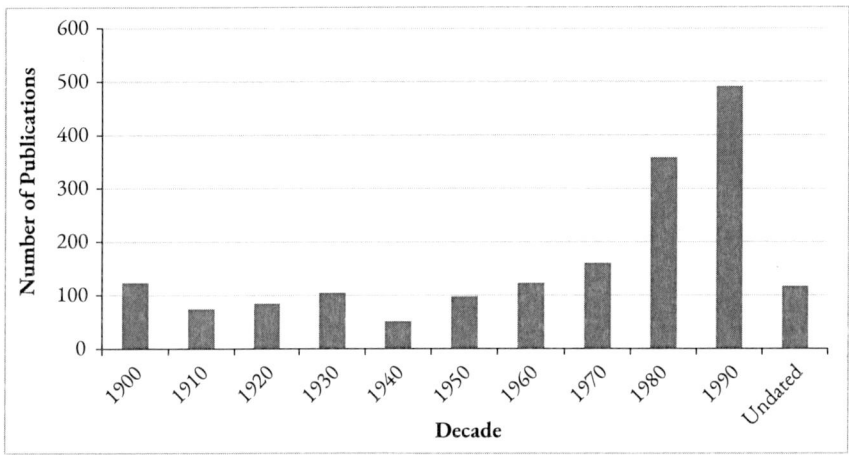

Figure 1.5 Twentieth-century book-length travel accounts in Urdu by decade
Source: Author's personal database, 2021. For further details, see pp. 18–20.

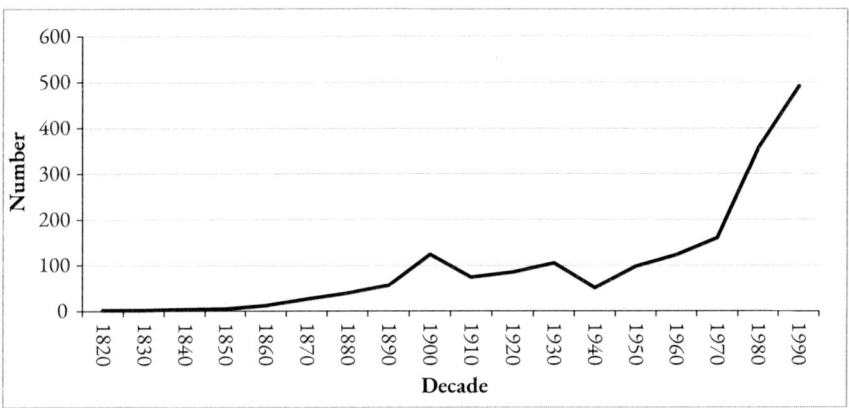

Figure 1.6 Urdu travel account publication in book form by decade, 1820–1999
Source: Author's personal database, 2021. For further details, see pp. 18–20.

While guidebook-style travel accounts were once common, they gradually disappeared in the 1950s. The obvious exception here are pilgrimage guidebooks for hajj, *'umra*, and the holy sites of Iraq and Iran. The publication rate of Urdu travelogues in book form in the twentieth century are shown in Figure 1.5. Figure 1.6 shows growth over the period 1820–1999.

Travel Writing in Other Indian Vernaculars

No major South Asian vernacular had a recognizable travelogue tradition before the nineteenth century. By 1910, all of them did. Travelogues were readily available in Urdu (the first account appearing in 1824),[92] Telugu (1830),[93] Tamil (1832), Bengali (1850), Nepali (1853), Gujarati (1860), Marathi (1863), Punjabi (1881),[94] Hindi (1841/1871),[95] Odiya (1875), Kannada (1890), Assamese (1890), and Malayalam (1903).[96] Through travel writing, authors in each of these languages cultivated their own aspirations and imaginations. In the case of Hindi, for instance, Charu Gupta argues Swami Satyadev "Parivrajak" (1879–1961) was responsible for "shaping the vernacular intellectual and literary history of the modern Hindu political imaginary.... His imagination of the nation [in his travelogues] ... exercised considerable influence in early twentieth-century India."[97] Ideas traveled easily and freely between literatures and languages, in part because many people spoke multiple languages. Further cross-pollination came in the form of translation.[98] Some travelogues were published in multiple languages simultaneously. Jagjit Singh, Maharaja of Kapurthala, published his travels in Urdu, Hindi, and English. The Begum of Bhopal, Shah Jahan Begum, had her travels published in five languages, gifting copies to visiting dignitaries. This type of multilingual exchange is often forgotten in a world increasingly imagined to be monolingual or mediated by English.[99]

Urdu's Travel Writers

Urdu travel writers defy easy categorization. They belong to no single social class, region, ethnicity, or nationality. Unlike Persian or English, the use of Urdu has never been restricted to the elite. Nor is it bound geographically, as with Telugu or Bengali. Historically (though less so today), it did not have an exclusive affiliation with Muslims—Bhavani Singh is proof of that.[100] Instead, for much of the nineteenth and twentieth centuries, Urdu was the most prominent language of the public sphere in northern India and several neighboring regions. Regardless of one's "mother tongue," knowing Urdu was the mark of a well-rounded education.[101] It served (and serves) as a link language across South Asia, the Persian Gulf, and beyond, particularly in its spoken form.[102] Urdu was a primary language of communication and literary expression at every level of society. In many regions, it was (and is) used by non-native speakers in literary, public, or trans-regional contexts.[103] Not everyone used it, by any means, but the range and diversity of its speakers nevertheless defy any attempt at clean categorization.

Grappling with this diversity, scholars have proposed various terms to refer to this sprawling communicative and literary space. Jennifer Dubrow speaks of an

"Urdu cosmopolis." Sarah Waheed proposes the word "Urduphone," while Amy Bard offers the term "Urdu-wāle."[104] Each of these terms capture something of this diversity, but not all. At a more abstract level, and in the context of Punjabi literature, Farina Mir coins the broader term "literary formation" to refer to a group of individuals "who shared the practices of producing, circulating, performing, and consuming" literary texts in a single linguistic tradition.[105] This term circumvents the question of identity while pointing to the social space in which texts and ideas circulated among its participants. Rather than coin a term for those who participated in Urdu's literary formation, I refer to them as simply Urdu speakers. However, I do so with the caveat that participation in this literary formation is not reducible to the act of "speaking," and it certainly does not refer only to those who used Urdu as a first language, or even a second. Some participants in this space might have understood written Urdu, but not spoken it. Others might have consumed Urdu aurally without being fully fluent.

While the identities of those who consumed Urdu travel literature are difficult to trace, the travel writers themselves have left more clues, and they are remarkably diverse. The sources employed in this book reflect the social, economic, and religious heterogeneity of Urdu travel writers. They range from queens to housewives, from renowned intellectuals to underpaid draftsmen. Alongside prominent figures, I give ample space to authors whose names or travel writing are unknown today. These relatively marginal travelers are almost never studied, but they contributed in significant ways to the discourses about the world that circulated in Urdu. Obscure writers played a crucial role in imagining the world according to their own positionalities and aspirations. For all their differences, Urdu travel writers were united, ultimately, by their choice of Urdu to record their travel, and by their contribution to Urdu's literary and intellectual episteme.

Many of them hailed from major cities like Delhi or Bombay or intellectual centers like Aligarh or Lucknow, but a significant number came from smaller towns, called *qasba*s, located in agricultural areas, the *mufassal*. Despite their relative remoteness, agricultural qasbas were fertile terrain for the development of the safarnama. Culturally, qasbas were dominated by a small group of land-owning Muslim elites with family histories in administrative work and cultural and intellectual attainment. They had relatively stable incomes and often ample leisure time. Many qasba residents dedicated this time to intellectual and literary pursuits and to promoting access to knowledge in their environs.[106] Even small qasbas could boast impressive libraries.[107] Many had printing presses whose publications commanded a nationwide readership and inflected national debates.[108] The qasba "sustained distinctive and generative forms of public life." Despite being "remote … its people were never isolated or passive."[109] In colonial India, urban elites did not impose a global imagination on the countryside.[110] These productive spaces were already deeply linked to Urdu's literary networks.[111] Travel writing from qasbas and other small towns was not limited to men either. Women's magazines were peppered with articles and letters from small-town women.

While Urdu's travel writing community was diverse, it did not include everyone; the act of writing or composing depended on access to leisure time. Urdu travel writers were rarely train attendants, soldiers, or sailors. They did, however, travel for business, pilgrimage, education, politics, to accompany family, and, sometimes, for pleasure. Before the 1970s, most did not travel as "tourists," in the modern sense of leisure travelers.[112] Instead, as throughout much of the Muslim world, travelers "mixed commerce, study, travel, and religious devotion."[113] Though many travel accounts were engaging, most authors were not literary maestros. Charu Gupta describes the quality of the average Hindi-language travelogue as "middling"; the same is true for Urdu as well.[114] Most authors had only moderate financial resources. A smaller group of authors had money, but little influence. Some, like the novelist Intizar Husain, had wide social recognition, while others only had status within their small communities or regions. Some authors had illustrious titles, but few resources. Bhavani Singh was a crown prince, but he traveled in cramped train carriages and bargained like the dickens.[115] Of course, travel had the power to change one's status.[116] Terms like "vilayat-palat" (England-returned) acknowledged those who had traveled to Europe. "Hajjan" or "Hajji" honored those who had performed the hajj. As the nineteenth-century draftsman Manzur 'Ali of qasba Badaun put it:

> Without travel, one has neither respect nor status
> Truly, what value has the babe in the doe's womb?[117]

Writing and publishing turned a journey and its unique experiences and insights into public knowledge. In this sense, travel writing let individuals promote not just their visions and global imaginations, but also themselves.

The average Urdu travel writer's middling status means most are now forgotten. Collectively, though, they fashioned a global imagination for the Urdu-reading and Urdu-speaking public and shaped Indian discourse about the larger world. They constituted what C.A. Bayly describes as "local, decentralized networks of knowledgeable people on the fringes ... [that] carried the deepest power of social change."[118] S.A. Zaidi similarly attributes this power to Urdu's "second-tier" writers who joined an Urdu "press and publication industry [that] held sway over the beliefs, minds and actions of many Muslims who could read and write Urdu."[119] These travel writers responded to colonial messaging and the zeitgeist of colonial India but, ultimately, they wrote and imagined according to their own preference and ideals.

Materiality, Circulation, Reception

Periodicals

From an archival perspective, printed books are the most visible and best-preserved form of Urdu travel writing, but the genre was in fact primary published in periodicals: magazines, newspapers, and journals.[120] Periodicals in South Asia were not only sources of information, but also of community.[121] They functioned as print publics, shared spaces for discussion, debate, and the exchange of ideas.[122] It was here that the travelogue sank its deepest roots. There was no one kind of periodical that printed travelogues. Even periodicals with highly specialized content, like theological magazines, carried them. Periodical accounts were sometimes one-off pieces submitted as essays, letters, or poems. They might also be published serially, providing readers with weekly or monthly installments. Travel writing appeared alongside news reports and commentary, lending them contemporary relevance and creating an intertextuality with news reports. This mode of publication and circulation facilitated dialogue as readers discussed the day's travel account in person or via letters to the editor.

Travel accounts were commonly published even as the traveler was still abroad, inviting readers to follow along almost in real time.[123] In 1921, Khwaja Ghulam al-Hasnain, editor of the Lucknow theological monthly *al-Va'iz*, announced his departure for Iraq in his magazine with the promise of regular updates:

> Today ... I leave for Iraq.... I will compose an account of my travels and attempt, to the best of my abilities, to keep readers informed of all I encounter on this trip that is of interest.... Anyone wishing to write me a letter personally may address it, along with my name, to: Iraq, Exalted Karbala, Ma'rifat Postmaster.... I hope that all my friends and respected elders will pray for me and for the success of my trip.[124]

This announcement made readers into fellow travelers. By praying for his success they played an active role in it. As they followed along, they saw Iraq and Karbala synchronically, reading the installments as they were printed. For as long as Ghulam al-Hasnain was in Iraq, the magazine's readership traveled along with him. He also provided his address because readers often wrote in to share their commentary and feedback. Each successive installment of a travelogue could thus net suggestions, praise, or scorn; this feedback was often published in the periodical itself, where it could be read by the author mid-journey. Newspaper travel accounts were thus a dialogic encounter between travelers and the community.[125] The full extent of this dialogic literary ecosystem in Urdu is analyzed by Jennifer Dubrow, who shows how Urdu novels, which were also often published serially, shifted in response to reader feedback and published letters to the editor.[126]

Well-received periodical travel accounts garnered a particularly wide circulation because Urdu periodicals often reprinted content from other outlets.[127] One author, Nawab Muhammad 'Umar 'Ali Khan "Vahshi" of Basoda (r. 1864–96), noted in 1876 that his travel accounts that year appeared in newspapers in six cities between Bombay and Madras.[128] In the 1950s, installments of 'Abd al-Majid Daryabadi's travel account of Pakistan were reprinted repeatedly across South Asia:

> God knows what pleasure readers saw in it, but it was reprinted in a great number of Pakistani newspapers, and even a few Indian ones, almost as soon as each installment was first published. I received a constant flow of letters from those who enjoyed the account. These letters of appreciation were sent by readers of almost every class. Many of these kind people insisted that the various pieces be brought together in the form of a permanent book.[129]

As Daryabadi's readers themselves suggested, periodical accounts found greater permanence in book form. Indeed, many, if not most, Urdu travel accounts published as books were first serialized in periodicals.[130]

Short-form travelogues were always best suited to periodicals, and newspapers and magazines were always more accessible than books. Book-length travel accounts required significant time and expense, while mailing a short account to a magazine was cheap and easy. Women particularly found periodicals an accessible and socially appropriate outlet.[131] For these reasons, periodical publications came from a wider range of authors. It was even common for magazines to publish letters sent in by the letters' recipients, sometimes without the knowledge of the authors themselves! One Najm al-Nisa, for instance, sent a letter to 'Ismat magazine with this note: "My father, Sayyid 'Ali Akhtar sahib, has been transferred from Allahabad to British Somaliland in Africa. He often sends us interesting accounts of that place. I'm forwarding one of those letters now for my sisters [i.e., fellow readers] to enjoy."[132] In this way, magazines significantly reduced the barriers to producing and publishing travel writing. It took little more than writing a letter to become a published travel author, while the presses themselves thrived on these types of voluntary contributions.[133] Meanwhile, the country's sophisticated mail system allowed for timely distribution of periodicals across thousands of miles. The same system facilitated subscription payments.[134] Urdu's global imagination had a subcontinental reach.

Printed Books

The printed book is today the most accessible and well-preserved material form of travel writing. One reason for this was the British policy of collecting copies of every book published in India. A huge number of these works were catalogued and stored, and can still be accessed at archives in India and London today. A second reason is that, unlike diaries or letters, they were mass produced. Out of hundreds or even thousands of copies of a single book, perhaps only one copy may exist today—but that is enough. Large print runs thus increase the odds of preservation. Lastly, books tended to be more durable. They were often thick enough that even if a few pages were lost (a common occurrence), the core of the book yet survived.

Nevertheless, printed books took many forms, and not all were equally durable. The most expensive travel books might use heavy paper with fine inks, expert calligraphy, and even gold leaf. They might be bound in ornate and weighty covers. These qualities could make a book ideal for use as a gift or official state production. Sultan Jehan Begum of Bhopal's ornate travelogue, *Rauzat al-Rayahin* (The fragrant garden, 1906), weighed several pounds.[135] At the other end of the spectrum, the cheapest books comprised a dozen lithographed pages on low-quality paper. This was the case with Bhavani Singh's account. Books of this sort were economical but were quickly worn out if read or circulated frequently, often to the point that they no longer exist. Bhavani Singh wrote three travelogues, printing each as a book.[136] Two are lost entirely, and only two copies of his account of Badrinath are known to exist today, including the tattered copy I found at Subhan's. Only a single known copy exists of Fatima Begum's flimsy paperback travelogue, *Hajj-i Baitullah* (Hajj to the House of God, 1959), in a private collection on a farm in Pakistan's Punjab. Thus, while printed books had more longevity than newspapers or magazines, cheap volumes like these were still relatively perishable.

As for the print itself, lithography, rather than moveable type, was used almost exclusively until the 2000s, when computer-rendered text came to dominate. Images in books were not common, though some lithographed drawings appeared in travelogues as early as 1852. Photographs appear from the 1890s, sometimes depicting the author and sometimes destinations. Maps were, and remain, rare. Instead, geographical locations were expressed in words. The oral potentiality of travel writing is perhaps reflected in this preference for descriptive rather than visual mapping. Bhavani Singh's account included neither images nor maps. Like many books of its time, though, it boasted an ornate cover page. Typically, geometrical designs surrounded text distributed across the page. References to God appeared at the top, followed by formulaic Persian or Persianized phraseology. The title of the book was usually centered, and followed by the names of the patron who commissioned it, the author, and often their mentor. The press was named at the foot of the page.

The year of publication was only occasionally printed on the cover. Beginning in the 1920s, presses began experimenting with formal visual representation in cover art, such as a map or a drawing of a building. From the 1950s, covers typically displayed an abstract drawing, a photo, or white space.[137] Travel writing continues to appear regularly in book form today. Pakistani bookstores have sections dedicated to the genre; the larger stores might have dozens of recently published titles in stock.

Travel and Orality

Not all travel accounts were produced or circulated in print. One of the most memorable short stories in Urdu literature gives a glimpse into the way that travel narratives could be shared to a group of listeners, particularly by those who were not literate. The story is Rashid Jehan's *Dilli ki Sair* (A tour of Delhi, 1932), in which the female protagonist, Malika Begum, gathers her female neighbors together in the zenana to tell them the story of her journey to Delhi.

> Of all her friends, Malika Begum was the very first to travel in a train. And that too all the way from Faridabad to Delhi for an entire day. Every woman in the neighborhood had come to hear the tale of her journey. "Ae hai, come on then! I'm exhausted from speaking so much. As God is my witness, I swear I've already told this story a thousand times. I took the train from Delhi, and when we got there, he went to meet his friend, that damned stationmaster."[138]

Malika Begum, who, thanks to her husband's negligence, never managed to get past the train platform, regaled her friends with a telling of everything that she saw in the station. Though the trip was not very successful, she clearly relished narrating it, and her audience was patently enthralled. Malika Begum is just one example of the ways that Urdu's global imagination could spread through oral accounts.[139]

Though oral travel narratives are least accessible of all, they should not be dismissed. South Asian historiography demonstrates the folly of assuming "the hegemonic ascent of literacy over orality."[140] The social power of orality is best known in the context of religious literature, but it was equally privileged in secular spaces as well.[141] Literacy was not a prerequisite to access the Urdu travelogue's global imagination. Much of India was marked, in C.A. Bayly's famous phrase, by "literary awareness." Despite being illiterate, "most north Indians had access to literate people and knew the meaning and power of writing."[142] Urdu speakers could access writing via ubiquitous scribes, and they experienced literature through oral recitation, which occurred when an author recited from memory, or when an individual read aloud, as the purohit did with Bhavani Singh. Many travel accounts were recited but never published, while others initially circulated orally before moving to print. Those print copies inspired further oral recitations. Punjabi offers a comparative example. In 1932 the poet Nur Begum wrote a series of descriptive, versified letters home, specifying that they were to be read publicly: "Let this be read aloud to the people ['am loka'i] of Kandhvala." Another concludes: "Let this letter be read to my community [mera qabila]."[143] The letters were later included in a versified travelogue that was surely also read aloud. The enchantment of her words persists. When I shared some of my favorite passages with friends, they enjoyed them enough to pass them along to their families via Whatsapp voice notes. Similar practices would have spread Nur Begum's voice in the past, too, albeit without the convenience of the internet. Through all these types of orality, Nur Begum's poem, and her global imagination, have had a wide social reach.[144]

Oral travel accounts also circulated in formal venues in the form of speeches.[145] Poetic gatherings offered another venue. Traveler poets could read their compositions to small groups of listeners and poets called nishists. They might also recite them at formal poetic gatherings called musha'iras which function as "a point of 'collective discourse'" and which are spaces highly marked by audience interaction.[146] Zarif's poem, cited in the Introduction, could easily have been recited in a nishist or a musha'ira. It was clearly intended for oral recitation, and thus offers a sense of the emotive power and wide social reach of oral performance. In short, travel writing was not just consumed by the literate. A sophisticated understanding of literature cut across social classes.

Conclusion

While the Persian travelogue existed in South Asia for centuries, it had only a limited role in intellectual and literary life. In the nineteenth century, the travelogue suddenly blossomed in Urdu and other Indian vernaculars. Its rise was occasioned by the spread of literacy, colonial patronage, the availability of cheap print, and the increasing convenience of travel. Thanks to these and other social and intellectual shifts, travel became celebrated as a worthwhile personal undertaking. As the genre proliferated, it increasingly welcomed writers from across a wide cultural, religious, and socioeconomic spectrum. These shifts are exemplified by Bhavani Singh. Today, there is little conceptual space for imagining a Marathi-speaking Hindu from rural central India writing a Himalayan pilgrimage account in Urdu. Yet he surely did. Urdu today is typically associated with Muslims, but Bhavani Singh's Safarnama demonstrates that the world of Urdu print—and its global imagination—was diverse. This world is easy to forget, in part, because the textual record of Urdu travel writing is so precarious, as the tattered copy of Bhavani Singh's account demonstrates. Reclaiming this history means historicizing conceptions of travel, reading against the grain, and stepping outside the formal archive. Few Urdu readers today, most of whom are Muslim, are interested in Jain or Hindu pilgrimage accounts and, resultingly, texts like Bhavani Singh's are not always preserved. Women's writing, too, is more likely to be lost or irregularly archived, obscuring women's role in producing Urdu's global imagination.

The remaining chapters of this book explore the formal and informal travel archives to ask how Urdu travel writers used the genre to create in words the world they wished to see. Following on Bhavani Singh's account, Chapter 2 continues the focus on India's princely rulers, exploring how this influential group used the travelogue to imagine a place for themselves in a colonial world. A close reading of two princely texts from the early 1850s shows how genre hybridity helped produce this imagination. The chapter is preceded by a selection from one of these travel accounts, Nawab Ghaus Muhammad Khan's *Sair al-Muhtasham* (The tours of al-Muhtasham, 1852). Ghaus Muhammad was the ruler of the small state of Jaora in central India, a hundred-odd miles west of Khilchipur (Figure 2.3). In 1852 he traveled through northern India before returning home to record all he had seen. In the following passage, he displayed his willingness to improve his abilities as a ruler while suggesting, implicitly, that diligent and perspicatious rulers like him had a future in British India.

Notes

1. In a comparable context, Rian Thum writes that in Altishahr (today's Uyghur heartland in western China) most of the books "that reach the market today come from the heirs of copyist-owners who have died." Thum, *Sacred Routes*, 77.

2. By contrast, other antique booksellers work on a much larger scale, selling books via Facebook or Whatsapp. The biggest players in this market sell books in bulk for hundreds of thousands of dollars at a time, primarily to Western institutions such as Stanford or Harvard University. Venkat Mani's concept of bibliomigrancy (defined as "the physical and virtual migration of literature as books from one part of the world to another") is a key term in thinking about this movement. Mani, *Recoding*, 10–12.

3. For a set of compelling case studies, see Boyk, "Provincial Urbanity"; Mandhwani, "The Hindi Library"; Kirk, "Books."

4. For a fascinating comparison of the book trade and informal archives, see Thum, *Sacred Routes*, 28.

5. Pernau, "Virtuous Individual," 170.
6. Singh, *Safarnama*, 47. This may have been a work published in Urdu three years earlier, Ganga Prasad, *Rasta Jatriyan*.
7. Singh, *Safarnama*, 115.
8. Siddiqi, *Pandit Ratan Nath*, 27.
9. Singh, *Safarnama*, 134.
10. Singh, *Safarnama*, 143.
11. Sinha, *Communication*, xxiv.
12. The term is Mary Louise Pratt's. Pratt, *Imperial Eyes*, 8.
13. Wheeler, "Introduction," xx. The quote refers specifically to Bengalis but was clearly meant broadly.
14. For two studies, see Sharma, *Mughal Arcadia*; Gommans, *Mughal Warfare*.
15. Brittlebank, *Tipu Sultan's Search*, 131. The practice of travel for hunting (*shikar*) was also related to legitimacy and mobility. Hughes, *Animal Kingdoms*, 7.
16. Faruqi, *Urdu Literary Culture*, 25.
17. 'Abd al-Rasul, *Nairang*, 1; Eaton, *Social History*, 78–104; Subrahmanyam, *Three Ways*, 73–132.
18. Relevant studies include: Eck, *India*; Khera, "Picturing India"; Schaflechner and Bergmann, *Ritual Journeys*.
19. The literature on this topic is immense and varied. Important works include: Kolff, *Naukar*; Digby, "Some Asian Wanderers"; Pearson, *Pilgrimage*; Bose, *Hundred Horizons*; Markovits, Pouchepadass, and Subrahmanyam, *Society and Circulation*; Das Gupta and Pearson, *Indian Ocean*; Strauch, *Socotra*; Levi and Alam, *India and Central Asia*.
20. Pollock, *Language*, 530; Ricci, *Islam Translated*, 8–13. Literary links between these regions revived in the nineteenth century as the movement of people between India and Southeast Asia led to the translation of significant amounts of Urdu literature into Malay. Braginsky and Suvorova, "Urdu in Malay," 115–53.
21. In Sanskrit, the most proximate type of writing is the *tirtha* genre, which is typically a collection of praise poems to deities worshiped by the author while on pilgrimage, as in Sri Vadiraja, *Theerthaprabandha*. Some scholars have posited a medieval Indian travel writing tradition outside Persian, but cited texts are typically either devotional or geographical surveys of temple complexes. Chaudhuri, "Indian Travel Writing," 160. That said, precolonial vernaculars, particularly from the eighteenth century, are chronically neglected by scholars who either study "colonial modernity, or … leap over the intervening centuries to classical India." Rao, *Text*, 125. See also Pollock, "Introduction," 5. Bengali *mahakavya*s, for instance, may hold as-yet undiscovered accounts. A reconsideration of what constitutes travel writing, as argued in this book,

and more attention to these literatures may ultimately help scholars in regional South Asian languages to identify earlier forms of travel writing. At present, though, there is little indication of a sustained precolonial travel writing tradition.

22.   For a discussion, see Bhattacharji, "Indian Travel Writing," 127–28.

23.   Relevant scholarship includes Williams, "Sacred Sounds," 162–67; Behl and Weightman, "Introduction," xxxi–xxxix; Ghalib Lakhnavi and Bilgrami, *Amir Hamza*, ix–xiv.

24.   Brief travel narrations were occasionally included in works that are not about travel. For example, Banarasidas's autobiography in Braj includes several journeys. Banarasidasa *Ardhakathanak*. The *Baburnama*, a rare instance of autobiography in the sixteenth century, is dominated by narratives of travel. Babur, *Baburnama*, xvi; Sharma, *Mughal Arcadia*, 68–72.

25.   Azad, *Unnisviñ*, 32–38; Ahmad, *Azadi*, 33–38.

26.   Indeed, classical Arabic travelogues like those of Ibn Jubair or Ibn Battuta are almost never cited in Urdu or Persian travelogues before the 1880s.

27.   Metcalf, "Pilgrimage," 187. Houari Touati argues that the travelogue's role in Islamic intellectual life briefly flowered but then died by the fourteenth century. Touati, *Islam*, 221–65.

28.   Two early works sometimes considered travel accounts that had a wide influence were Shah Waliullah's *Fuyuz al-Haramain* (Reports/Secrets from the Holy Places, 1731) and 'Abd al-Haqq Muhaddis Dihlavi's *Jazb al-Qulub ila Dayar al-Mahbub* (The attraction of hearts to the home of the Beloved, 1589). The first relates the author's mystical visions in Mecca. The second is a detailed study of Medina. Neither discusses the author's travel, though some Urdu scholars have suggested they are precursors to hajj writing. Nadvi, "Dibacha," 3.

29.   These figures are based on my own database of travel accounts held in libraries or described in handlists, as described in the Introduction.

30.   Kashifi, *Anvar*, 42.

31.   Kashifi, *Anvar*, 46.

32.   Bayly, *Empire*, 22.

33.   Bayly, *Empire*, 21.

34.   Sinha, *Communication*, 92; Pernau, "The *Delhi Urdu Akhbar*," 1–2.

35.   Mathur, "Geography," 8–10, 14; Raj, *Science*, 214–22; Sharma, "Mohan Lal," 82–86; Khazeni, "Sand," 133–36.

36.   Muzaffar Alam and Sanjay Subrahmanyam describe many such Persian travel accounts from or about South Asia. Many, though, were written by Central Asians, a reflection of the genre's limited use in India. Alam and Subrahmanyam, *Indo-Persian Travels*. Sunil Sharma also discusses some previously unstudied

Persian-language travelogues in *Mughal Arcadia*. See, for example, Sharma, *Mughal Arcadia*, 157–59.

37. A remarkable exception is Anand Ram "Mukhlis," *Safarnama-i Bangarh*. See Alam and Subrahmanyam, "Discovering the Familiar," 131–54.
38. Nenzi, *Excursions in Identity*, 1.
39. Jahanara Begum, "Jahanara Begum," 389.
40. 'Abd al-Karim [Abdulkurreem], *Memoirs*, 121–22. Spelling edited for clarity.
41. Singh, *Safarnama*, 75.
42. Malhotra and Lambert-Hurley, "Gender," 1–30.
43. Leed, *Mind*, 7–8.
44. Nenzi, *Excursions in Identity*, 2. Similarly, in Malay, *Kisah Pelayaran Abdullah* (The story of Sea Abdullah's Voyage, 1854), one of the earliest Malay memoirs to use the first person, is "an individual's journey.... [Abdullah] describes personal moments, such as a conversation with a ship captain, another pilgrim's actions and demeanor, and specific events he experienced while on the journey." Tagliacozzo, *The Longest Journey*, 97; 'Abdullah, *Kisah*.
45. Nenzi, *Excursions in Identity*, 2.
46. These figures are based on my own database of travel accounts. See p. 18–20.
47. For several studies of early Indian travel writing in English, see Fisher, *The First Indian Author*; Fisher, "From India to England"; Tavakoli-Targhi, *Refashioning Iran*, 35–76.
48. Orsini, "*Qasbas* and Cities," 69.
49. Jagjeet Lally, for instance, shows how the arrival of maritime colonial powers did not displace robust trade and travel networks between India and Central Asia in the eighteenth and nineteenth centuries, but rather transformed them, typically through Indian and Central Asian intermediaries. Lally, *Silk Roads*, 7–8.
50. For a detailed exploration of these themes in a global context, see Gelvin and Green, "Introduction," 1–13.
51. For example, Husain, *Haramain*, 2.
52. Khan, *Dala'il*, 3.
53. Danapuri, *Sair-i Dihli*, 3.
54. Relevant studies include Deloche, *Circulation en Inde*; Wagner, *Thuggee*.
55. For a specific example, Digby, "Bāyazīd Beg," 160.
56. Sinha, *Communication*, xx.
57. Goswami, *Producing India*, 107–8. For full studies of this issue, see Kerr, *27 Down*; Prasad, "Tracking Modernity." For complicating views, see Arnold, *Science*, 110–11.
58. Rathi, *Bagh*, 157–58.

59. Singh, *Safarnama*, 22.

60. Singh, *Safarnama*, 38–39.

61. See Mukhopadhyay, *Imperial Technology*, 41.

62. Begum Hasrat Mohani, *Khutut o Safarnama*, 102. See also Majchrowicz, "Begum Hasrat Mohani," 178–81.

63. Goswami, *Producing India*, 124.

64. On Dwarkanath Tagore's brush with communal exile in the 1830s, see Kling, *Partner in Empire*, 181. On criticism of Mohandas Gandhi's overseas journeys, see Guha, *Gandhi before India*, 33. On the Maharaja of Jaipur's purification ceremonies, see Saksena, *England Yatra*, 23. On the "seavoyage controversy" among the Kayasth community, see Carroll, "Seavoyage Controversy," 169–99.

65. Sayyid Ahmad Khan faced significant disapprobation for his trip to England. Khan, *Musafiran* (1961), 11–12.

66. See Shervaniya, *Zad al-Sabil*, 20; Shibli Nu'mani, *Safarnama*, 16.

67. Working-class women faced less social stigma, or traveled simply because there was no other choice.

68. Goswami, *Producing India*, 121–26; Qaisari Begum, *Kitab-i Zindagi*, 454.

69. Mu'in, "Safar," 27.

70. Fatima Begum, *Hajj-i Baitullah*, 47. For another inventive solution, see Qaisari Begum, *Kitab-i Zindagi*, 459.

71. Robinson, "Technology," 232.

72. Megan Robb argues that printers used lithography to mimic both manuscript books and earlier, handwritten newsletters that preceded the popularization of print newspapers. Robb, *Print*, 92.

73. For a technical and British-focused history of lithography's proliferation in India, see Shaw, "Calcutta"; Shaw, "Lithography, Part I"; Shaw, "Lithography, Part II." For a more culturally focused exploration of its adoption for Urdu and Persian books, see Lanzillo, "Translating the Scribe," 281–300; Robb, *Print*, 90–125.

74. Stark, *Empire of Books*, 46.

75. Stark, *Empire of Books*, 65. A reduction in the price of paper also helped the industry grow. See Stark, *Empire of Books*, 67.

76. Stark, *Empire of Books*, 19.

77. Bailey, *Urdu*, 80–83; Ahmad, *Urdu Nasr*, 11–15; Dubrow, *Cosmopolitan Dreams*, 5.

78. Metcalf, *Islamic Revival*, 48; Robinson, "Technology," 240–41; Farooqi, "Changing Literary Patterns."

79. Cohn, *Colonialism and Knowledge*, 33–53.

80. King, *One Language*, 54–57.

81. Dodson, "Translating Science," 823. See also Pernau, "Delhi College," 15–19; Datla, *Secular Islam*, 56–81.

82. Early modern European travel writing on India was also translated, particularly accounts by François Bernier, Jean-Baptiste Tavernier, and Jean de Thévenot. Translations were also made for Osmania University's Urdu curriculum.

83. Shibli Nuʿmani, *Turkey*, 221.

84. Metcalf, "Pilgrimage," 171; Shackle and Majeed, *Hali's Musaddas*, 22. Thus, a travel author like Barlas Sahiba could write, "There was once a time when Muslims had an insatiable passion for travel, because of which Muslims can now be found in every corner of the world today. There is no telling why Muslims lost their daring." Barlas Sahiba, "Japan," 281.

85. It also finds backing from the equally erudite Barbara Metcalf, who locates the genre's proliferation squarely with the arrival of colonialism. Metcalf, "Pilgrimage," 171–72.

86. Shibli Nuʿmani, "Dibacha," 7.

87. Orsini, "Detective Novels," 435–36. For individual studies of shifts in fiction and the epic romance, see Dubrow, *Cosmopolitan Dreams*; Khan, *Broken Spell*.

88. Chatterjee, "Introduction," 10–11.

89. On the travelogue and imperialism, see Thompson, *Travel Writing*, 52–53.

90. Travelogue production was reduced during wartime; travel was not. As Radhika Singha shows, over a million Indians were drafted to serve in World War I alone. Singha, *Coolie's Great War*, 3. Anand Yang points to the longer history of Indian involvement in British conflicts abroad, and highlights the unique production, in Hindi, of a text by a soldier sent to fight against the Boxer Rebellion in China in 1900. Yang, "Introduction," 1–32.

91. Afzal Ahmed, personal communication, September 13, 2012.

92. Hashmi, *Tin Musafir*, 19–74.

93. On one of the earliest Telugu travel accounts, Enugula Veeraswamy's *Kasiyatra Caritramu*, see Mitchell, *Language*, 53–55.

94. Travel writing in Punjabi is voluminous and almost totally unstudied. I encountered this material regularly. Early Punjabi accounts appear in brief *kafi*s, but longer writing appeared much later. The first prose account was published in 1881, but the genre was most common in popular verse forms ideal for recitation. For a brief overview of travelogues in the closely related language of Siraiki, see Raza, "Saraʾiki Safarname." On the wide popularity of verse narratives in colonial Punjab, see Mir, *Language*, 38.

95. Hindi represents an exceptional case in that the first print account appeared as a colonial school textbook in 1841, but following this, further titles did not appear until the 1870s. In Hindi, the genre was pioneered by the "father

of Hindi literature," Bharatendu Harishchandra, before whom "there was practically no model" for personalized travel writing in Hindi (though, of course, it is important to acknowledge that Urdu—a language and script which Harishchandra himself knew fluently—itself offered several possible models and cannot be bracketed off). For a succinct introduction to his travel writing, see Dalmia, *Nationalization of Hindu Traditions*, 322–28. On his childhood mastery of Urdu, Dalmia, *Nationalization of Hindu Traditions*, 126. Gadhadhar Singh (1869–1920) and Swami Satyadev "Parivrajak" are also considered founding figures.

96. The Malayalam date excludes an eighteenth-century account of a voyage to Rome. Tommakkattanar, *Varthamanappusthakam*. Dates given here are based on a survey of current research for each language and may change as attention to the genre in South Asian vernaculars increases.

97. Gupta, "Histories," 837.

98. For instance, see Scott, "Translated Liberties," 3.

99. On this topic, see Orsini, "*Qasbas* and Cities," 68.

100. Dubrow, *Cosmopolitan Dreams*, 9–11.

101. Waheed, *Hidden Histories*, 33.

102. For example, Green, "Trans-Border Traffic," 483–87; Green, "Africa in Indian Ink," 176–82; Desai, *Commerce*, 77–80.

103. As Christina Oesterheld rightly points out, "although in Pakistan Urdu is the mother tongue of only a small part of the population, Urdu publications ... by far outnumber those in all other languages, including English." Oesterheld, "Mirza Athar Baig," 229.

104. The challenge of accurately capturing the diversity of Urdu speakers over time is reflected in these various scholarly attempts to find a word that refers to those who participate in this literary formation—particularly a word that is not shaped by religious or nationalist political identities. Bard, "Desolate Victory," xii; Waheed, *Hidden Histories*, 34.

105. Mir, *Language*, 6; Dubrow, *Cosmopolitan Dreams*, 2.

106. Rahman, "*Qaṣbas* as Place," 671–75. More broadly, see also Rahman, *Locale*.

107. Boyk, "Bound for Home," 495.

108. Robb, *Print*, 1–2.

109. Boyk, "Bound for Home," 495–96.

110. Jones, "Amroha," 873.

111. Williams, "Songs," 605.

112. MacCannell, *The Tourist*, 3.

113. Can, *Spiritual Subjects*, 85.

114. Gupta, "Histories," 842.

115. Singh, *Safarnama*, 42–45. On taking loans, see Singh, *Safarnama*, 119.

116. In a European context, Eric Leed argues that modern travelers, particularly in the age of "discovery," were marked by their "freely chosen opportunity to demonstrate an identity—as freedom, self-display, and self-discovery." Leed, *Mind*, 13.

117. Manzur 'Ali, *Safarnama*, 2.

118. Bayly, *Empire*, 314.

119. Zaidi, *Making a Muslim*, 16, 18.

120. Similarly, Yoruba travel writing was cultivated through experimentation in newspaper columns. Jones, *Crossroads*, 57–58.

121. For a discussion of the transition from precolonial news reports (*akhbarat*) to colonial newspapers, see Pernau, "The *Delhi Urdu Akhbar*," 2, 31–33.

122. Pernau, *Ashraf*, 105. The role of periodicals in creating publics has been closely studied. Work on print publics emerged in the context of Europe, as exemplified by the work of Jürgen Habermas. Scholarship on South Asia has complicated this work through a study of colonial Indian print publics. Early work focused on Bengal, but a new generation of scholars has built up a sophisticated understanding of print publics in Urdu and Hindi. For key moments in this debate, see Orsini, *The Hindi Public Sphere*; Boyk, "Collaborative Wit"; Joshi, *Fractured Modernity*; Perkins, "From the *Mehfil*"; Robb, *Print*; Ingram, *Revival*. For an overview of academic approaches to the concept of a public in South Asia, see Scott and Ingram, "Public."

123. For instance, in the 1910s, Abul Kalam Azad published his own regular travel updates in *Al-Hilal* newspaper, through which its 25,000 subscribers learned from his observations and movements. Pernau, "Virtuous Individual," 180.

124. Ghulam al-Hasnain, "Shazrat," 1–2.

125. One traveler between Pakistan and India wrote: "On my return [to Pakistan] I presented a serialized tale of my journey to my countrymen in my column '*Mushahadat o Ta'surrat*' ["Observations and impressions"] in *Jang* newspaper. Without any exaggeration, I received response letters [to each column] by the score." Niyazi, *Naqsh*, 9.

126. Dubrow, *Cosmopolitan Dreams*, 53–58.

127. In 1906, 'Abd al-Qadir, the founder of the Urdu magazine *Makhzan* and the English daily *Observer*, visited Istanbul. He mailed home letters for publication in the *Observer*. These were popular enough to be translated and republished "in the biggest Urdu newspapers." 'Abd al-Qadir, *Maqam-i Khilafat*, 3.

128. Khan, *Zad-i Safar*, 1–2.

129. Daryabadi, *Dha'i Hafte*, 5.

130. The lack of attention to the literary and social influence of periodicals is being ameliorated by scholars who are now bringing much-needed attention and methodological innovation to the study of Urdu literature. Pernau, *Ashraf*; Robb, *Print*; Dubrow, *Cosmopolitan Dreams*; Perkins, "Partitioning History."

131. Majchrowicz, "Malika Begum's Mehfil," 873–74.

132. Sayyid 'Ali Akhtar, "Somaliland se Khat," 258.

133. Robb, *Print*, 46.

134. Perkins, "South Asian Print," 144–51.

135. Sultan Jehan Begum, *Rauzat al-Rayahin*.

136. Singh, *Safarnama*, 20, 143.

137. Information in this paragraph is based on my archival research and personal database. For a discussion of visual representation in Urdu hajj travelogues, see Metcalf, "Pilgrimage," 181–88.

138. 'Alavi, *Angare*, 163. For a full English translation of the story, see Chughtai, "Dilli ki Sair," 107–10.

139. Francesca Orsini has shown that literature in early Indian print cultures was heavily shaped by aurality and often written for public recitation. The same is true of the travelogue. Orsini, *Print and Pleasure*, 106–97.

140. Novetzke, *Namdev*, 126.

141. For an excellent overview, see Novetzke, *Namdev*, 124–27.

142. Bayly, *Empire*, 35.

143. Nur Begum, *Mazahir*, 8, 11.

144. The inaccessibility of her account today may, ironically, indicate its popularity. I have located two copies of the third edition, which had a remarkably large print run of 1,000 copies. The poor quality of the printings may mean the other copies were read to oblivion.

145. Some speeches were later reprinted. Azad, *Sair-i Iran*. Others remain preserved in private archives, like a draft of an 1894 speech in Urdu on England by Amena Tyabji prepared for the "ladies' club" 'Aqd-i Suraiyya. Lambert-Hurley, *Elusive Lives*, 166. Another example is provided by unpublished notes from a speech by Iqbalunnisa Hussain on "My Experience at an English University," delivered in Mysore in 1935. Iqbalunnisa Hussain, "Iqbalunnisa Hussain," 335.

146. Tabor, "Local Apocalypse," 70.

The Book of Beneficence, the Exemplar of Beneficial Instruction, The Travelogue of Pure Delight, entitled, The Tours of al-Muhtasham

composed by the exalted and revered Nawab Muhtasham al-Daula, Ghaus Muhammad Khan Bahadur Shaukat Jang and published on the State Press of Gulshanabad, also known as Jaora [1852]

The next day we arrived in Mandsaur. Mandsaur is a large and ancient town in the region of Malwa, located on the banks of the Shivna River. It is surrounded by a strong wall. At its center is an old, dilapidated fort. The shops here are lively. There are Muslims and Hindus, and people from every community. Although the conditions of Mandsaur have not been passed down in any book of history, I learned the following from the oral traditions of its oldest inhabitants. This place was first settled by Raja Jasrat, the father of Ramchandar. It was called Jasratpuri. After a long existence it was suddenly destroyed.

The reason for its destruction is this. Once, a *faqir* named Dhundhari Dhamal started living nearby. He was a master of miracles and revelations. He would send his disciple into the city to beg so that they would have something to subsist on. However, the people of this city were so stingy that they would not give him even a pinch of flour or their scraps, much less deign to open their doors for him. With no other choice, the poor disciple ended up going to the forest to cut wood, which he then sold. He would then arrange with the oil woman for his master's repast. He never told his master about this.

One day, the dervish happened to glance at his disciple's head, which no longer had a single hair on it. "What happened to all your hair?" he asked. The disciple evaded his questions, but his master persisted. He finally recounted the entire story. That dervish, whose prayers were always answered, flew into a rage. He brought a curse to his justice-seeking tongue and the entire town was immediately annihilated, save the oil woman's home. For ages afterward, the town remained desolate.

May God protect us! Avarice is such a negative quality and one of the vilest of human characteristics, worthy only of scorn and disgust. The wise have written that greed in the pursuit of a little profit leads to even greater loss. In saving a paisa, a thousand rupees are lost. A greedy person is like a pool that is fed water from all sides, filling it up. If there is a path for the water to flow out as it comes in, that pool will remain strong and full. But if there is no outlet, the pressure will increase until cracks appear everywhere. The walls will be destroyed, and all the water will wash away. By the same token, the people of Mandsaur were so greedy for a pinch of flour that they ultimately lost everything, even their lives.

Couplet:
> If the parsimonious do not make use of their wealth
> The hand of God will snatch it all away from them[1]

There is a saying of Plato that "avarice is cursed and despised in this world. And it brings damnation in the next." And this is quite right. The miser has no friend; the generous man has no enemy.[2]

Notes

1. A verse from *Anvar-i Suhaili.*
2. Khan, *Sair*, 1014–17 (Figure 2.1)

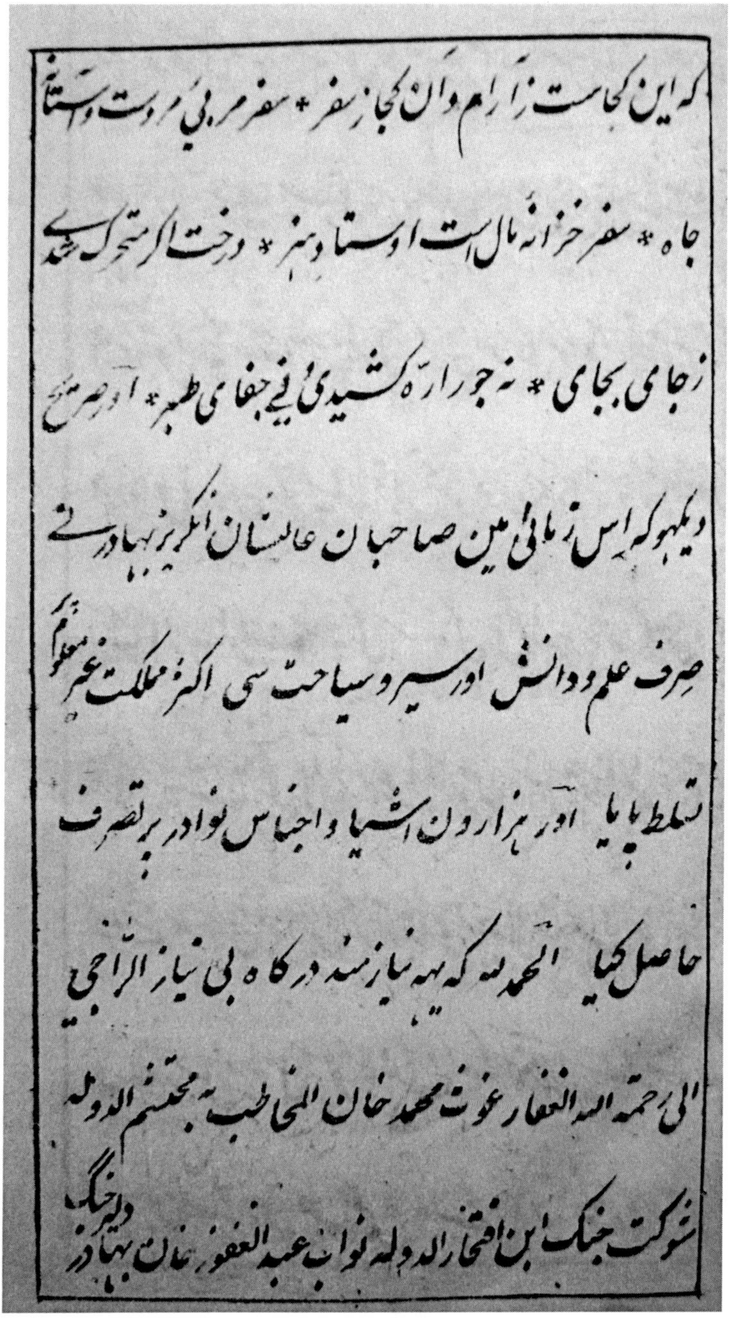
که این کجاست ز آرام و آن کجا ز سفر * سفر مربی مردست و آستانهٔ
جاه * سفر خزانهٔ مال است و استاد هنر * درخت اگر متحرک شدی
ز جای بجای * نه جور ارّه کشیدی نه جفای تبر * اور صریح
دیکھو که اس زمانی مین صاحبان عالیشان انگریز بہادر نے
صرف علم و دانش اور سیر و سیاحت سی اکثر مملکت غیر معلوم پر
تسلط پایا اور ہزارون اشیا و اجناس نوادر پر تصرف
حاصل کیا الحمد لله که یه نیازمند درگاه بی نیاز الراجی
الی رحمة الله الغفار غوث محمد خان الملقب به محتشم الدوله
شوکت جنگ ابن افتخار الدوله نواب عبد الغفور خان بہادر دلیر جنگ

Figure 2.1 Page from *Sair al-Muhtasham*

Source: Author.

2

A Future Fit for a King

Sair al-Muhtasham (The travels of al-Muhtasham, 1852) by Ghaus Muhammad Khan, Nawab of Jaora, was among the earliest Urdu travelogues and just the second full-length account written in Urdu by an Indian court. Its publication helped inaugurate a tradition of princely travel writing that would sweep the subcontinent. Precolonial rulers had shown little interest in the genre, but the politics of sovereignty in nineteenth-century India made the travelogue appealing to "princes" like Ghaus Muhammad. He and his fellow Indian rulers were tightly bound by treaties with the British that limited their ability to command their armies, control their finances, or regulate their foreign relations. These limitations forced them to find new ways to assert legitimacy and project their continued relevance. Travel literature let them present themselves as competent actors, and as legitimate, efficient, and just rulers with an irreplaceable role. Through it, they even aspired to augment their status in a colonial system designed to control, minimize, or terminate indigenous rule.

When Ghaus Muhammad wrote *Sair al-Muhtasham* in 1852, princely travel writing hardly existed, and no sitting Indian ruler had ever left the subcontinent. Nor had precolonial rulers claimed princely travel benefited the populace. By the late nineteenth century, though, India's indigenous rulers were constantly on the move, traveling and writing, they said, in the service of their subjects. They were such frequent travelers that they regularly encountered one another at hotels and on steamer decks. The Nawab of Basoda wrote at least nine book-length accounts in Urdu chronicling his many travels around the world, from China to Morocco.

Jagatjit Singh of Kapurthala published five accounts in multiple languages on Cuba, Java, and Brazil, among other destinations. The queens of Bhopal maintained a nearly century-long tradition of princely travel writing that began in 1863.

One of the wealthiest and most prolific traveling princes was Nawab Hamid 'Ali Khan (1875–1930) of Rampur. By the age of seventeen, Hamid 'Ali had seen and written about much of the world, including such distant places as Sitka in the Alaskan panhandle. Throughout that trip—part of a world tour (Figure 2.2)—he had had his scribe note down his observations for publication in a two-volume travelogue, *Masir-i Hamidi* (The voyages of Hamid, 1893). He did so not for pleasure, he said, but for patria:

> I do not publish this account to grow in fame or in name, nor because I believe that I have seen wonders that have never before been known.... Rather, my intention is to ... present before the reader those things which our own country may require, those matters which may be desirable for the improvement of its craft and industry or natural productions, and all that a traveler will encounter in these places. My countrymen may then adopt, with moderation, those things they find appropriate and useful and reject instantly those they consider foolish and useless, and, in short, take from my notes all that is beneficial.[1]

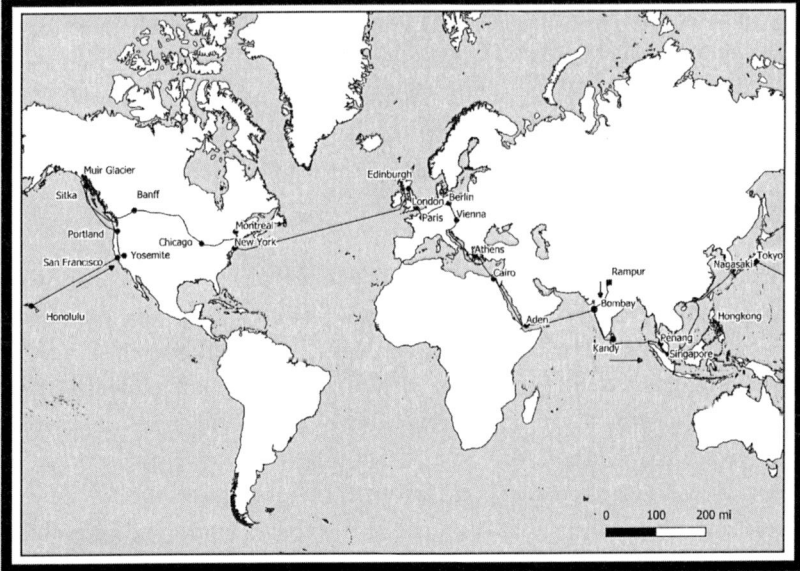

Figure 2.2   Hamid 'Ali's global tour

Source: Author.

In 1852, the princely travelogue was novel. By 1893, the notion of the teenager ruler of Rampur writing about Alaska for his subjects' benefit was pedestrian.[2]

Princely travel writing was pan-Indian and spanned the subcontinent's many written languages. The Jaipur court published in Hindi and Urdu. Hyderabad's *nizam*s preferred Persian. The Raja of Bhor typically published in Marathi but also wrote in English because, although travel accounts were "pouring in in the Marathi papers," English would also allow him to share his "experiences" with readers "in India and abroad."[3] Whatever the language, he believed, the point was to write; anyone who traveled but did not publish would have "entirely wasted their money."[4] Travel, he implied, was not an indulgence; it was an investment. But an investment in what? What were India's rulers supposed to gain from writing about travel?

The answer lies in the political structure of colonial India.[5] While the British controlled nearly the entire subcontinent, they ruled much of it indirectly. Forty percent of India's area was administered through "native princes" who had varying degrees of autonomy and who had to constantly guard against their own obsolescence. Before 1858, princely states were often dissolved and brought under direct rule on dubious charges of "mismanagement." This threat compelled Indian rulers to constantly reaffirm their legitimacy and efficiency. Even after Queen Victoria guaranteed the states' continuity in 1858, rulers themselves could still be deposed, and states could often only advance by carefully managing their relationship with the British. This was a game of optics. The British imagined the princes as inept and inferior. The princes, in turn, projected their own competence, legitimacy, and value through public displays. They established charitable works and patronized sites of pilgrimage. They adapted ideas of kingship to fit the new politics of the age.[6] They sought legitimation through political association, divine injunction, photographic portraiture, and patronage of the arts.[7] And, like Hamid 'Ali, they wrote travelogues.

Princely travel writing and the promotion of a princely global imagination was an act of legitimation and an exercise of power. To be a king, "one had to look like a king."[8] Rulers had to "adopt the trappings of kingship and carry out certain acts which augmented and emphasized" their royal nature.[9] In the colonial era, the performance of legitimacy meant touring beyond one's own borders and claiming a space on the global stage. This type of visibility was a modern take on an old concept. Precolonial rulers had long "adopted the practice of *darśan* [viewing] and regularly toured their domains, making themselves visible and accessible to their subjects."[10] In an era of expanding mobility, new forms of travel and visibility reconfigured legitimacy and the optics of sovereignty. Printed travel literature offered a sort of modern darshan, a global imagination in which the princes were legitimate rulers with a global relevance.

In this, Indian princes were participating in a global practice. Every Indian ruler knew that British royalty and nobility visited their possessions in India—indeed, the princes were summoned to pay obeisance at imperial *durbars*.[11] Accounts of the British royal family's movements appeared in many Indian languages.[12] Travelogues by other world leaders were also available in India.[13] The travel accounts of Iran's Qajar rulers circulated widely.[14] The travelogues of Naser al-Din Qajar (1831–96), published in the 1870s, for instance, were sold in both Persian and Urdu, even accompanied by published vocabularies to help readers understand unfamiliar Iranian usages.[15] Qajar accounts functioned similarly to the aspirational princely accounts studied in this chapter. In his travels, Naser al-Din sought to "recast monarchical power through the medium of the written narrative" and to "project a new public image of monarchy in Iran."[16]

Fascinatingly, the strategic travel writing practices of India's indigenous rulers finds a strong corollary in northern Nigeria. This region was remote from everyday Indian experience, but, critically, its political structure broadly mirrored that of the Indian princely states: in colonial Nigeria, Hausa-speaking rulers were officially independent but in fact controlled by the British colonial state, including by administrators who had cut their teeth in India. Perhaps it was not coincidental, then, that Nigeria's princely states themselves became prodigious travelers and producers of travel writing in the colonial period. There, "northern Nigerian Muslim aristocrats ... leveraged metropolitan travel to negotiate their roles in the empire, reinforce their positions as imperial cultural brokers, and translate and domesticate imperial modernity in a predominantly Muslim society." Faced with the diminution of their power, these rulers "strategically navigate[d] the imperial system for their own ends" through travel and the production of travel writing.[17]

These writings prompt a reconsideration of the political valences of royal travel in the British Empire. Twentieth-century scholars once characterized the princely states of colonial India as static and apolitical, with "no hope of achieving either fame or distinction." On this view, they were "confined to their own territories and [had] no prospects of advancement."[18] This view has now been turned on its head. Careful archival work and attentiveness to the subtle functioning of power in colonial India has shown how courts adapted and innovated to survive and prosper. This agility allowed them to continue to wield "significant power in local, regional, all-India, and imperial politics during the British colonial period."[19]

Questions of sovereignty and aspiration lay at the heart of this chapter's analytical orientation, which explores how two early princes used travel writing to promote their global imaginations in the first two major princely travel accounts written in Urdu: *Bagh-i Nau Bahar* (The garden of new spring, 1851), produced by the court of Maharaja Tukoji Holkar of Indore, and *Sair al-Muhtasham* (The tours of al-Muhtasham, 1852), by Nawab Ghaus Muhammad Khan of Jaora. A comparative reading reveals the relationship between legitimacy, literature, and travel at one of India's most turbulent moments, just before the uprising of 1857 and the restructuring of power in British India. Through their travelogues, Ghaus Muhammad and Holkar adapted a marginal form of writing—the travelogue—to their own needs and aesthetics. Ultimately, they laid the foundation for the emergence of the princely travel account, showing how the genre could help reimagine what it meant to be a subordinated Indian ruler in an imperial world.

Sovereignty, Rivalry, and the Princely Travelogue

Viewed in the light of contemporary expectations around Urdu and historical perceptions of the location and directionality of intellectual and cultural innovation in northern India, the facts behind the production of the two travel accounts studied in this chapter are remarkable. These were landmark publications, among the very first travelogues to be published in Urdu. With very few exceptions, they are preceded only by colonially sponsored accounts published expressly for use in government educational institutions (see Chapter 3). Yet they were not written or published in what is considered to be Urdu's heartlands in northern India; nor did they emerge from the celebrated intellectual centers of Delhi, Lucknow, or Hyderabad that are typically associated with Urdu literary culture. Instead, they came from relatively remote central India, where they were published by courts that were not even primarily associated with Urdu (Figure 2.3). Jaora was ruled by a Persian-speaking Afghan, while Indore was home to a Hindu Maratha successor state that emerged from the disintegration of the Peshwa. And yet, it is to this region, and to these courts, that we must trace the earliest beginnings of what would soon become one of Urdu's most popular genres and a favorite tool of soft power for India's rulers. This unexpected genealogy serves as a reminder of the vitality of Urdu outside of its traditional centers and attests to the rapid growth of its popularity even among those who did not speak it as a "first" language.

The story of these groundbreaking accounts begins in the years 1851–52, when the rulers of these two states crossed beyond their borders to undertake touristic tours of northern and central India. At seventeen years of age, the younger, but also the more powerful, was Maharaja Tukoji Holkar II (1835–86), king of Indore, a large state with a grand military past. The second was Nawab Ghaus Muhammad Khan (1825–65) of Jaora, a diminutive and relatively new state bordering Indore. Holkar was the wealthy scion of a Maratha Hindu political dynasty; Ghaus Muhammad, an ethnic Afghan, was only the second sovereign of Jaora.

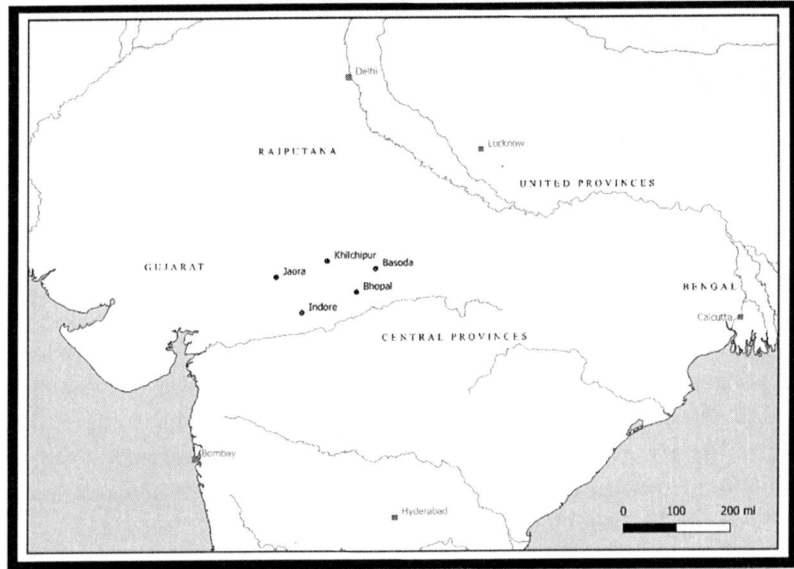

Figure 2.3   Location of central Indian states mentioned in Chapters 1 and 2
Source: Author.

Despite these differences, both their courts seized on the same revolutionary strategy to promote their position in colonial India: they bought printing presses, adopted Urdu prose, and took up travel and travel writing to promote their views of the world before the widest possible audience at a particularly precarious time.

In 1851, the British were rapidly expanding their control of South Asia. These gains came at the cost of indigenous rulers. Some saw their states dissolved entirely, while others managed to remain in place only with severe restrictions on their independence. These deprecations were justified in colonial discourse by dismissing the princes as prodigal despots who tyrannized their subjects. British administration, the line went, would bring peace, prosperity, and happiness. This discourse is on full view in the following description of Indore from an Urdu travelogue, also written in 1851, by an Indian, Aminchand, who worked in the colonial administration:

> Mister Hamilton is the resident [the official colonial representative in Indore and Jaora]. He excels in bringing administration to the city and is very accomplished. His demeanor wins immense praise from the city's leaders. Meanwhile, his foresight and unstinting effort have ensured that every state under his supervision is well-managed. The populace now sleeps in cradles of peace without fear of disturbance....

Previously, mismanagement in these regions was so rife that travelers wouldn't dare
to pass here.... [Hamilton] has organized the government to establish a college to
spread knowledge. They teach in English, Persian, and Marathi.[20] There is also a
hospital and a press, which prints the [bilingual Urdu and Marathi] *Malwa Akhbar*
[newspaper]. All of this is thanks to the resident.[21]

This passage demonstrates the battle of perceptions over legitimacy in
mid-century colonial India. Aminchand's travelogue was used by the colonial
school system as a geography textbook for students across northern India. Through
it, one of India's most renowned states was introduced to generations of students
as a failed kingdom returned to prosperity by British management. Travelogues
like Aminchand's portrayed an India where indigenous rulers were footnotes to
the grand narrative of colonial order. For their part, Indore and Jaora rejected this
projected irrelevance. Holkar's travelogue, *Bagh-i Nau Bahar*, reversed the roles
outlined above: yes, the British resident was intelligent and perspicacious, but the
true glory of Indore was Holkar himself.

India was a complex political space, though, and Indore was fighting many
battles at once. Colonial dominance did not mean the end of rivalries between
Indian princes. Jaora and Indore were party to a long-running dispute dating to
1818. In that year, Indore lost a devastating war with the British. At a pivotal
moment in battle, Ghaus Muhammad's father, 'Abd al-Ghaffur, seemingly
abandoned Indore's forces, resulting in the Holkars' defeat.[22] As a reward, the
British revoked control of Jaora from Indore and crowned 'Abd al-Ghaffur. This
enraged the Indore court, which argued incessantly for Jaora to be returned to
its subordinate position.[23] Holkar's travel account accordingly emphasized
Jaora's selfishness and perfidy and complained of Ghaus Muhammad's failure
to respect his superiority.[24] In his own account, Ghaus Muhammad rejected this.
He insisted that the people of Jaora were better off under his enlightened rule,
rather than under the rule of an outdated dynast.

Despite their formal split, Indore and Jaora were still bound together in
the colonial administrative structure, sharing a British resident, Robert Collie
North Hamilton (1802–87). Residents like Hamilton represented the colonial
government at Indian courts, where they wielded immense influence. Major state
decisions typically went through them, but they also exerted soft power, acting
as court advisors. Hamilton arrived in 1844. He personally supervised Holkar's
education, hiring an English-speaking *munshi*, Ummid Singh, to be his tutor.[25]
The capstone of Holkar's education was a tour of the subcontinent, an Indian
Grand Tour.[26] Hamilton was himself deeply interested in Indian history.[27]
He encouraged both Holkar and Ghaus Muhammad to travel, and probably
also to write travel accounts.[28] He may have even suggested they write in

Urdu rather than Persian: Urdu was the preferred language of administration in the colonial state, while Persian was still dominant in the princely states. However, he probably did not participate in their actual production. The accounts draw on Indian literary practices and aesthetics and include critiques of the British and their effect on India's social structure. Also indicative of their freedom is their difference: Each court took a completely unique approach to the genre. Their divergent paths underline one of this book's arguments, namely, that under the broad rubric of "travel writing," authors participated in the literary forms most conducive to their global imaginations and social aspirations. The following two sections consider each travelogue in turn.

Bagh-i Nau Bahar (The Garden of new Spring)

In late December 1850, Maharaja Tukoji Holkar set off on a clandestine tour of northern India. He and his party ultimately traveled as far as Haridwar, some 800 miles away. This was no quick jaunt in an era before train travel. Indian rulers typically traveled with pomp, but Holkar did not: his journey had been approved by the resident on the condition that he travel incognito. He and his friends were thus compelled to conceal their identities and wear costumes.

> On Wednesday, the nineteenth of December 1850, at an auspicious moment, when there was still darkness in the sky, [the maharaja's companions] joyfully opened their tent flaps and snuck out of the [military] camp. Making their way to Munshi Ummid Singh's tent, the party gathered to wait for the maharaja. When he arrived, they removed the royal garments from his blessed body and replaced them with a rider's uniform. They tried to conceal his face, but it was like the moon, the light of which can never be obscured. When the group set off the atmosphere was heavy with sorrow. All were despondent, their emotions uncontrollable. Pearls of tears began to well and flow from their oyster-like eyes. They were leaving their homeland. They were restless, uneasy. Their speech became halting; truly, they were unable to speak at all. Their teardrops were tumbler-pigeons that took flight only to fall back onto their own breasts. It took two hands to steady their trembling hearts. The pen quivers to write of their dreadful state. Their fists trembled. The inkwell of their hearts blackened. They sobbed freely. They were all travelers now, but they were sad to leave their homeland.

Their sorrow, though, quickly turned to mirth:

> For a time, they were afflicted by the sorrow caused by travel. But then, they … began to laugh and play. They changed their clothes and selected new aliases. One became a cavalry officer. Another became captain of the infantry.

One became the master, another his servant. Only Munshi Ummid Singh was immune; he remained a munshi. Everyone else devised their own story, but all were to be close friends through thick and thin [*nadim-i ranj o rahat ke sahim*].[29]

They retained these false identities until they returned to Indore. Once home, Holkar took his throne, and the court immediately set to publishing a travel narrative. Authored by Munshi Sayyid Karim 'Ali Rathi, the text was based on Munshi Ummid Singh's Persian journal and conversations with Holkar himself. At five hundred pages, composing the text was a major project, but Karim 'Ali had to work quickly: the book began to be printed even while he was still writing it.[30] Copies were sent to British officials and to other princely states, including to Ghaus Muhammad in Jaora.[31]

In his introduction, Karim 'Ali offered an extended justification for princely travel. He had to convince a British readership skeptical of princes, whom they often considered profligate pleasure-seekers, but also Indian rulers who might be unimpressed to see Holkar endlessly riding through the wilderness with just a few attendants to uncertain ends.

> Travel is the key to wisdom, a source of greater intelligence. Travel is a touchstone that separates humanity's worthless coinage from pure gold. Travel bestows experience. It matures the naïf. Observing this colorful world swings open the gates of learning. It offers salvation from depravity and bad breeding. It makes one good-natured and veracious. [In the Qur'an] God commands *sairu fi al-arz* (travel the world). Look, and look carefully! Travel is written into the Qur'an. When commoners travel, they profit individually. No other gains. [But] when the upper classes travel, all of society benefits. What benefits? The travels of one elite benefit commoners seven times over. When a nobleman resolves to travel it is a great day for society. Humanity's destiny is awoken.... Justice dawns, tyranny subsides.[32]

He went on to argue that travelers gain bravery and skill. They converse with the wise, and thus improve their domains. "Travel teaches you how to serve your subjects." Those who do not travel have no experience. They are cruel and clueless:

> Unfortunately, noblemen are unfamiliar with their own cities. They consider travel a useless absurdity. If you mention it, or ask them to see the world's colors, to leave their domain, they reply, "Come to your senses! What an idea!" This is a shame. If the kings of the past never left home, how could they acquire territory? What raja or padishah attained fame without travel? ... Ramchandra and Lakshman were of impeccable lineage, and they traveled through every valley and city from Ayodhya to Lanka. Raja Yudishthara, Lord of the Dharma, was a great king. There is not a place on Earth he did not visit. Krishna traveled so much![33]

Karim 'Ali countered the prevailing notion that kings should only travel with armies and grand retinues. Citing "historians," he argued that kings had always traveled, and that many, from Vikramaditya to Alexander the Great, traveled alone. He challenged the skeptical to "read a book" if they did not believe him.[34]

At the same time, Karim 'Ali acknowledged that travel was difficult, and that "very few have attained the rank [of traveler]."[35] Among those who had was Tukoji Holkar, who had "traveled in foreign lands, seen the ways of every kind of ruler, and adopted what he found beneficial."[36] In Karim 'Ali's telling, Holkar had been personally inspired to travel. He felt that the world was filled with wonderful, instructive sights and people from whom he could learn. He confided his wanderlust to Munshi Ummid Singh, who relayed the request to Hamilton, who sent to the imperial capital of Calcutta for formal permission. Holkar's journey was approved, but the idea was unpopular with Holkar's guardians in Indore. Thus, the trip was organized without their consent. Ummid Singh arranged to smuggle the prince out of a military camp unnoticed, as described above. On the road, the group was always at risk of detection as they visited, in disguise, Haridwar, Agra, Delhi, Jaipur, Panipat, and a host of central Indian cities (see Figure 2.4).[37] Once the tour was completed, Holkar changed back into his royal attire, mounted

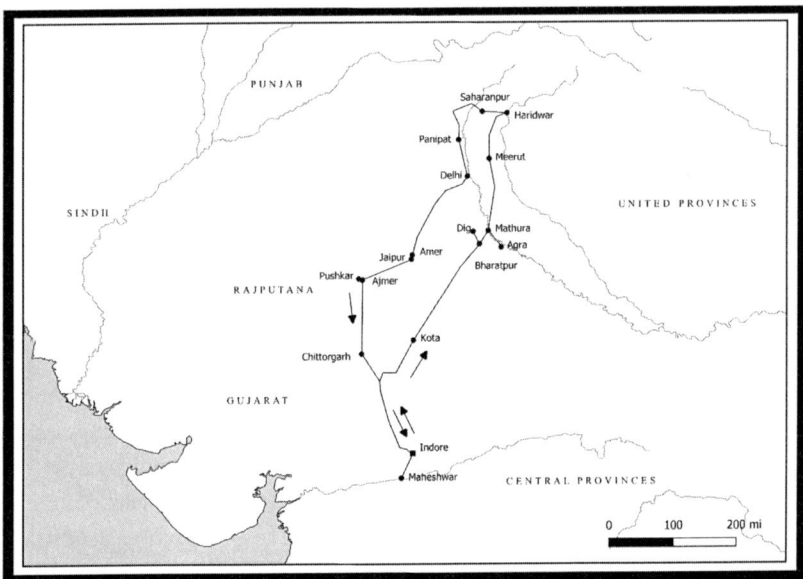

Figure 2.4   Maharaja Tukoji Holkar's tour

Source: Author.

an elephant, and triumphantly re-entered his kingdom, assuming full control from his regent shortly thereafter. Meanwhile, his courtiers produced an official account of the journey, showing a young but energetic and precocious ruler whose claims to rule over central India were legitimate. The book implicitly set him against local rulers like Ghaus Muhammad in Jaora. The remainder of this section explores how Holkar's travelogue helped him project this imagination.

Genre and legimacy

When *Bagh* arrived at the British Library, it was catalogued as a travelogue. But in the text itself its author had called the book a history (*tarikh*). This distinction offers a path to understand how *Bagh* functioned within the political world of mid-century colonial India. Genre, after all, "tells us about the worldview of the time in which it was instituted."[38] The travelogue was a marginal genre in the Indo-Persian world, but the tarikh was a well-established court literature, and the production of histories was a state obligation. Blain Auer and Stephen Dale both argue that in precolonial India the tarikh was a means of setting the record and a "symbol of authority," "part and parcel of empire-building."[39] Karim 'Ali positioned his work among India's best-known histories, claiming that his book was "a new type of history." He offered specific points of comparison, writing, "The author of this book compared it to the *Akbarnama* and *Jahangir-* and *Shahjahan-nama*s, *'Ibratnama, Siyar al-Muta'akhirin, Asar al-Sanadid, Rajavali, Tughluqnama, Rauzat al-Safa*, etc., and did not find a hair's-breadth of difference between them."[40] The books listed here are not travel accounts. Except *Asar al-Sanadid* (1847), they are famous histories produced by India's greatest rulers. Karim 'Ali added *Bagh* to the list, suggesting "readers will call this *Tukoji's History*, or perhaps *Tukoji's Spring Garden*."[41] The book's final line echoes this claim, referring to the text as a "tarikh-i nau," or "a new history."

While writing about travel was certainly new, calling his book a "new kind of history" offered continuity with the long tradition of court histories. This continuity was further underlined in several ways. *Bagh*'s physical appearance mimicked a manuscript style, lacking the line breaks, periods, or headings typical of colonial productions. Its orthography was distant from emerging standards of Urdu spelling.[42] This is not because these developments had not reached Indore. Karim 'Ali and Ummid Singh were well versed in the latest literature coming out of colonial India. Rather, this strategic classicism signaled a relationship with the past.

And yet, this was no typical history. Karim ʿAli emphasized that his was a new take on an old genre. Its "newness" manifested in several ways, including through his use of the printing press, the Urdu language, and also in that he wrote about travel. Colonial modernity was also slyly embedded in the book's title, which references Mir Amman's *Bagh o Bahar*, a famous work of Urdu literature written at Fort William College in Calcutta in 1801. *Bagh o Bahar*, a tale of four wandering dervishes that marked the arrival of "modern" Urdu prose, contains the year of its publication within its title. Every letter in Urdu has a numerical value, and *Bagh o Bahar* (باغ و بہار) totals 1217, the *hijri* year corresponding to 1801 CE. *Bagh-i Nau Bahar* (باغ نو بہار) was published precisely fifty years later. The titles are accordingly distinguished by a single letter, ن, whose value is fifty. The title thus refers to a work of Urdu literature from colonial Calcutta. Another nod to colonial modernity is the citation of two early and acclaimed Indian travelogues to England by Abu Talib Khan and Yusuf Kambalposh, both discussed in Chapter 3.[43]

Francesca Orsini points out that "while we tend to think of late-Mughal Delhi and Nawabi Lucknow as 'premodern' and colonial Calcutta as 'modern,'" in fact "they were part of a coeval, two-way traffic."[44] *Bagh-i Nau Bahar*, written when the nawabs still ruled Lucknow, exemplifies this coeval-ness and even invokes it directly. In gesturing toward both the Mughal tarikh and the colonial travelogue, it clearly addressed two sets of readers, those who preferred Persian literature and those who were conversant in British norms. For the former, it offered continuity with a respected and recognizable genre. For the latter, it conjured an inquisitive and enlightened raja who traveled for self-improvement and participated in a celebrated colonial genre. *Bagh* thus brought both traditions together.

Karim ʿAli played with more genres than just the tarikh and the *safarnama*. He also drew particularly on the *dastan* (epic romance), a genre that Pasha Khan argues was itself typically read as a form of history writing.[45] Like a good romance, *Bagh* has multiple narrators, dramatic scenes, dialogue, and foreshadowing. Consider the use of expressive storytelling, wordplay, and the generic flexibility in the passage earlier recounting Holkar's departure. The lines are dramatic and playful, clearly inspired by departure scenes of the romance genre's questing hero. This section of the account even quotes directly from Urdu's most famous verse romance, Mir Hasan's *Sihr al-Bayan* (An enchanting narrative, 1785).

The dastan structure gives rise to a plotline that will run throughout the text. If the maharaja is detected, he will fail in his quest. Time and again, the party must devise a ruse to escape detection. These moments, which occur frequently, bring levity and suspense to the chronicle, echoing the cadence of dastan. This play is enhanced by a revolving cast of characters: courtesans sing *ghazals*, bawdy entertainers tell explicit anecdotes, comic negotiations with traders give voice to the bazaar, and visits to local villages introduce wary farmers and alms-seeking brahmins. Incidents stack on top of one another, stories within stories. Passages from the *Ramayana* illustrate Holkar's emotional state. Quotations from medieval historians bring occasional gravity to the text (Firishta, Tabataba'i, Abu'l-Fazl, 'Inayat Khan, Barani). The text is filled with poetry, sometimes in Persian (Sa'di, Va'iz, Ghani Kashmiri, Hafiz, Brahman), sometimes in Urdu (Mir, Atish, Nasikh, Sauda).[46] Citations and retellings envelop one another in layers.

All these voices inflect the narrative arc of a young prince who overcomes incredible odds to reach his objective (namely, to see and learn from the world) before coming home to take the throne. This epic framing is strategic in four ways. First, the narrative compels the reader to root for Holkar's success. The prince becomes an underdog, traveling in weather-beaten clothes on a quest to know the world.[47] This framing is not unique to India; travel writing around the world often draws on the quest romance.[48] Second, the framing masks the jarring contradiction of a powerful ruler traveling in secret. Social expectations demanded Holkar travel with a large retinue, but colonial authority acted as a constraint. The narrative turns this contradiction on its head, casting Holkar as the archetypal king-in-the-bazaar. Rather than focusing directly on questions of status and protocol (as did neighboring ruler Sikandar Begum of Bhopal in her travelogue a decade later), the text calls on readers to enjoy this clandestine quest with suspenseful scenes reminiscent of the *Thousand and One Nights* or *Jodhaa Akbar*.[49]

Third, the epic form creates space for shrouded dissent. British power made it difficult to openly propose alternative political futures. Even still, Karim 'Ali wove alternative political imaginaries into his narrative in creative and disarmingly humorous ways. At one juncture, he related a conversation between Holkar and a headman in Mewar where alternative political possibilities were put in the mouth of a bumbling old man:

> Perhaps thinking that Maharaja sahib might be among this party, he asked "Who are you, where are you going and why have you come here? ... Maharaja Holkar sahib has disappeared somewhere; do you know anything about his whereabouts?"
>
> Munshi Ummid Singh answered, "Is this Holkar of yours some sort of raja? Where does he live? What a pity, we have no idea who he is. You're the only one who seems to know anything about this man. What will we get from hearing such a story?"

This irreverence incensed the man:

> "Holkar's state is glorious! It is located in Indore. I once saw Indore myself, twenty years ago. It was splendorous. It is a large state. It wants for nothing. It has thousands

of sword-wielding, brave soldiers ... constantly standing guard. If this raja and the Rana of Udaipur were to band together and make peace with one another, then they would become the rulers of all of India, and who could stop them then...! I've been so sad since I heard [this news] that I have stopped eating entirely: some munshi working for the English fed him a pill, a bitter pill that makes you crazy, makes you lose your senses. Well, the raja lost his senses and started to do every little thing the munshi commanded him to! Next thing you know, he's bundled the raja into a palanquin and carried him off to Calcutta with ten of his henchmen."[50]

The comical scene whispers an ambitious alternative political topography.

Finally, epic emplotments enable a symbolic territorial reconquest.[51] With the princes bound by colonial treaties, literal conquest was impossible, but literary conquest was still on the table. *Bagh* turns Holkar's journey into a narrative *digvijaya*, a "conquest in every direction." At the beginning of the account, Holkar departed with his army in full regalia, astride an elephant (before sneaking away from the camp), and that is also how he returned. Holkar's symbolic military campaign took him through the very regions Indore had once controlled (Jaora included). As he traveled, the account reflected on Indore's earlier hegemony over the country. On his return, Holkar terminated his journey at the shrine of Jaswant Rao, a celebrated Indore military leader, surrounded by jubilant masses, as though he had come back a conqueror.[52] He was victorious, just as Ummid Singh had predicted at the start of their trip: "Travel is hell, but with you [Holkar] by our side, it is the means to victory."[53]

This symbolic conquest relied on reading Indore's past against its present. Passages narrating this history appear constantly and extend for as long as ten pages at a time, almost always returning to the subject of Indore's hegemony. Ultimately, *Bagh* contains a full history of Indore told in short passages throughout the book, ordered not chronologically but geographically. The reader learns of Indore's historical expansion as Holkar advances. As Holkar moves through British-controlled India, *Bagh* finds in the landscape evidence of the enduring glory of his state, not its contemporary political subjugation. And thus, it stakes a claim for Indore's enduring legitimacy, with Holkar at its center. *Bagh* does not have a geographical telos; readers do not know where Holkar is going, leaving them with little to anticipate. They are forced instead to focus on his person and his dynastic history. The effect is to create a chronotope in which there is no destination but home, where Holkar returns with a ceremony at Jaswant Rao's shrine that symbolized his readiness to continue the Holkar dynasty. Thus, *Bagh* opens with an invocation of Holkar's legacy from the Puranas, sees him traverse the physical geography of his state's expansion, and closes with a symbolic ceremony at the site of his martial ancestor. He had fulfilled his dynastic destiny.[54]

A Rival Responds: Jaora's *Sair al-Muhtasham* (The tours of al-Muhtasham)

Seven months after Holkar returned to Indore, his neighbor and rival, Ghaus Muhammad Khan, Nawab of Jaora, traveled to Agra, Kanpur, Lucknow, and Qannauj before returning home via Delhi, Alwar, Jaipur, and Tonk (Figures 2.5 and 2.6). He was twenty-nine years old.[55] On his return he converted his travel journal into a travelogue of over 1,150 pages titled *Kitab-i Faizyab Ma'ab, Nuskha-i Afadat-Intisab, Safarnama-i Farhat-i Tamam, Musamma bi Sair al-Muhtasham* (The book of beneficence, the exemplar of beneficial instruction, the travelogue of pure delight, entitled, The tours of al-Muhtasham).[56] It was published on his state press in 1852.[57] The travelogue focused almost exclusively on cities and towns, often compressing three days' of travel into three lines of text. Most of the account was dedicated to contemporary descriptions of just three cities: Agra (116 pages), Delhi (325 pages), and Lucknow (154 pages). Ghaus Muhammad had by this time already read *Bagh*, but he charted his own course.[58] *Sair* differed from *Bagh* in its genre associations, its style of Urdu, and above all in its rejection of dynastic rule. Ghaus Muhammad's travelogue instead emphasized his superiority as a self-made ruler.

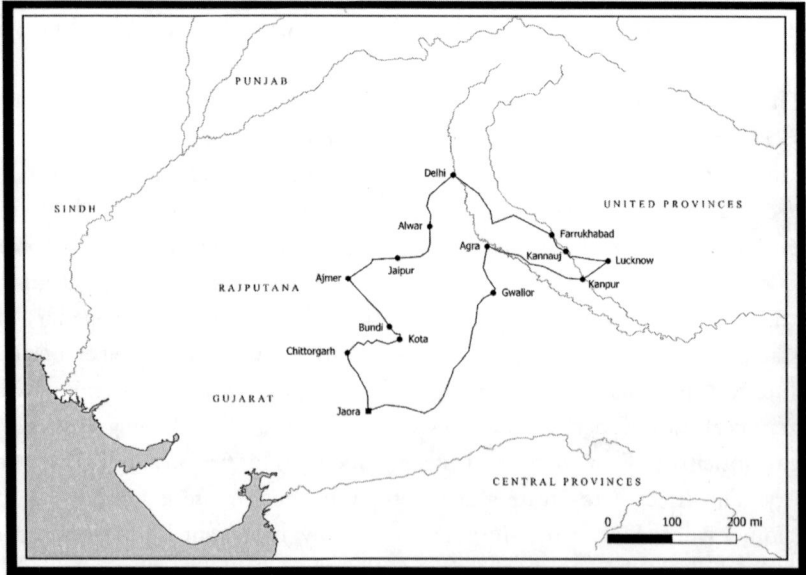

Figure 2.5   Ghaus Muhammad Khan's tour

Source: Author.

Figure 2.6 Ghaus Muhammad Khan on tour

Source: Author.

Ghaus Muhammad wrote in the first person and only rarely mentioned his servants or companions. Heteroglossia is minimal. Interlocutors are paraphrased, rather than directly quoted, as when Ghaus Muhammad had an earnest chat with an American missionary about life in the United States.[59] The language of the account is Urdu, but so heavily influenced by Persian that a knowledge of Persian is practically a prerequisite for reading it. Verse quotations, typically in Persian, abound. His location is given at the head of every page, making for easy perusal and offering a more "modern" layout than *Bagh*. The book also includes dozens of line drawings.

Like *Bagh*, *Sair* underlined its author's legitimacy as an Indian ruler. It made the case for his rule to be perpetuated and bolstered by the British (who themselves had created Jaora state). If *Bagh* asserted Holkar's legitimacy based on his dynastic past, Ghaus Muhammad instead asserted his right to rule by drawing on long-standing Islamic and Persianate notions of kingship and justice. In classical Persian moral texts,

> the most important question is not how to rule, but who to become in order to rule well. It is only within the framework of a polity and through sociability that the civilizing process and the cultivation of virtues can take place—in solitude and without the constant interaction with others, an individual cannot develop his ethical potential and his humanity.[60]

Ghaus Muhammad demonstrated that he was an ideal ruler through the embodiment of these classical ideals. At the same time, he put his own mark on them by integrating them with an emphasis on travel as a marker of civilization and accomplishment.

In his introduction, Ghaus Muhmmad asserted the Islamic idea that humans are superior beings (*ashraf al-makhluqat*) charged with maintaining order in the world and dividing it into kingdoms. But not all men may rule: only the wise deserve this role. Wisdom must be consciously cultivated by legitimate rulers, who must acquire a "knowledge of philosophy and religion and study the history of our predecessors." They should also "tour and travel and engage the conversation of all who possesses wisdom and insight."[61] Finally, wisdom is cultivated through the contemplation of God's wonders. "Gaining experience of every person, good and bad, and of comfort and pain, gives man maturity and makes him capable." To give finality to these ideas, he cited the thirteenth-century poet Sa'di: "Earthly man attains greatness through travel/Just as the clay goblet is fashioned by constant rotation."[62]

This discourse on just rule ultimately frames his travel account. Ghaus Muhammad shows himself as a legitimate ruler whose journey is a quest for knowledge:

"Having completed my mandatory studies, including *fiqh* and hadith, and after years of study of mathematics, philosophy, and books of advice and morals, and books on the lives of great figures of the past, [I] had long desired to travel. I thought about it night and day."[63] This desire distinguished him from his princely peers, most of whom, he argued, did not travel: "Man cannot realize his value if he remains sedentary, nor will he acquire divine knowledge, nor ... become aware of the wonders of God's creation."[64] Immobile individuals—a reference to other Indian rulers—are like stagnant water or veiled women. They are unlike the English: "Look clearly, in this era, the ... English have conquered unknown realms and mastered countless wondrous things through their application of knowledge, their wisdom, and their travels."[65] Ghaus Muhammad followed their legitimating model.

Bagh emphasized Holkar's dynastic history, while *Sair*, in turn, chided rulers who clung to their lineage. Ghaus Muhammad cited the caliph 'Ali's supposed saying that "nobility lies not in lineage or provenance, but in superior wisdom and social virtue."[66] Ghaus Muhammad did not mention his lineage, but instead used his travelogue to cultivate the image of a responsible sovereign. On every page, he demonstrated his commitment to studying the world and learning to be a better ruler. Thus, for instance, in the passage that introduced this chapter, Ghaus Muhammad saw in the history of Mandsaur an example of the impoverishing impact of avarice. Mandsaur's sad state taught him not to fall prey to these negative qualities.

Sair's genre associations underline this emphasis on self-improvement, just rule, and morality. *Sair*'s travel narrative is shaped around three genres: advice literature (*nasihatnama*), the account of wonders (*'aja'ib*), and the *shahr-ashob*, a systematic description of a city. Advice literature and moral tales were mainstays of classical Persian literature. The account of wonders had roots reaching back to the tenth century. The shahr-ashob genre, meanwhile, was a primarily aesthetic inclusion that highlighted poetic dexterity. Ghaus Muhammad was an innate urbanite who enjoyed wordplay, poetry, music, and other refined pleasures. Collectively, these three genres allowed Ghaus Muhammad to display his status as a learned ruler, emphasize his legitimacy, and counter Indore's claims on his territory. Each is considered in turn below.

Of the three, advice literature dominates. Advice literature typically conveyed its lessons through short stories called *hikayats*.[67] Ghaus Muhammad's travel hikayats pepper the narrative liberally. They pause the action to relate a situation or experience and reflect on its lessons. Advice sections—often explicitly marked with the heading "advice"—begin by describing a situation or experience. The text then explicates its moral lesson and summarizes it in a single pithy verse or statement (*qaul*). These hikayats draw an implicit distinction between Ghaus Muhammad and other Indian nobles and rulers who were his foils. In the excerpt at the beginning of this chapter, he lamented the avarice of the wealthy. In other sections he bemoaned Indian rulers' unwillingness to learn or travel. He called them "corner-sitters" and suggested they frittered their time in useless pursuits.[68] However, he was probably not just taking other rulers and nobles down a peg. Rather, his travelogue was truly a book of advice for the Indian elite. Ghaus Muhammad's global imagination saw princes and nobles as an important part of Indian political and social life, and his travelogue held out an aspirational path to retaining and reinvigorating their role. He repeatedly reminded his readers that the British attained their dominant position through travel; to return to prosperity, Indian nobles would have to travel as well.[69]

Consider his hikayat on a small town called Sunahra, near Gwalior. This was once a prosperous town filled with nobles. "Now, it is a wasteland."

[Seeing this place,] one learns the reality of prosperity and destruction and turns toward the acquisition of godly knowledge. I learned that the destruction and ruined state of the place was occasioned by the oppression and excess of its rulers and administrators and the negligence and carelessness of its nobles. *Observation*:

> The world sees destruction from injustice
> >   Like the joyful garden from the autumn wind;
> Do not allow tyranny in any situation
> >   Lest the sun set on your country.[70]

The destitute condition of the nobles of Sunahra was a warning and a lesson:

Statement: In reality, worldly goods are temporary and relying on them is foolish. Man should not be attached to or proud of his wealth or the high station of his ancestors. He should acquire knowledge and skills, for these are the wealth which never depreciates. The wise find respect everywhere. If for some reason you should no longer have worldly wealth, even then you will not be looked down upon by the eyes of creation.

Hemistich: Acquire greatness so that you may become dear to the world.[71]

Here Ghaus Muhammad demonstrated how he learned to be a moral person and thus a prosperous noble and successful, legitimate ruler by traveling and observing the failings of others. He shared those lessons with readers to instruct them, but also to distinguish himself. Reproducing the advice genre within his travelogue made this possible.

He likewise invoked the account of wonders ('aja'ib), which were similarly tied to moral instruction and mastery. Wonder accounts, which Sunil Sharma calls "catalogue[s] of wonders or curiosities," once "made up an entire sector of knowledge and participated in both edifying literature and literature for entertainment."[72] Wonders were an important demonstration of kingship and sovereignty and signs of God's universal order.[73] The role of wonders was so central to travel writing during this era that "Muslims of the Middle Ages ... considered that such a work had missed its target if it did not include some 'aja'ib."[74] Ghaus Muhammad made a clear reference to the genre, calling his book a "collection of wonders."[75] He suggested that wonders were central to a moral education: "Neither does the [stationary man] value his self, nor does he obtain a knowledge of God, nor does he learn the reality of things, and nor does he become aware of God's wonders."[76] Ghaus Muhammad collected together many wonders in his account, including descriptions of superhuman Sufi feats and beautiful artifacts and buildings. He marveled at the variety of God's creation and reflected on its lessons, as in this passage:

I saw a Hindu perfumer who had a strange form and was a sight to behold. On seeing him, one is both frightened and warned [as by a sign]. He proved the existence of the fashioning of men by the Sculptor of Creation. His odd shape and strange appearance had been with him since birth. *Statement*: The wise say that men's sperm contains the essence of all the limbs, and if any limb has in it a bad substance or a defect or an imbalance then it will certainly have an effect such that it will be manifest in the shape of the body from birth, but God knows best.... I made a picture of that person for those interested in the wonders of creation.[77]

The book is filled with line drawings of wonders like these, a rarity at the time.[78] Wondrous objects and creatures had long been collected by princes to demonstrate their power and reach.[79] Ghaus Muhammad's account did something similar, showing his own influence and authority through his eyewitness descriptions and pictures. He also responded to them emotionally, sharing his own feelings, in this case fright and astonishment. This demonstrated his morality, and his ability to learn from God's wonders.[80]

Finally, there was the shahr-ashob genre, which historically often consisted of a poetic catalogue of a city's beautiful boys, and later, its craftsmen and women, though it could also become a lament for the destruction of a city.[81] Ghaus Muhammad's shahr-ashobs are written in praise of three cities, Lucknow, Agra, and Delhi (tragically, two of these cities would be virtually destroyed a few years later as a result of the uprising of 1857, after which period they would become the subject of lamenting shahr-ashobs).[82] Ghaus Muhammad's shahr-ashobs are not in verse but in semi-rhymed prose (*saj'*), listing and praising members of virtually every profession in the city, from vegetable sellers to candlemakers to cobblers to poets. There was little specificity in this praise. Rather than, say, name individual poets in Lucknow (as literary scholars might have hoped), he instead spoke to the city's poetic prowess in general terms. This section also allowed him to compose Persian poetry and showcase his literary abilities and his eye for aesthetic beauty.[83]

Collectively, Ghaus Muhammad Khan's use of advice literature, wonders, and the shahr-ashob within the framework of his travelogue allowed him to draw on classical Persian literary norms to present his own vision of the future and to offer a justification for his legitimacy as the ruler of Jaora. Persian had long been a language of prestige, of eloquence, and, especially, a moral language unmarked by ethnic or religious affiliation. All of this made it integral to the symbolic structures of legitimacy and authority in India's Islamicate courts. Ghaus Muhammad relied on that symbolic prestige, but by transporting it into Urdu. His literary style is overwhelmingly Persianized. This is easily seen in the following sentence which describes his administrative preparations for departure from Jaora (**non**-Perso-Arabic words have been bolded below):

> Avval ba-nazar-i ri'ayyat-i khair khala'iq **aur** ba-khayal hifazat o hirasat-i ra'iyat o intizam o ahtimam-i ta'luqat **aur** bandobast-i mahalat **ke**, kar-guzaran-i haqiqat agah **aur** muntaziman-i havakhvah **aur** 'amilan-i kifayat shi'ar **aur** mustahafazan-i tahavvur-asar **ko** muqarrar **aur** muvakkad **kiya** wa ahl-i saif o sahib-i qalam ko **apne apne** 'uhde **aur** mansab **par** khabardar o musta'ad **kiya**.[84]

This ponderous style, full of recondite vocabulary, *izafa* possessives and *waw-i 'atifa* compounds, is not the result of a difficult transition between two languages, but rather a conscious effort to carry into Urdu the ethos and symbolic valence of Persian. He claims that in his book, "the form of Persian has been adorned with the ornaments of Urdu and become the bride of the Indian [*Hindi*] language, which has itself been made fresh through the use of copious Persian vocabulary."[85] In other words: this is Persian, but in Urdu. This style is palpably different from *Bagh*, which, with its short sentences and simple vocabulary, is reminiscent of Mir Amman's *Bagh o Bahar*, as in this passage describing the benefits of elite travel:

> 'Sairu fi al-arz' khuda ne farmaya hai. Ba-chashm-i ghaur to dekho! Sair karna Qur'an meñ aya hai. 'Amm ka safar zat-i vahid ko behtar, ek ne naf' paya. Dusroñ ko kya fai'da hu'a? Kisi khas ne safar kiya, zamane ka bhala hu'a.[86]

Unlike Ghaus Muhammad's style, this language is generally familiar and easy to understand even for Urdu speakers today. Thus, it is not only the form of the travelogue, but also the style of the language itself that reflects the travelogue's aspiration and imagination.

For over a thousand pages, Ghaus Muhammad wrote about his travels through India in this heavily Persianized style, drawing on Persian literary genres, to show himself deserving of a place in the new colonial order in the face of an ongoing campaign by Indore to have his state dissolved. He wrote his account in Urdu, the new language of British administration (though many colonial officials continued to support and appreciate Persian), and had it published on his state press for wide distribution for both British and Indian readers. Like Holkar's text, he spoke to two possible audiences to reach both those who were at home in a Persian ecumene and those who preferred British or European thought. Ghaus Muhammad thus used traditional Persian literary forms, but also reflected the colonial obsession with travel writing, in the language now preferred by the colonial state.

Conclusion

The years before the establishment of Crown rule in 1858 demanded that princely states radically rethink their strategies for survival. Prospering under indirect rule required novel political approaches. Courts accordingly learned to repurpose precolonial textual techniques and practices of statecraft. *Bagh* and *Sair*'s strategic innovation was to reimagine the travelogue as a court literature. These texts were vectors for symbolic power. Lithograph stones replaced cannonballs; travel replaced conquest. The authors of *Bagh* and *Sair*, each in their own way, demanded the British recognize their right to exist and even their claims of superiority. They were also innovative in their adoption of the press, harnessing the benefits of mass circulation when indigenous printing was still in its infancy. Even more remarkably, they opted to write in Urdu when Persian was still the language of prestige in the princely states. In 1850 Urdu prose was still new, and it would be notable for anyone to write a prose history in Urdu, much less the princes themselves. Indore and Jaora both sensed the shifting sociolinguistic winds, adopting the language the British now preferred for use in justice, administration, and education in northern India. Writing in Urdu signaled their willingness to adapt to the conditions of the age. The decision also made their work widely accessible, particularly to a British readership of colonial administrators who were now being trained in this language.

India's indigenous rulers were also among the first to use Urdu travel writing to propagate their imaginations of the world. Travel writing was novel for the courts, but it emerged from a broader literary context in which court literature was central to the cultivation of symbolic legitimacy. Court literatures did not disappear in the colonial period, but continued to evolve as the princes attempted to maintain their roles and preserve their wealth and territory. Even as British rule foreclosed many possible arenas for aspiration and advancement, the printing press offered new ways to project legitimacy, at the same time revolutionizing how states conveyed those visions to their subjects and rivals. If, in this period, "Indian rajas legitimated their ruling status by religious and social rituals and symbols of sovereignty," this legitimation now included travel, which marked out a ruler as modern, advanced, and progressive.[87] That was precisely the impression Nawab Hamid 'Ali Khan had hoped to convey by writing about his travels to Alaska. Acting and looking like an independent sovereign and world leader became ever more important to the maintenance of symbolic power. Travel and travel writing were both part of these optics.

In the years after the Indore and Jaora courts published their accounts an increasing number of states began to take up the genre to promote their own global imaginations at home and abroad. Rulers increasingly published their travels because "in a more settled society, ruling houses needed to exalt their lineages before a wider audience."[88] As tangible power waned, symbolic power took its place.[89] This was a key lever in balancing relations with other kingdoms and the British in a situation where "rulers had to use every possible strategy to reconcile disparate interest groups and associate valuable allies and client communities with their regimes."[90] This strategic politicization of travel writing is reflected in the writing of Raja Bhavani Singh of Jhalawar (1874–1929) who claimed in his 1912 English-language account that he had written it "primarily for the benefit of my people in Jhalawar, whose ideas of European civilization are of the vaguest."[91] What precise benefit he might have had in mind for those people is not clear. The book was dedicated to King George V, written in English, and published in London, thousands of miles away from Jhalawar. In fact, it is more likely that the book was a political bid meant to curry the sympathy and support of British readers. Princely travelogues were all about political power and competing visions.

Perhaps these strategies did not always work, but princely travelogues did catch the attention of at least one powerful British administrator. About fifteen years after *Bagh* was first published, the Governor of Bombay Presidency, Bartle Frere (1815–84), was giving a speech to an assembly of rulers and aristocrats. He chided the group for being so sedentary; if they truly wished to improve their domains, he scolded, they needed to start acting more like the Maharaja of Indore. That is, they needed to travel. And they needed to do so quickly, for students in British India were quickly catching up.[92] Those students were being hurried along by British administrators and reformist Indians who saw promise in the pedagogical project of promoting travel. Many colonial officials argued that Indians would benefit from being introduced to travelogues from an early age. They began to commission travelogues and translations for use as textbooks in colonial schools, paying Indian authors, many of them who worked within the British administration, to produce the literature their syllabi called for.

These textbooks contained new global imaginations, representations of the world that emerged from the complex interactions of Indian writers and their British patrons. Their travelogues embraced colonial objectives, but also prioritized their authors' views and interests. They became standard reading in schools across the subcontinent. The following excerpt comes from the most widely read textbook of all, Aminchand's *Safarnama*. Aminchand traveled at the same time as Holkar and Ghaus Muhammad, but he espoused very different views. He imagined India as a single territory that had yet to realize its unity. He saw it as primarily Hindu, dotted with temples, and organized by a benevolent and efficient administration. This vision sounds familiar today, but when Aminchand wrote his travelogue, only a handful of Indians would have thought to imagine the world in this way. Aminchand's travel textbook meant to change that.

Notes

1. 'Ali Khan, *Masir-i Hamidi*, 1:2–3.
2. Previous to the nineteenth century there are only limited instances of official court literatures reproducing accounts of royal travels. These include Abul Fazl's annals of Akbar's court, the *Akbarnama*. In Rajasthan, the Udaipur court sponsored paintings that represented the king's pilgrimages visually. Khera, "Picturing India," 243–71. In the nineteenth century, early instances of court travelogues appeared in verse. These include a brief verse poem in Urdu by Nadir, a poet at the court of Nawab A'zam Jah, ruler of Arcot in southern India. Hashmi, *Tin Musafir*, 19–74. The journey was also recorded in Persian. Ghulam 'Abd al-Qadir Nazir, *Bahar*. In Persian, an exiled ruler from Rampur produced a versified account of his flight to Mecca called "Sair-i Karimi" (1826). Karimullah Khan, "Sair-i Karimi." The earliest book-length travel account by a ruler in Urdu is *Bagh-i Nau Bahar*, discussed later.
3. Shankarrao, *Twenty-One Weeks*, xx.
4. Shankarrao, *Twenty One Weeks*, xxi.
5. For a full account of the system of indirect rule in India, see Fisher, *Indirect Rule*.
6. Ramusack, *Indian Princes*, 6.
7. Princely sovereignty in colonial India has been studied from many angles. Relevant works include: Archambault, "Becoming Mughal"; Khera, "Picturing India"; Bellamy, "Alternative Kingdoms"; Segura-Garcia, "Picturing Indian Kingship"; Hughes, *Animal Kingdoms*.
8. Shulman, *The King*, 368.

9.   Brittlebank, *Tipu Sultan's Search*, 113.

10. Brittlebank, *Tipu Sultan's Search*, 131.

11. For a book-length study of the imperial durbars, see Codell and Ryan, *Power*.

12. See, for instance, a detailed account of the visit of the Prince of Wales to India in 1905–06 by a Rampuri officer: 'Ali Khan, *Sair*.

13. For instance, the travels of the Amir of Afghanistan. See Bismil, *Siyahat-i Habib*.

14. Sohrabi, *Wonder*, 72–103.

15. Khan, *Sharh*.

16. Sohrabi, *Wonder*, 88.

17. Ochonu, *Emirs in London*, 2–3. Other regions of British Africa possess similar literature, including from rulers in southern Africa and Uganda. Relevant works include: Mukasa, *Katikiro*; Parsons, *King Khama*; Jabavu, *India and East Africa*.

18. Keen, *Princely India*, 10.

19. Ramusack, *Indian Princes*, 8.

20. Note the lack of Urdu in this list.

21. Aminchand, *Safarnama*, 177–78.

22. Wilson, *History*, 2:288.

23. Holkar spent his entire life attempting to reclaim Jaora. The court cases stretched into the twentieth century, as recounted in a court history of his life. Burway, *Life*, 457. Jaora, naturally, contested this claim. That state's version of key events leading to its creation can be found in an 1895 history of Jaora. See Khan, *Darbar-i Jaora*, 47–76.

24. Rathi, *Bagh*, 49.

25. Ummid Singh's father was employed by Nawab Ahmad 'Ali Khan of Karnal, grandfather of Pakistani prime minister Liaquat 'Ali Khan. Ummid Singh, though, took up colonial service. Burway, *Life*, 145. He also ran the Indore City School and presumably stayed on in Indore after Holkar was an adult, as suggested by a reference to him in one of Ghalib's letters. Ghalib, *Ghalib ke Khutut*, 11. On Holkar's education, see Burway, *Life*, 146.

26. Burway, *Life*, 146.

27. Troll, "A Note," 141.

28. Both *Bagh* and *Sair* credit him as inspiration. Khan, *Sair*, 10; Rathi, *Bagh*, 14.

29. Rathi, *Bagh*, 40–41.

30. Rathi, *Bagh*, 495.

31. Khan, *Sair*, 1106. Remarkably, five copies of *Bagh* are extant today. Two are in the British Library in London, two in Rampur, and a fifth in a private archive in Gujranwala. It was only at Saulat Library that I was able to make a digital copy of the book. This copy, though, was missing the critical first fifteen pages. These missing pieces were supplied to me in the form of a photocopy from Raza Rampur Library.

32. Rathi, *Bagh*, 2–3.
33. Rathi, *Bagh*, 5–6.
34. Rathi, *Bagh*, 3–6.
35. Rathi, *Bagh*, 8.
36. Rathi, *Bagh*, 7.
37. A detailed summary of the tour is available in Burway, *Life*, 147.
38. Khan, *Broken Spell*, 20–21.
39. Auer, "Persian Historiography," 37.
40. Rathi, *Bagh*, 494.
41. Rathi, *Bagh*, 495.
42. Key differences include the lack of a distinction for retroflex sounds, *kaf/gaf*, and nasalized and palatized /n/, nor any differentiation between *bari ye* and *chhoti ye* and *he* and *do-chashmi he*.
43. Kambalposh, *Tarikh*; Abu Talib Khan, *Masir-i Talibi (1812)*.
44. Orsini, "*Qasbas* and Cities," 75.
45. Khan, "Marvellous Histories," 527–56; Khan, "The Romance Genre," 105–40.
46. These lists are not exhaustive.
47. This device has a long history in South Asian literature. In Urdu, it dates to as early as Mulla Vajhi's (d. 1659) *Qutb Mushtari*. Maratha court literature, too, would winnow "factual elements from royal lives in order to emplot a narrative of royal triumph consummated by union with a queen who embodied the glory of the kingdom." Guha, "Speaking Historically," 1088.
48. Fussell, *Abroad*, 208.
49. Sikandar Begum, "Tarikh."
50. Rathi, *Bagh*, 414–16.
51. Fabian, "Time, Narration," 5.
52. Rathi, *Bagh*, 436.
53. Rathi, *Bagh*, 38.
54. His coronation did not spell an end to his travels. The maharaja apparently enjoyed this voyage so much that he began planning a second one the moment he returned. This trip took him to Puna and Bombay, probably in 1853, where he traveled on the newly installed railway line from Thana. He also visited Ahmadnagar and Nasik, according to the travel diary of a friend and fellow traveler on both trips. Burway, *Life*, 151–52. His journey was recorded in a diary by his friends. I have been unable to trace these texts, though citations show that they existed at least as late as 1925.
55. For a locally produced history of his life and major political events, see Khan, *Darbar-i Jaora*, 94–153.
56. Khan, *Sair*, 12.

57. Now lost, his first book was on the nature and care of horses. Khan, *Sair*, 469. Copies of *Sair al-Muhtasham* are now rare. Unlike *Bagh*, it is not present in the British Library, suggesting he may have had less success at sharing his vision with the colonial state. There are, though, two copies in Rampur, suggesting that he did reach a princely audience, as well as at a private collection in Gujranwala. My reading is based on a digital copy I made at Saulat Library.

58. Khan, *Sair*, 1106.

59. "Father Scott spoke to me at length with the greatest kindness and courtesy. The rapturous tales and engrossing stories he told me about his homeland, America, fascinated me and made me desirous to visit that land." Khan, *Sair*, 31.

60. Pernau, "Virtuous Individual," 170.

61. Khan, *Sair*, 5–6.

62. Khan, *Sair*, 7.

63. Khan, *Sair*, 10.

64. Khan, *Sair*, 7–8.

65. Khan, *Sair*, 9.

66. Khan, *Sair*, 22.

67. On uses of the hikayat in South Asia, see Kia, "Adab."

68. A group also critiqued in *Bagh*, though less scathingly. Rathi, *Bagh*, 5 and 25.

69. Khan, *Sair*, 8. See also Chapter 3.

70. Khan, *Sair*, 19–20.

71. Khan, *Sair*, 20–21. The hemistich is Sa'di's.

72. Sharma, "Delight and Disgust," 114. Touati, *Islam*, 227.

73. Brittlebank, *Tipu Sultan's Search*, 115–19.

74. Touati, *Islam*, 230. This, of course, was not exclusive to travel writing by Muslims either.

75. Khan, *Sair*, 1157.

76. Khan, *Sair*, 4.

77. Khan, *Sair*, 30.

78. In fact, *Sair* appears to be the first printed travelogue to include extensive illustrations. Though it is slightly predated by *Bagh-i Nau Bahar*, the latter text only has a single drawing, while *Sair* incudes dozens by the artist Husain Bakhsh.

79. Jasanoff, *Edge of Empire*, 77–78, 184.

80. Pernau, "Virtuous Individual," 171. The influence of the wonders genre on colonial-era Islamicate travel writing is affirmed by a study of Hausa travel writing, where indigenous Nigerian rulers similarly invoked wonders to bolster their claims to sovereignty. Ochonu, *Emirs in London*, 8–9.

81. Sharma, "City of Beauties," 77.

82. Khan, "Lament," 88–89.

83. This display of aesthetic sophistication was typical of the genre. Sharma, "City of Beauties," 73.
84. Khan, *Sair*, 14.
85. Khan, *Sair*, 1149.
86. Rathi, *Bagh*, 2–3.
87. Ramusack, *Indian Princes*, 3.
88. Bayly, *Empire*, 42.
89. The travelogue was even taken up by dethroned rulers, again for at least partly political objectives. In 1858, Wajid 'Ali Shah, the deposed ruler of Avadh, wrote a long *masnavi* that included a description of his journey of exile from Lucknow to Calcutta. Sharar, *Jan-i 'Alam*, 73–177. From there, he sent family members, including his mother, to London to plead his case before the queen. The mission was a failure, but that too resulted in a travelogue, likely composed in 1865. 'Alavi, *Safir-i Avadh*.
90. Bayly, *Saints*, 173.
91. Singh, *Travel Pictures*, vii. Singh made a second global tour in 1925 and ultimately died while sailing to Europe in 1929.
92. Frere, *Speeches*, 10.

Aminchand's *Safarnama*

Munshi Aminchand sahib, resident of Punjab....
As requested by the Aristotle of the Age, Janab Robert Curst sahib bahadur
Printed at the Nur Press, Lahore, under the direction of Manager
Pandit Surajbhan, 1859 [second edition]

Next comes the city of Cuttack, which is very ancient and well known. I describe it now. This city has no equal in all the land of Orissa. There is a cantonment here. One famous place, located in the center of town, is the building housing a footprint of the Prophet. It is located very close to the jail. The courthouses are located on the shores of the Katchori [Kathajori] River. Commissioner sahib's mansion is located beside the Mahan River. It is situated such that it can be seen from afar. The city is something like an island, for the Mahan flows to the north and the Katchori to the south. The Katchori splits from the Mahan upriver from the town but the two join together again downstream. This means that no matter which way you go in town, you will have to cross a river. They say that in the rainy season these rivers have huge floods, with the water sometimes even flowing into the city itself. This is why, when the Marathas ruled here, they built a barrier along the Katchori that still exists today. After Cuttack comes Balanta, which is along the banks of the Katchori. Until here, the road is excellent and lined on both sides by mango trees. After three *kos* comes the Balkhani River.[1] There is a village here called Bamsami. From here a road goes west to the holy place of Bhuvaneshwar Maharaj. I went there to take a darshan. I will describe it now. The name of this god is Ling Raj. He is called Bhuvan-ishwar because [he is] *prithvi ka ishar*, meaning Lord of the World. There is a large tank near this temple for ritual bathing. The temple here is exactly like that of Sri Jaganath-ji. The Brahmins here say that in the forests for five kos all around the temple there are *kota-kot*, meaning, crores of deities. This temple is older than Jagannath-ji's. Truly, it appears to be very old indeed.[2]

***

Conclusion [to the book]: Praise be to God that I have been preserved from the dangers of this unreliable world and have now completed my second journey. I have recorded here all that I saw, and all that I learned about the countries, cities, and various peoples that passed before my eyes. Through this journey, I have gained a knowledge of the various customs and practices of every country, places whose name had never even reached my ears heretofore. [I saw] many magnificent buildings and fascinating rural areas, places that I could not have imagined, not even in my wildest dreams. I see now that people in different lands have different practices, and that their rituals and habits do not all agree with each other. Especially among those of our Hindu faith, every region has its own gods and goddesses, its own traditions, its own family systems, and ways of distinguishing between castes. I noticed that the ways of the Muslims vary as well. For example, in Kashmir and Peshawar, the Muslims are not at all careful when it comes to matters of food and drink. On the other hand, the Muslims of Hindustan [northern India] are completely sincere in attending to these matters as concerns their Hindu fellow-travelers. Nevertheless, not all people [in any one region] can be regarded as equal. Goodness and evil, justice and tyranny, indiscretion and wisdom, diligence and negligence—these qualities are to be found everywhere.

But the most astonishing thing is that the inhabitants of one land are so unfamiliar with those of other lands that it seems as though someone has constructed a great, firm wall across which no one may pass. Thus, the people of the Deccan would ask me about Punjab, saying that it must be an enormous city with a great fort. They do not know that Punjab is a land [*mulk*]! That is why, in this book, I have tried to fully examine every place that I was able to observe. If, by studying this book, my fellow countrymen can familiarize themselves with other lands [mulk] and their practices, then my labors will not have been in vain. I request my readers to forgive me should they find any errors here, or any passages that are incomplete. Soon, if I am given the opportunity, I intend to make another journey, this time via Madras and Ceylon, to the land [mulk] of Europe. I will write about that journey after I have completed it.

I now conclude this book. Salam.[3]

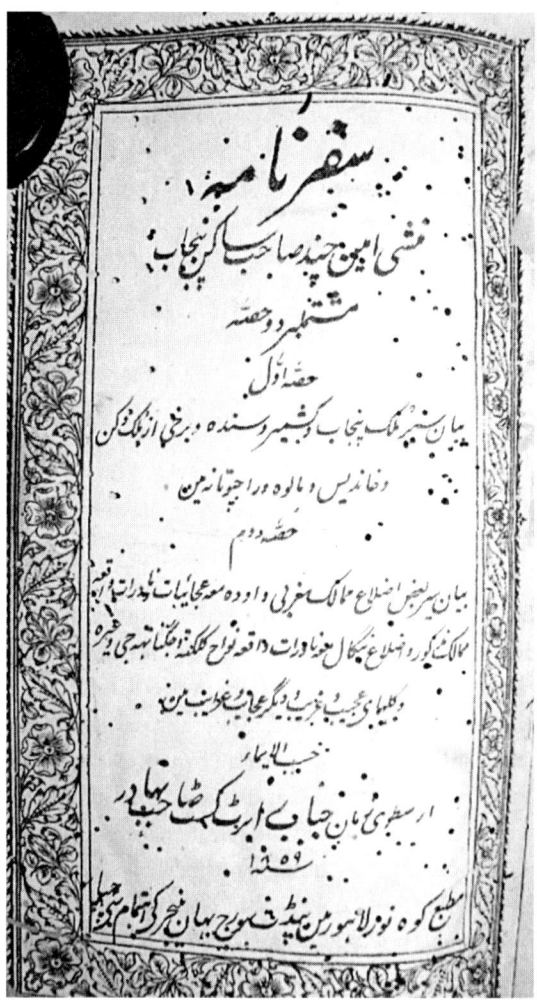

Figure 3.1 The second edition of Aminchand's *Safarnama*
Source: Author.

Notes

1. A kos is approximately two miles.
2. Aminchand, *Safarnama*, 335–36.
3. Aminchand, *Safarnama*, 423–34. Figure 3.1.

The Travel Lesson

Aminchand's *Safarnama* was not just a travelogue. It was also a textbook, mandatory reading in schools across much of northern India. Generations of students in colonial schools of the 1850s and '60s read it. Through it, they learned not just about the political and topographical geography of India, but also about how they should imagine it. Rather than seeing India as a variegated territory populated by different groups and divided into independent regions and kingdoms, students were asked to imbibe Aminchand's aspirational vision that India was indeed a single country united under British rule. At the same time, Aminchand taught students that travel was a valuable and critical component of a sound education. Through books like his, travel and travel writing played a central role in the curriculum from the moment colonial schooling began in 1835.

Travel was important enough that it featured in students' final exams, too. In 1844, for instance, the English Department at Delhi College asked students to write an essay on "the effects of intercourse with foreigners." One successful student, Ramchund, answered that these effects were "very beneficial and ennobling":

> A knowledge of the manners of the inhabitants of foreign countries has a tendency to make men liberal, and to generate in them those generous feelings of which man is capable, but which are smothered by the pernicious influence of local prejudices and partialities. *It is this very reason why travelling has been recommended, as a necessary part of a liberal education.* The mind of the traveler is, as it were, unchained from prejudices, is enlarged and freed from narrow views and considerations, his thoughts

take a wider range, and are not confined exclusively to the concerns of the small community in which he lives. He is, as it were, a citizen of the world.... Civilisation and knowledge are the natural offspring of such an intercourse.[1]

Ramchund had learned his travel lesson. He could reflect critically on his society's shortcomings and aspire to a better life. Ramchund argued, to the approval of his examiners, that Indians were less worldly and less civilized than Europeans in part because they did not travel.

This chapter asks how travel and travel writing were integrated into colonial Indian school systems with the objective of changing the way Indians saw, and acted in, the world. The British imagined Indians to be uninterested in and uninformed about the wider world. Teaching travel and travel writing, they hoped, would change this, and thus they recommended travel as "a necessary part of a liberal education." Revolutionizing Indians' geographic knowledge of the world was considered so essential to the colonial civilizing mission that Sumathi Ramaswamy terms its advocates "cartographic evangelists."[2] From the earliest experiments in colonial and missionary education to its broad institutionalization in the second half of the nineteenth century, every student learned the importance of geography. A strong knowledge of the subject became a prerequisite for government employment. Educationists believed geography would fashion Indians into modern subjects, wean them from idolatrous beliefs, and fashion them into subjects who saw the world in ways consonant with colonial discourse. If this was the "geography lesson," to use Ramaswamy's term, students were also given a "travel lesson." Geography was important, but students were encouraged to also learn directly themselves. They were encouraged to become travelers. The colonial education system promoted the discourse of beneficial travel by assigning travelogues like Aminchand's account as textbooks. Colonialists believed travel would revolutionize India, create modern, rational subjects, and, as via train, "overturn prejudices, uproot habits, and [change] customs as tenaciously held and dearly loved as life itself."[3]

The travel lesson was reformist. It sought to ameliorate social woes—namely, India's supposed backwardness and isolation—by encouraging students to travel, gain knowledge, and become productive members of a colonial empire. A mobile India held out numerous benefits for the colonial state, allowing it to facilitate trade, strengthen the administration, increase state integration, de-localize loyalties, and introduce consistency and cohesiveness to an uneven political topography. Educated and worldly Indian travelers willing to see the world in colonial terms were likewise critical to the functioning of empire outside South Asia, as exemplified by the countless Indians who traveled to Africa and Southeast Asia for the purposes of administration, trade, and labor.[4]

The promotion of travel was also simply a product of its time and a reflection of the growth of tourism and leisure travel in Britain itself.[5] The British saw themselves as a nation of intrepid travelers, and they wished for Indians to emulate these qualities too. If the education system sought to encourage Indians to adopt British morals, aesthetics, and practices according to MacCaulay's widely cited "Minute on Education," that meant inculcating in Indian students a traveling spirit. Thus, even before Aminchand's travelogue was published Indian students were already being taught how travel could bring to them the benefits of modern European civilization. In 1852, a Bengali student at Hooghly College named Nobinchunder Dass answered an exam question on the "effects upon India of the new Communication with Europe by means of Steam" by noting:

> Nothing tends so much to advance society, to humanise the manners, and elevate men in the scale of civilization, as intercourse with different nations. It encourages commerce, by supplying the wants of one country with the superfluities of another; the knowledge of one people may be made the common property of all by its means; what the people of the remotest regions discover or invent, can be communicated everywhere.[6]

A thousand miles apart, Ramchund and Nobinchunder produced remarkably similar answers because the travel lesson encouraged Indians to see British India similarly no matter where they lived.

In Urdu, the travel lesson was initially imparted through translated travelogues, but in time original accounts by Indian authors came to dominate. Alongside the princely accounts studied in the last chapter, these works were among the earliest travelogues in Urdu. Travel textbooks were unabashedly didactic. They were not meant to bring pleasure to readers or appeal to their aesthetic sense. The accounts that found sponsorship were patently outside the reigning aesthetics and preferences of the time. They instructed students in the history and geography of unfamiliar places and taught them how to live in the world on largely colonial terms. As Kamran Rastegar notes, "from the European perspective, travel writing was often considered one of the duties of the colonial subject; the writing of the travel experience was a conscious self-interpellation of the productivity and scientific empiricism that the colonial project claimed for itself."[7] This chapter examines the history of how this duty was inculcated in students through the travel lesson before turning to an analysis of early travel textbooks.

Teaching Travel in British India

The travel lesson in India dates to the colonial period. While references to travel sometimes appeared in precolonial syllabi, it was never systematically discussed or studied. It is sometimes thought that Sir Sayyid Ahmad Khan, an educationist and author of two didactic travelogues, was among the first Indian Muslims to establish a link between education, social reform, and travel in the 1860s. Alternatively, one study conjectures that the educational aspect of Bengali and Hindi travel accounts emerged as authors "borrowed" from translations of British travel guides to India during the mid-nineteenth century.[8] In fact, the travel lesson appeared several decades before the era of the vernacular guidebook, and well before Sayyid Ahmad Khan began his educational project.

Gauri Viswanathan argues that India's colonial education system was based on a curriculum designed for a ruling elite whose lessons and expectations were misaligned with the subordinate administrative roles that Indians were generally offered.[9] For that elite, travel played an important role in their educational training. Touring as a form of education had been celebrated by Francis Bacon, while the Grand Tour was once encouraged as a capstone experience for young aristocrats after the completion of their formal education. By the nineteenth century, though, the formal Grand Tour had grown obsolete as modern tourism emerged in its place.[10] But in India, the older idea of travel, or a Grand Tour (whether in Europe or elsewhere), as crucial to a well-rounded education was suggested for Indian students, even for those who were not particularly wealthy and who had no hope of joining the governing elite. Some colonial educationists accordingly found these expectations unrealistic. In a convocation speech at the University of Madras in 1873, W.A. Porter lamented:

> The critics of the Hindu student set up too high a standard. They compare him not with the graduates of England or Scotland or Germany, but with an ideal man who loves culture purely for its own sake and into whose mind there never enters, in connection with his studies, any idea of personal aggrandisement in the shape either of money or fame.[11]

Another influential colonial figure, Sir Bartle Frere (1815–1884), the governor of Bombay and chancellor of Bombay University, called on Indian students to embody the ideal of educational travel. In an 1864 speech at Bombay University, he asked them to follow the example of the example of Ulysses as he was imagined by Tennyson:

> I cannot rest from travel: I will drink
>   Life to the lees: All times I have enjoy'd

> Greatly, have suffer'd greatly, both with those
>> That loved me, and alone, on shore, and when
> Thro' scudding drifts the rainy Hyades
>> Vext the dim sea: I am become a name;
> For always roaming with a hungry heart
>> Much have I seen and known; cities of men.

Citing "Ulysses," Frere argued that travel was an educational and civilizational ideal. By traveling, not only would the student learn and advance, but all of India would rise up and grow, too. The student's travels would inspire those around them. A "passion for foreign travel," he argued, only grows as a nation develops.[12] Travel thus became a key component of the ideal colonial education and a keystone for India's development.

"Ulysses" was a poem about Europe's bravery and exploratory spirit. By invoking it, Frere suggested to his students that Europeans—the offspring of Odysseus, who harbored an "insatiable passion for travel which the ages and years could not obliterate or satisfy"—were an ideal model.[13] He painted a mythical picture of Europeans borne to greatness by their peripatetic willingness "to strive, to seek, to find, and not to yield." While Frere argued that travel would help Indians advance, mere ambulation was not enough. Movement must be accompanied by a reorientation of character. Frere did not discuss the difficulties, risks, or costs of travel. Nor did he address the ridicule that well-traveled Indians were subjected to in colonial society as "brown sahibs." His advice was unequivocal: to succeed, students must travel.

A few decades earlier, a similar view was endorsed by one of India's most influential administrators, the infamous Thomas Babington Macaulay (1800–59). Macaulay took a dim view of all "Oriental" literature, but also argued that travel itself could provide an education as sound as that one might derive from a full study of European literature. The mind of the tourist, he wrote in 1828, "is enlarged by contemplating the wide diversities of laws, of morals, and of manners." But to harvest this bounty they must "see ordinary men as they appear in their ordinary business and their ordinary pleasures."[14] It was Macaulay who helped pass the English Education Act of 1835, letting the travel lesson take a firm hold in the colonial syllabus. This Act, which legally bound the British East India Company to provide education in India, marked a shift toward a British-inspired educational system emphasizing "useful learning." And thus, the travel lesson was born. Of course, colonial education was far from universal or homogeneous. Literacy remained low throughout the nineteenth century, but schools nevertheless reached substantial numbers of individuals. As more and more people learned to read and write, many of them began to use their new skills to make their own contributions to travel writing and Urdu's global imagination. But first, they had to be introduced to travel writing at school.

Promoting Travel

Well before students had the opportunity to journey in person, they were asked to travel in their minds. Geography was taught in the classroom through "the use of ideal journeys." One teaching guide suggested instructors propose an imaginary journey from Calcutta to New York via London. The teacher would ask a series of questions about the trip to "excite the student's interest."[15] Geography and map reading were thus vivified through a connection to lived experience. These imaginary journeys eventually made their way into Indian literature, as with a book of popular cultural geography, *Dunya ki Sair* (A tour of the world, 1897?) by Pyare La'l, a textual tour of the globe complete with lithographed images. In the final chapter, having completed his imaginary tour, Pyare La'l suggested that "having read this book, many readers will now surely be filled with an immense desire to see foreign countries for themselves."[16] He then got down to practicalities, offering travel tips and cost estimates to help them begin. In this way, textual travels became a stepping stone for actual travel.

Similarly, when parents visited a school, education officials would extoll to them the virtues of worldly knowledge and experience. One strategy involved placing world maps on classroom walls during open houses. When these displays caught a visitor's eye, the deputy instructor would then "seize on the opportunity" to demonstrate the advantages of study by pointing out and introducing individual countries. He would "describe the route from Calcutta to London, both overland and by the long sea-voyage. Most present would thereupon express regret that they were so far advanced in years and had not yet acquired a knowledge of these subjects." The instructor would then urge them to ensure their children were "duly taught such useful studies."[17]

Outside the classroom, officials encouraged travel in a number of ways, including through direct mentorship. Mid-nineteenth-century travelogues often attributed their composition to the aid of a British friend. To remove financial barriers for Indian student travelers, trips were sometimes funded by university patrons. An 1854 "Minute on Education" by the Governor-General of India called for the establishment of "'traveling scholarships' to encourage our advanced students to visit various parts of India."[18] In 1862, Munguldass Nathoobhoy donated twenty thousand rupees to establish a traveling fellowship at the University of Bombay.

These funds were explicitly *not* for travel to an educational institution, but were for general travel, in keeping with the "great advantages of foreign travel as a part of University education."[19]

Further enticement came in the form of employment. Travel experience was an extra qualification on graduates' resumes. Just a few Indians, Frere had remarked, were "beginning to be stirred by a consciousness that all knowledge is not comprehended in the teaching of a single master, and that it cannot be grasped by one who never quits the limits of the hermit's cell." Only graduates who "improved their minds through travel," he argued, would be "destined" for greatness in government service.[20] The implications were clear: in British India, the government would reward the well traveled. A knowledge of geography was mandatory for government employment from the 1840s, but many, like Frere, found experience preferable to book learning.[21]

To this end, Frere advocated for travel to be taught in schools and for travel writing to be made widely available in Indian vernacular languages.[22] In response, the Gujarati newspaper owner, businessman, and social reformer Karsandas Mulji (1832–71) published an account in Gujarati of his travels in Europe, *Englandamañ Pravas* (A journey to England, 1866). The book was soon translated into Urdu and Marathi. Mulji, who had spoken alongside Frere at the lecture cited earlier, gave a "literal translation" of Frere's remarks:

> In the advanced countries of Europe, the passion for travel is unparalleled. The wise and accomplished men in Europe's universities spare nothing to travel as much and as widely as possible. They desire to gain the maximum results from the knowledge that they collect by engaging in travel.... The type of knowledge possessed by one who has never left his little corner, but who has obtained intelligence and comprehension by the ceaseless reading of books—that type of knowledge may be gained by merely strolling the paths of Europe.[23]

Mulji claimed that scholars felt "contempt" for Indians who pretended to be well educated but were untraveled. For him, a complete education required travel even where social or religious restrictions forbade it. J. Barton Scott neatly summarizes Mulji's view: "Hindu tradition prevents travel; British modernity requires it."[24]

Similar exhortations proliferated across India wherever students encountered a colonial education. As one administrator put it, "if education is essential to good 'travel habits,' travel itself is essential to that fuller education which generates good citizens."[25] At a University of Madras convocation in 1882, another travel advocate, Justice Muthuswamy Iyer (1832–95), pronounced:

After the close of your college career, you should travel at least through India and acquire some practical knowledge of the country in which you live and of the various peoples that inhabit it. I would advise those of you who can afford to pay a visit to Europe to do so and add to your knowledge the benefit of that social education which residence in civilized countries for a time, with a view to self-improvement, is likely to ensure. While I urge you to further progress, let me advise you not to merit the reproach that the knowledge of Indian students is only book-knowledge and that their observation does not extend beyond the precincts of their village or town or district.[26]

Justice Iyer's reference to costs acknowledged that not everyone could travel, and certainly not everyone could go to Europe.

While all students were expected to travel, rank and financial status shaped access. Princely elites, in particular, were warned that by not allowing their children to travel they would fail to "fit them for their future rank in life." Frere— functioning now as governor of Bombay Presidency—advised his royal listeners that commoners and non-Brahmins were acquiring knowledge which was "the key to wealth and power." He promised to facilitate their journeys, though he also warned that their preferred modes of travel were inappropriate to this educational mission: "One great obstacle is the expensive custom of traveling with a retinue as large as in the days when an armed force was needed for defense in traveling. This is no longer necessary, and if you would reduce your escorts ... the expense of a long journey would cease to be an obstacle to your enjoying the pleasures and advantages of travel."[27] Frere even warned that young students might topple the social order unless its princely rulers began to travel, setting the groups as antagonists in a race to complete their travel lessons. He first advised them:

[By] education I do not mean mere reading and writing. Without these elementary means of acquiring knowledge there can be no perfect education. But much may be learnt from travel—from seeing other countries and conversing with men of wider experience and more knowledge than can be met with at any one place.

Then he threatened them:

You know that it is the earnest desire of Her Majesty the Queen, and of the government of India, to maintain the class of nobles to which you belong with undiminished hereditary property and influence and to see them act as leaders of the people in the moral and physical advancement which it is the eminent desire of the British nation to encourage in this country. But this is simply impossible if you neglect all opportunities of learning.[28]

Other officials were even more strident. One proposal even suggested royal pupils be forced to spend their holidays touring India accompanied by British guardians, following the model of the aristocratic Grand Tour.[29]

Many Indians were convinced. There are copious examples of prominent figures making public their travels, even in the face of social approbation. An early instance involved the reformer Ram Mohun Roy (1772–1833), who famously traveled to England in 1831. Perceived risks to his caste purity made this controversial.[30] Still, he found support from the Native Literary Society of Calcutta, which declared that the "chief causes of our depressed situation may, we think, be regarded as the following wants: that of social and mutual intercourse; of mutual agreement; of travel."[31] Another supporter of educational travel was Dwarkanath Tagore (1794–1846), who, on his return from England in 1842, thanked the Royal Asiatic Society for promoting education in India and spoke of rising Indian interest in foreign travel. The Society praised Dwarkanath's willingness to travel "solely to acquire information and indulge a laudable curiosity; and not from any political motive."[32] Lesser-known Indians supported travel in subtler ways. Some authors in 1860s Bengal, for instance, wrote travelogues and then had them printed and distributed free of charge.[33]

Travel Textbooks in British India

The first travelogue by an Indian to be used as a colonial school textbook was probably Abu Talib Khan's (1752–1806) Persian-language *Masir-i Talibi* (Talib's travels, 1804) on England. Abu Talib's account originally circulated in manuscript. It subsequently became India's first explicitly pedagogical travelogue even before the creation of formal colonial schools when, in 1812, the Bengal government commissioned a print edition of the original Persian text for Indian readers.[34] This eight-hundred-page original was published in two more editions, including by the Calcutta School Book Society and the Baptist Mission Press.[35] It later appeared in an abridged edition published by Abu Talib's sons in the 1830s.

By the 1840s, though, the book was falling out of favor. Delhi College did publish an abridged Urdu translation in 1843, but it was not widely read.[36] Abu Talib's work may have been discarded because it did not reflect the emerging colonial discourse on India's supposed civilizational backwardness. His travelogue showed him meeting Europeans as moral equals. Abu Talib did believe India lagged behind Europe, but he blamed the situation on India's material conditions and limited scientific knowledge. British ideologues, though, increasingly understood India's backwardness to be due to its people's character and lack of morality. Accordingly, beginning in the 1830s, the travel lesson impressed upon its pupils that their shortcomings were not material, but cultural. As Ramchund's essay suggested, nobility, generosity, wisdom, and civility were British qualities that must be taught to Indians—not at all the position espoused by Abu Talib.

Early colonial school libraries also plied students with travelogues in English.[37] Students at Delhi College in 1836 read both volumes of John Malcolm's travels in Persia, in addition to the Indian volume of Josiah Condor's *The Modern Traveller*, a series dedicated to geography and topography.[38] In the North-Western Provinces and Bengal, students read Oliver Goldsmith's "The Traveller" and "The Deserted Village," both long poems with extended ruminations on travel.[39] Top students were awarded copies of George Anson's *A Voyage around the World* or Mungo Park's *Travels*.[40] Students also read the Ottoman traveler Evliya Çelebi's *Siyahatname* (Voyages), certainly in English, and possibly also in Urdu translation.[41]

The first Urdu travelogue to find a firm place in the colonial syllabus was *Safarnama Mungo Park Sahib ka Bayan meñ Mulk Habsh Ke* (Mungo Park's travelogue describing the land of Africa, 1842), a translation of Mungo Park's *Travels to the Interior of Africa* (1799). At first blush, the dated story of a Scottish explorer's journey to West Africa seems an odd choice for an Indian curriculum in 1842. A first-person account of Park's failed search for the source of the Niger River, the book was a blockbuster on its publication in Britain and served as a model for generations of later European travel writers. Forty years later the Urdu version was published by the Agra School Book Society (ASBS) for use in colonial schools. A second edition was printed by the Calcutta School Book Society in 1853.[42] These bodies, which produced educational materials for Indian primary schools, were based on a "massive translation venture, in which textbook knowledge from English and other language sources was transferred into Hindi and Urdu." Because these efforts relied on Indian translators, "early textbooks constitute an important site of the discursive encounter between colonial empiricism—with its underlying concept of 'useful knowledge'—and Indian learning and literary forms."[43]

The question remains: Why would a largely uninformative work about West Africa hold such an important place in Indian colonial education? The intention was not to teach Indian students about West Africa. In fact, the geography hardly mattered. As Mary Louise Pratt argues, Park's *Travels* is remarkable precisely because it is not scientific or geographical. Instead, it was a "personal experience and adventure," the work of a "sentimental hero."[44] His account is not shaped by facts and figures, but by people, and, above all, by Park himself. His experiences and emotions are always at the center of the narrative.[45] He is appealing for his mundaneness as the "non-hero of an anti-conquest."[46] He was a daring and tireless protagonist who used his skill to navigate a dangerous and difficult landscape.

What made his book worthy of becoming the first travel account translated from English into Urdu was the fact that Park was a model traveler, one who did not pursue political or financial objectives but traveled to further scientific knowledge. Park embodied the myth of the British as benevolent and understanding. His account was marked by bravery, principle, and nobility of character. Openminded and inquisitive, Park's humility affirmed European superiority. He was a selfless, apolitical traveler, neither wealthy nor remarkable. His account offered a "combination of humanism, egalitarianism, and critical relativism anchored securely in a sense of European authenticity, power, and legitimacy."[47] It displayed the qualities that Indian readers were meant to cultivate—who would not be struck by Mungo, naked, imprisoned, and starving, yet ever willing to persevere? Park himself remarked that Africans "thought it impossible ... that any man in his senses would undertake so dangerous a journey merely to look at the country and its inhabitants."[48] The narrative reminds us constantly that he survived not through his connections or because of his access to material wealth, but as a "naked, essential, inherently powerful White man."[49] He was the ultimate colonial ideal.

In the Urdu translation, an unnamed translator proclaimed the book's benefits in a brief introduction:

> The wise and sensible know that the benefits of travel are without limit. From it, man's understanding and comprehension are enriched, while his prejudice and ignorance—two qualities that frequently afflict those who remain cloistered—are repulsed from his heart. The arts and science of one nation become known in another, and the trends and industry of one country become current in others. Trade is increased, and the congruity and intercourse between the communities is strengthened.

Then the author turned grave:

> But the residents of the land of Hindustan [northern India], owing to their homeland being far from the sea, and because they usually follow the customs and traditions of their religion, and also because, in keeping with the verse [of the Persian poet Sana'i], "Love of the homeland is sweeter than the country of Solomon," they prefer the place of their birth, think it better than other countries, [and] are generally devoid of the benefits of travel. For this reason, this ignorant one ... [has translated this book] into the Urdu language to lighten this deficiency.[50]

This pedagogical travelogue, in other words, was meant to change how Indians engaged with the world, to encourage them to imagine it as a space for selfless and apolitical travel and exploration.

This objective was helped along by the looseness of the "translation," which is more accurately a third-person interpretive abridgement, with the translator summarizing and analyzing Park's text. The following comparison of the two books' opening passages shows how Mungo Park's work was adapted into a pedagogical and didactic example for Indian students. In the English original, Park begins by explaining how he was selected for this mission to Africa:

> Soon after my return from the East Indies in 1793, having learned that the noblemen and gentlemen associated for the purpose of prosecuting discoveries in the interior of Africa were desirous of engaging a person to explore that continent, by the way of the Gambia River, I took occasion, through means of the President of the Royal Society, to whom I had the honour to be known, of offering myself for that service.[51]

The Urdu translator, though, offered an interpretation of these lines that moved beyond Mungo's specific circumstances to underline Britain's civilizational superiority and selflessness:

> The English [angrez] sahibs are always desirous to learn the nature of every country of the world, and to become familiar with the ways and laws of every community in the inhabited portions of the world; and, having ascertained the products and profits of every land in the seven climes, to open up avenues for trade, to spread knowledge, and to teach backward nations the principles of humanity. Thus it was that fifty years ago, an intrepid group of sahibs formed an association to explore the interior of the Land of the Black People [Balad al-Sudan]. For some time, they sought a talented and brave man who was strong enough to explore that immense region. It was around then that Mungo Park sahib arrived from the land of Hind and learned of their desire. He enthusiastically volunteered.[52]

By exposing Indian students to this literature, reformists hoped to inspire them to see global travel as an ideal and even to imagine themselves as one day being able to occupy a similar role as Mungo through their own mobility and writing—in Africa if not in Europe.

As Urdu students were reading *Safarnama Mungo Park Sahib Ka*, Hindi students were presented with another travelogue. Pandit Ratneshvar's *Patramalika* (Letters, 1841) was an epistolary account describing a journey from Sehore through present-day Maharashtra to Bombay, all while showcasing a colony-approved orientation toward knowledge, travel, and British greatness.[53] Published by the ASBS, the text was to be read from in class once a week.[54] It presented a community leader eager to travel and to share knowledge.

C.A. Bayly argues that the book was "suffused with the western ideology of improvement" even as it "left space for Indian reconstructions of their own world."[55] As with Aminchand, Ratneshvar does remark on temples and other religious sites, but his focus is on the contributions of the British. These views are presented in simple, clear sentences that glorified Europe and lamented Indians' limited knowledge of geography:

> Major Winfried sahib introduced me to Major [unclear] Baisley sahib, the Principal Assistant. This gentleman showed me some European cows and bulls. One strange thing about these cows is that is that there is a very thick hair on their bodies.... Then the great sahib took me to visit the garden, which looked splendid with its many European fruits and flowers. It was filled with coconut, areca, rubber trees, etc. The sap of the rubber tree is used to remove pencil marks from paper.... After this we went to Madhav Rao's school and quizzed the students there. A few of the students were able to answer questions about math and geography, but despite the presence of a scholar like Madhav Rao, the people here do not encourage their children to study anything apart from some math.[56]

Pandit Ratneshvar's pedagogical travelogue is reminiscent of an entire genre of colonial textbooks that foregrounded European accomplishments while using travel to instruct students. In French West Africa, for instance, one of the most widely used textbooks for primary school students was *Moussa et Gigla: Histoire de Deux Petit Noirs* (1916), a book that followed two boys from Senegal and Benin on their travels through French West Africa.[57] Like *Patramalika, Mousa et Gigla*'s "'pedagogical' aims ... include encouraging the 'moral' and practical education of young colonized African students. This [was] to be achieved by helping them to 'discover' the resources of the country in which they live as well as showing them how France represents the pinnacle of civilization."[58] The travel lesson was a colonial staple.

In India, travel texts continued to appear. In 1847 the Delhi Vernacular Translation Society, which provided textbooks in northern India, printed Yusuf Kambalposh's *Tarikh-i Yusufi* (Yusuf's history, 1847), one of just two texts used for Urdu reading classes across the region.[59] That made this travelogue about England one of the most studied books in northern India's colonial schools.[60] Over time, pedagogical travel books written by Indians became increasingly common, relieving the "anxiety" of officials for locally produced pedagogical travelogues.[61] The remainder of this chapter briefly examines the fate of three such travel textbooks written between 1851 and 1861: Munshi Aminchand's (b. 1827) *Safarnama*, Kali Rai and Tulsi Ram's (n.d.) *Sair-i Punjab* (Travels in Punjab, written 1851, published 1872), and, in Gujarati, Dosabhoy's Framjee's (1829–1902) *Gret Britain Khate ni Musafiri* (A journey to Great Britain, 1861).

These diverse authors each invoked the importance of travel and knowledge acquisition for individual and communal advancement. All three linked travel to moral rectitude and aimed to write in clear, accessible language. Fully aware of the government's desire for travel textbooks, they sought government sponsorship by emphasizing the utilitarian benefits of travel literature.

The first author, Munshi Aminchand, enjoyed significant British patronage. He was fluent in English and trained within the colonial system. So-called new *munshi*s like him preferred English and Urdu to Persian, and frequently worked in the Department of Public Instruction, where they drafted and translated textbooks.[62] Originally a government employee, Aminchand left his post in 1850 to travel with Robert Needham Cust, a commentator on Indian affairs with whom he had worked since 1846. The pair traveled through Punjab, Peshawar, Kashmir, and Sindh with a cavalcade that included "six pack mules, and the requisite number of servants"—though in keeping with the travel lesson's emphasis on practicality and economy, Aminchand never told his student-readers this![63] From Karachi they sailed to Bombay, with Aminchand "taking notes of all he saw under my guidance," Cust recalled. The two men eventually parted ways in Bombay. Cust wrote up an account of his journey, as did Aminchand, "telling the story in his own way."[64] Aminchand then continued his travels independently (see Figure 3.2), before resuming government service.[65] Later in his career he wrote additional books on local culture, customary law, history, and mathematics. He was honored with a title for his distinguished service and was well respected in his native Punjab.[66]

Safarnama was written in simple Urdu and focused on "useful information." Aminchand muted his own presence in the text, eliding commonly discussed matters like living arrangements, bowel movements, and logistics. His account gave no sense of how he traveled, where he stayed, or what he did. Because his travelogue was intended to present an ideal model of the selfless pursuit of knowledge and experience, he falsely told the reader that he had retired from service because of an abiding passion for knowledge and travel, and that he was in no way motivated by "trade or government work."[67] Rather than constitute a meaningful aspect of the narrative, Aminchand's movements serve only to segue between cities and regions. *Safarnama* is both a sourcebook of Indian geography and custom and a model for ideal, educational travel. Its first edition is the first known Urdu travelogue to include a map, offering a visual representation of the India that Aminchand wished for students to imagine as their homeland.

Safarnama was a success, netting a government sponsorship. The review committee was pleased that the book was written by a "well-educated man, who makes no pretense to be a scholar, according to the narrow views of the Hindoo or Mahomedan..., [with] no pretention to elegance of style."[68]

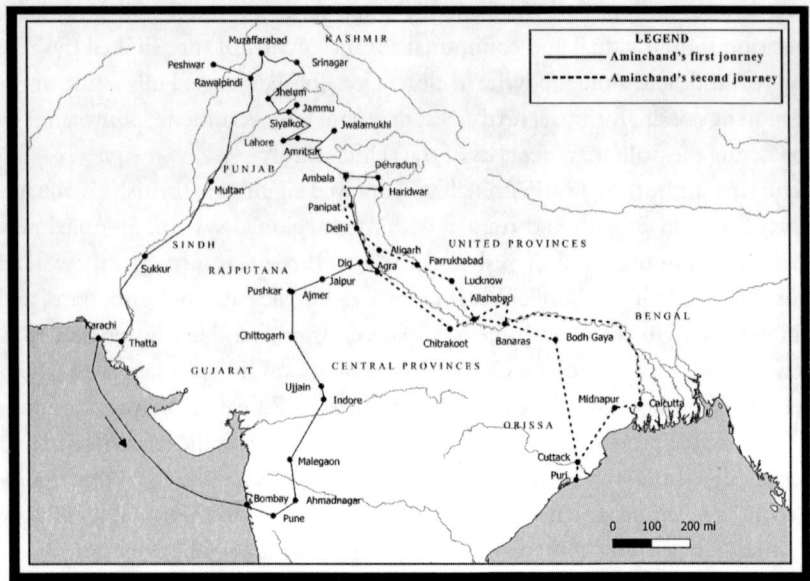

Figure 3.2   Aminchand's travels in India
Source: Author.

It cultivated the idealized image of an Indian Mungo Park: well-traveled, apolitical, unprejudiced, and fully committed to the pursuit of knowledge and the success of British India. His travelogue is filled with didactic suggestions for reimagining India. He particularly expressed disappointment at Indians' inability to recognize one another as fellow countrymen. "Everyone should be aware of the conditions of their country," he wrote.[69] For perhaps the first time, Punjabis were being told that Orissa, too, was their "own country" (*apna mulk*).[70] As this proto-nationalist language might suggest, though, Aminchand's imagined audience was Hindu. He referred to "our Hindu religion," often contrasting it with Islam (thus, he understood the audience for this Urdu textbook to be primarily Hindu). He particularly included descriptions of Hindu pilgrimage sites and temples. In this, Aminchand's travelogue prefigured the Hindu-inflected nationalism that would soon emerge in Bengali travel writing.[71] As seen in Chapter 2, Aminchand underplayed the role and importance of India's princely rulers, and rarely commented on the practicalities of travel between different states. And, of course, just as the reformer-novelist Nazir Ahmad (1830–1912) popularized the government-sponsored pedagogical Urdu novel, Aminchand promoted travel writing.[72]

Similar lessons were taught through pedagogical travel writing in all of India's major languages. In Gujarat, students were assigned Dosabhoy Framjee's travel textbook *Gret Britain Khate ni Musafiri*.[73] Like Aminchand, Framjee spent his life in close contact with the colonial government. In 1857–58 he served as a media censor before traveling to England. For the next half-century he worked in the colonial government as a magistrate, tax collector, and councilman.[74] Also like Aminchand, his travelogue was adopted for study in government schools. The book met a long-standing desire for original travel writing: the Director of Public Instruction of Bombay Presidency had been "anxious for the publication of such a work."[75] Framjee claimed to travel "with the view of obtaining information which he could lay before his countrymen in a useful as well as entertaining form." Emphasizing the "advantages to be gained in point of education and enlightenment," he encouraged readers to judge from his book "the room which exists for improvement in their own [country]" and "obtain a knowledge of the means by which the sought ends could be accomplished." While he initially wrote in English, these utilitarian ends inspired him to instead employ Gujarati so that a greater number of students and general readers would be able to learn from his account. He also hoped, like his fellow Gujarati Karsandas Mulji, that his more accessible account would encourage Indians to travel to Europe.

With the market for travel textbooks booming, many authors submitted proposals for consideration, some of which inevitably failed. One such reject was *Sair-i Punjab*, by two brothers, Kali Rai and Lala Tulsi Ram, who composed a travelogue while in government service.[76] They prepared an initial draft in 1851, but it attracted no interest. They prepared a second draft around 1859 but failed again. The book never made it into Punjab's curriculum. It was ultimately printed, fifteen years later, at a commercial press. By the 1870s, there was enough general interest in travel writing for the book to be sold without government support. The travel lesson had moved out of the classroom and found its way onto the popular market. Despite the government's repeated rejections, *Sair-i Punjab* managed to spread widely across India as a commercial production and is widely available in South Asian archives today.[77]

Conclusion

In colonial India, the travel lesson taught students how to see the world and move within it. Through pedagogical travelogues and classroom activities like map reading, pupils were instructed to approach the world as a space of movement, a space for imagination and ambition. Early efforts to promote travel drew on translated accounts from English like Mungo Park's *Travels in the Interior of Africa*. Soon, though, Indian writers began with government support to supply original travel textbooks that offered models of ideal, apolitical travel for the sake of knowledge. These colonially approved travel accounts often celebrated European civilization and asked students to imagine India as a prosperous land under a single British administration. A host of travel textbooks emerged, some successful, others not. The comparative examples of Aminchand and Dosabhoy Framjee show how official sanction and government support allowed Indian travel writing to proliferate across India's colonial education system.

Colonial efforts to translate and publish vernacular travel writing for Indian students persisted at least into the 1880s, when the Madras School Book and Vernacular Society translated Sami'ullah Khan's *Safarnama* of Europe into Telugu and Tamil.[78] Travel writing remained a part of the syllabus well into the twentieth century. By then, though, the travel lesson was widely familiar to Urdu readers. Through the colonial school system, generations of students were exposed to the writings of model travelers like Aminchand and Mungo Park. They had been taught the ideology of "useful travel" and its benefits. They apprised from the writings and speeches of men like Sir Bartle Frere that the government would offer greater employment opportunities to apolitical travelers.[79] Meanwhile, Indians convinced of the benefits of travel themselves promoted the link between travel, education, and success. Some attempted to write their own pedagogical travelogues. Others designed their own initiatives, like one school instructor, Rai Bahadur Pyarelal in Delhi, who encouraged "traveling and promotion of education amongst his countrymen" by having students write travel narratives themselves, even if only based on a school field trip.[80]

As popular interest in travelogues grew, travel writing increasingly became the domain of commercial publishers. The government-sponsored Delhi Vernacular Translation Society lamented this shift, complaining that their books could not remain competitive with native presses.[81] Increasingly, Indians produced and bought travel accounts themselves without the need for government involvement. The 1860s and '70s saw the emergence of an entirely new generation of travel writers who were able to publish their works and even turn a profit. But as this chapter shows, the travelogue's sudden flowering was not simply the work of the zeitgeist, but the product of decades of concerted effort to promote the travel lesson and foster the practice of reading travelogues. Though popular travel writing was influenced by the travel lesson and its discourse of beneficial travel, commercial works were not beholden to official ideas and aesthetics. Indians were now able to imagine the world and write about it as they pleased. As they did, the genre became increasingly accessible. The geographical range of Urdu travel writing grew, as did the diversity of its global imaginations.

Chapter 4 begins with an excerpt from one such work. Dr 'Ali Sabzvari was a dentist and big game hunter who lived in a small *qasba* town in Bihar. His three extant travelogues cover Borneo, Kenya, and New York City. In the following passage, Dr Sabzvari describes his arrival in Kenya in 1899 and his plans to make money while enjoying the country. Dr Sabzvari's text imagines a world filled with pleasures and possibilities. Like Kazim Barlas, discussed in the introduction, he saw the world through his own version of colonial capitalism. He suggested Indians could become wealthy by trading with Africans, who are imagined to be ignorant and gullible. In his account, Indians acted in Africa much as the British did in India, enjoying the pleasures of the land, hunting animals for sport, keeping servants, and growing rich. They made themselves at home in a foreign land, setting up their own neighborhoods, eating their own food, playing their own music, and befriending their expatriate compatriots. Dr Sabzvari's imagination showed his readers new possibilities of Indian aspiration, ambition, and pleasure.

Notes

1. *General Report, Bengal Presidency, 1843–1844*, appendix F, xli. Emphasis added.
2. Ramaswamy, *Terrestrial Lessons*, 61.
3. Prasad, "Tracking Modernity," 9.
4. Mongia, *Migration*, 1–3; Green, "Africa in Indian Ink," 131.
5. Zuelow, *Modern Tourism*, 60–90.
6. Cited in Viswanathan, *Masks of Conquest*, 139.
7. Rastegar, *Literary Modernity*, 107.
8. Mukhopadhyay, "Wheels," 17. See also Sadid, *Urdu Adab*, 127.
9. Viswanathan, *Masks of Conquest*, 56.
10. Zuelow, *Modern Tourism*, 29.
11. Porter, "Convention," 88.
12. Frere, *Speeches*, 129. Of course, every British administrator in India had themselves undertaken foreign travel!
13. Frere, *Speeches*, 130.
14. Macaulay, *Miscellaneous Works*, 1:193.
15. *General Report, Bengal, 1856–7*, appendix C, 81.
16. Pyare La'l, *Dunya*, 142.
17. *Report on the State, 1858–9*, 30.
18. East India Company, *Correspondence*, 88.

19. Frere, *Speeches*, 88. Several more instances of community support for overseas travel as a form of education among the Kayasth community are given in Carroll, "Seavoyage Controversy," 266.
20. Frere, *Speeches*, 130–31.
21. Ramaswamy, *Terrestrial Lessons*, 74.
22. Ranade, *Sir Bartle Frere*, 144.
23. Mulji, *Sairistan*, 117–18. Translation from the Urdu.
24. Scott, "Translated Liberties," 8.
25. Quoted in Prasad, "Tracking Modernity," 113.
26. Iyer, "Twenty-Fifth Convocation," 121. For similar discourses among 1920s Yoruba-speaking travelers, see Jones, *Crossroads*, 82.
27. Frere, *Speeches*, 10.
28. Frere, *Speeches*, 2.
29. Commission on Education, *Abstract and Analysis*, 88.
30. Roy intended to publish a travelogue, though it is unclear if he ultimately did so. Carpenter, *Last Days*, 101.
31. *Asiatic Journal* (1823), 550.
32. *Asiatic Journal* (1842), 336.
33. Mukhopadhyay, "Wheels," 18.
34. Abu Talib Khan, *Travels* (2009), 58. The original print version referenced is Abu Talib Khan, *Masir-i Talibi* (1812).
35. Abu Talib Khan, *Masir-i Talibi* (1827); Abu Talib Khan, *Travels* (1836).
36. *General Report, Bengal, 1833–1843*, cxx.
37. *Report Bengal, 1836*, 142.
38. Malcolm, *Sketches*. This text was also translated into Urdu. See Malcolm, *Halat-i Iran*.
39. *Accounts and Papers*, 24, 1:400.
40. *Report Bengal, 1836*, 160.
41. *General Report, Bengal, 1846–7*, 46.
42. Park, *Safarnama* (1842); Park, *Safarnama* (1853). The ASBS was founded in 1838 on the model of the Calcutta Schoolbook Society. Both were run by boards with a majority of Europeans. Support for these bodies came from the government and community members who promoted colonial Indian education. Srivastava, *The Province of Agra*, 246; Ramaswamy, *Terrestrial Lessons*, 267; Ahmed, *Social Ideas*, 21.
43. Stark, *Empire of Books*, 50.
44. Pratt, *Imperial Eyes*, 73.
45. Pratt, *Imperial Eyes*, 75.
46. Pratt, *Imperial Eyes*, 77.
47. Pratt, *Imperial Eyes*, 82.

48. Cited in Pratt, *Imperial Eyes*, 81.
49. Pratt, *Imperial Eyes*, 79.
50. Park, *Safarnama (1853)*, 1–2.
51. Park, *Travels in the Interior*, 1.
52. Park, *Safarnama* (1853), 3.
53. Pandit Rataneshvar, *Patramalika*.
54. *General Report, Bengal, 1833–1843*, c.
55. Bayly, *Empire*, 235.
56. Pandit Rataneshvar, *Patramalika*, 3.
57. Trnovec, *Conquest*, 38.
58. Ní Loingsigh, *Postcolonial Eyes*, 179.
59. For a brief account of the Translation Society, see Minault, "Master Ramchandra," 97; Anonymous [R. Temple], "Village Schools," 187–88. On the *Tarikh-i Yusufi* in school syllabi, see *General Report, 1845–1846*, xix.
60. For an account of time dedicated to various subjects, see *General Report, Bengal, 1852–3*, 203.
61. Framji, *Musafiri*, 7.
62. Bayly, *Empire*, 229–30.
63. Penner, *Robert Needham Cust*, 135. See also Cust's papers at the British Library, particularly journals three and four. Letters from Aminchand to Cust are also preserved in this collection. I thank Irfan Khan for this reference.
64. Cust, *Essays*, 231.
65. Aminchand, *Report*. See also Stark, "Associational Culture," 16.
66. Massy, *Chiefs and Families*, 140. *Punjab District Gazeteer*, 28A:209. A school in Punjab still bears his name. Thanks to a recorded interview with his great-great-granddaughter, his descendants can be traced to present-day Seattle and the Bay Area. Vasishth, "Interview," 25.
67. Aminchand, *Safarnama*, 1–2.
68. Aminchand, *Safarnama*, n.p.
69. Aminchand, *Safarnama*, 2–3. Yet his idea is inchoate: he speaks of India as "our land" (*apna mulk*) but calls its various regions "other lands" (*aur mulk*).
70. Anderson, *Imagined Communities*, 47–66.
71. Chatterjee, "Discovering India," 200.
72. Nazir Ahmad's approach to India's cities, though, is radically different: "Nazir Ahmad's catalogue of towns is a claim staked for the irreducible particularity of places and their associated textures of life, existing alongside and negotiating the new globalizing experience that were influencing both trade and textbooks." Siddique, "Worlds of Advice," 184.
73. Framji, *Musafiri*.
74. Buckland, *Dictionary*, 229.

75. Framji, *Musafiri*, 7–8.

76. Kali Rai and Tulsi Ram, *Sair-i Punjab*, 6.

77. I have found copies at various libraries in Delhi, Hyderabad, Patna, and London.

78. Khan, *Musafiran* (2012), 16.

79. The constant emphasis on "apolitical" travel pointed to the very real British concern that Indians were traveling for anticolonial or subversive purposes. Seema Alavi's work on the travel patterns of "Indian Arabs" shows that, from a colonial perspective, there was certainly a "wrong way" to travel. Alavi, *Muslim Cosmopolitanism*, 7–8. See also Alavi, "Fugitive Mullahs," 1338.

80. Shankar, *A'ina*, 2.

81. *General Report, Bengal, 1846–7*, 3.

Part II

A Terrifying World

Dr ʻAli Shah Sabzvari
Barakat-i Akbari Press, Allahabad, 1935

[Mombasa, 1899]

I had set my heart on going to Nairobi, and Qasim bin Mansur [my Swahili servant in Mombasa] had set his on traveling to Nairobi with me. He said, "I will be your servant there, and I will accompany you on your hunting expeditions in the jungle." I really did need someone courageous, and Qasim was a brave and fearless young man. His faithfulness and service had found him a place in my heart, and so I happily agreed to hire him on a monthly salary. He eagerly prepared for the journey with me.

The plan was to go to Nairobi and make it my base. From there I would make regular trips into the surrounding jungle to go hunting and make tours through the encampments of the wild tribes, where I would acquire elephant tusks and rhinoceros horns. Back then, you could collect thousands of rupees' worth of the stuff from these people for just a few pennies. In those days, the biggest ivory trader in Mombasa was Seth Isma'il.[1] I spoke with him about what all I might need. On his advice I bought fake pearls, spools of thick copper, iron wire, and cloth for the savages. Once I had gotten a small tent and everything I needed for my meals, I was prepared to travel to Nairobi with Qasim and [my Punjabi servant] Mi'raj.

Finally, on the 14th of August, 1899, we boarded the train to Nairobi and left Mombasa and Kalindi behind. Ten miles after Kalindi jungle began to appear on all sides. The sight was breathtaking. It was not so much a wilderness as a garden in the full bloom of spring. You couldn't look away. The light winds felt delightful. If you looked behind you, you would see a gorgeous range of blue hills, and, at their center, the white buildings of Mombasa and Kalindi. You could clearly make out the ocean sparkling in the golden sunlight. This view remained for some time, but, just as the world turns, this pleasing sight soon began to slip away until the garden was replaced by desert and wild wasteland on either side of the track. Ahead of us, the peaks of the Rabai Hills came into view. There were copses of dry trees here and there, and rows of small bushes as well. Otherwise, there was nothing but glistening sand as far as they eye could see.

After twenty miles a change took place. The train entered a large, dense jungle that appeared to be filled with animals, though they were not immediately visible to the eye because the jungle was so thick. And also because any nearby animals took fright from the rumbling of the train and could only be seen as they bounded away. Sometimes we would spy huts belonging to the jungle people and their children. It was now late in the afternoon, and we had already traveled some eighty miles when wide plains replaced the thick jungle. We were gaping at these jungles and plains when suddenly we saw an unforgettable sight. The engine whistle and the rumbling of the train had startled a flock of ostriches, who began to flee in every direction. Some of them were so confused that they raced alongside the train for the longest time. Their manner of running was a wonderful sight, awkward but swift.... Was this a train journey or something from a bioscope?[2]

***

Nairobi is 347 miles from Mombasa. Since it has been made the headquarters of the Uganda Railway its population had rapidly expanded for miles. As in Kalindi, all the buildings being built here were temporary structures made of zinc sheeting. Here the population and energy were much greater than at Kalindi. The bazaars were bustling. Aside from the railway headquarters and workshops there were other government offices, a hospital, a police station, a court, and a post office. Everything was available in the bazaar. Itinerant vendors roamed about, crying out their wares. In the evening Punjabi coolies could be seen eating *alu chhole* and *chat.* There were all sorts of sweets, breads, and kebabs for sale. And to top it all off, the moment Nairobi was established no less than a dozen [Punjabi] prostitutes came to live here, each of them accompanied by their own musical ensembles. Their presence made the bazaar that much livelier. Group after group of Punjabi men milled outside their houses. The moment dusk fell you would hear the *thwack* of tablas and the warbling of vocal improvisations [*tans*], which quickly attracted crowds of people. Chanda *jan,* Moti *jan,* Bota *jan.* These women had presumably all taken loans from home to come here, and were now raking in the rupees. Their wrists and ankles dripped with gold jewelry....

This region had once been afflicted by the predations of lions and cheetahs, which took many lives. Many Punjabis became the prey of vicious people [*mardum-khor insan*] too.[3] At that time, the land around Nairobi was hilly and forested, with a river running near the populated area. The area was populated by two savage tribes, the Vakiko'ibu [Kikuyu?] and the Maasai. The latter tribe is warlike and bloodthirsty. Its members roam the bazaars in groups every day. The men are buck naked. Some hang animal pelts over their backs. They are never without a bow and arrow and spear, as though constantly prepared for war. They are always streaked in a type of red-colored grease and are loyal to their chiefs. They typically eat raw meat. They hunt every type of animal with their own hands and consume it raw. They file their two front teeth into sharp points, which makes it easier for them to tear into the meat. They are masters of archery and spear throwing; their hands never slip. They make houses of grass and leaves in the jungle and raise sheep and goats. Their women tie strips of leather around their waist to cover their privates. On their hands and legs they wear something like bangles made from fat loops of iron or copper wire. On their necks they prefer necklaces of fake pearls.[4]

Notes

1. A man presumably of Indian extraction, possibly Gujarati.
2. Sabzvari, *Khaufnak: Afriqa*, 23–25.
3. The Urdu might also be translated as "cannibals" or "man-eating," but the phrase seems metaphorical, not literal.
4. Sabzvari, *Khaufnak: Afriqa*, 29–32.

4

Worldly Pleasures

As noted in the introduction, *Khaufnak Dunya* was one of renowned Urdu writer and critic Naiyer Masud's favorite childhood reads. Of it he wrote, "I fell in love with this book. I would read it again and again, and every time I read it, I would discover a new kind of pleasure."[1] The book left such a deep impression on him that, decades later, he resolved to rediscover it and learn more about its enigmatic author. Eventually he managed to piece together the story. Dr 'Ali Sabzvari was a Punjabi with an insatiable love for travel and big game hunting. His first trip, in 1899, took him to hunt and trade in East Africa. Later, when he moved to San Francisco to study dentistry, he immediately availed the relative proximity to spend five months hunting in Brazil. On his return to Asia, he traveled, hunted, and traded in Borneo and across India, before settling in Bihar, where he could easily hunt in his leisure time.[2] He wrote at least three travelogues about these journeys, copies of which are today scattered across India and Pakistan. They are not high literature, but they are filled with excitement and astonishment. Masud remembered Sabzvari not for the beauty of his prose or the delicacy of his thought, but for how his writing fired the imagination, and, above all, for the way it evoked ever new kinds of *pleasure*.

Some of the travel accounts discussed in the previous two chapters also sought to evoke pleasure, but this was only a secondary concern. Chapter 2 showed how princely states used the genre to propose aspirational political visions for their own futures. The last chapter showed how pedagogical travel writing used in colonial schools projected a vision of British colonial modernity. A third strand of travel writing, which emerged in the 1870s, put pleasure at the forefront.

Authors often did so explicitly, telling readers that the primary mode of the account would be enjoyment. Examining the period between 1870 and 1935, this chapter argues that this pleasure emerged from these travelogues' familiar forms and aesthetics, but also because they allowed readers to imagine themselves gaining in respect, intelligence, and wealth while traveling to distant places. In the passage above, Dr Sazbvari painted a dramatic picture of East Africa as an enchanting land where visitors could grow rich, and that too without losing access to their favorite foods and musicians. This global imagination suggested readers think about the world as a space of play.

This chapter examines two aspects of this literature. The first half shows how pedagogy and pleasure merged in travel writing primarily meant for children. The second half considers travel writing explicitly for adult men that detailed the salacious side of life and asked readers to imagine the world as their playground, often one that focused on the visibility or accessibility of women's bodies. Both halves are united in their tendency to locate their aspiration and imagination in a derivation of colonialism meant for Indian travelers. Finding pleasure in the world, these texts sometimes suggested, meant mastering it in ways that mirrored British colonial practice and discourse. In Kenya, Dr Sabzvari reveled in the pleasures of life, enjoying nature and the performances of courtesans. Picturizing a Kenya oddly bereft of Europeans, he wrote with an air of civilizational and intellectual superiority. He delighted in his ability to enrich himself by swindling Africans, just as Europeans did in their own travelogues. In painting this bucolic picture of Indian colonial ease, Dr Sabzvari invited his readers to imagine themselves as potential colonizers.

These accounts emerged within a broader movement in vernacular literature toward enjoyable reading practices. In *Print and Pleasure*, Francesca Orsini explores a central puzzle in the history of Indian printing in the mid- to late-nineteenth century: "How could a diverse, diffuse and vibrant print culture emerge in the context of such low and sluggish increases in literacy and formal schooling?"[3] To answer this question, she turns to the development of a textual entertainment industry. On the one hand, neo- and non-literate groups were brought into literary culture through the inclusion of oral traditions in print. On the other, Urdu authors increasingly hybridized older genres with "new textual dynamics and new discourses," creating novel forms to entice new readers.[4] These forms were eagerly consumed by upwardly mobile individuals looking to claim their place in the colonial economy. The pedagogical bent of early Urdu travel writing, as described in the previous chapter, did not disappear as reading became an increasingly popular pastime; rather it made room for pleasure and entertainment alongside it.

This edu-tainment matrix was not always appreciated by colonial administrators. Nor did it impress those Indian elites who preferred a scholarly tone to Dr Sabzvari's dramatic tiger hunts. Ultimately, though, the emergence of popular print culture meant that it hardly mattered what stuffy elites and administrators thought.

A remarkable innovation critical to the evocation of a global imagination was that popular Urdu travel writers attempted not just to describe their travels, but to replicate them. Authors claimed their books would not simply inform readers about distant lands but would actually take them there. By reading a travelogue, they claimed, you could gain all the knowledge, experience, and enjoyment of travel for a fraction of the cost and none of the hassle. Travelogues of this kind became known as a "trip from home" (*ghar baitha safar*). The concept offered travel even to those whose financial or social position limited their mobility. From the comfort of home or the library, travelogues promised readers "experience" (*tajarba*) alongside "knowledge" (*ma'lumat*). Facilitating journeys from home inspired authors to experiment with new styles and forms of travel writing that engaged and entertained a wider audience. This chapter examines this diversification with a focus on writing on Asia and Africa.

Pleasurable travel writing like this is virtually unexplored. The best studied Urdu travel accounts of Asia are political or "scientific" accounts by "great men," including works like Sir Ross Masood's *Safarnama-i Rus o Japan* (Travelogue of Russia and Japan, 1923). Masood's writing was a noteworthy example of how "Japan provided newly globalized intellectuals with a template for empowering Muslim-ruled polities."[5] But these types of intellectual accounts do not make up the majority of Urdu travel writing, nor do they tell us what ordinary Urdu speakers wanted. Urdu speakers enjoyed reading about the world, but they were not all intellectuals bent on empowering Muslim-ruled polities. They wanted to be entertained. Even as Masood imagined a resurgent Asia fighting back against Europe, other Urdu authors imagined East and Southeast Asia as a region where empowered Indian men could go to enjoy themselves in supposedly libidinous spaces abroad. By turning to the politics and poetics of pleasure, this chapter offers a counterweight to the existing scholarly focus on accounts centered on anti-colonialism, nationalism, and other political orientations. Pleasure was the popular, softer side of Urdu's global engagement.

Performative and Imaginative Journeys

Chapter 3 showed how students in colonial schools were asked to imagine themselves traveling on a British ship to London. Soon these lessons began to

appear within travelogues themselves, which called on audiences to imagine they
were traveling with the author:

> Imagine we are in the Bay of Bengal, sailing in one of the large steamers that are so
> popular these days. We are on a journey. When we reach the mouth of the Hooghly,
> we look down from the side of the ship. The water, which had been so blue, has now
> turned light green. The steamer is being guided by a lightship which is anchored
> nearby. There are 120 more miles to Calcutta.[6]

Through these instructions, the use of vivid description, and the invocation of
emotion, Urdu authors suggested that, simply by reading, one could travel the world
from home. This idea first appears in Urdu in an 1861 book by Pandit Kanhaiyalal,
Sair-i Kashmir (A tour of Kashmir, 1861). As a young man, Kanhaiyalal worked at
the Government School in Delhi, but in 1840 his financial situation obligated him
to relocate to Lahore, then under Sikh rule. Fluent in English, he quickly found
employment with the British, and a few years later, when Punjab was annexed
to British India, Pandit Kanhaiyalal formally joined the colonial administration.
He was still new on the job when he was tasked with accompanying an Englishman
on a journey to Kashmir. So, "as ordered," he set off with the man.

> As I traveled, I kept a small record of every stage of the journey in the form of a daily
> diary. Once I returned, I was looking through this diary when it struck me that if
> I were to publish this account it would not be devoid of pleasure for those who
> are passionate about travel to other lands. Moreover, those who do not possess the
> ability to undertake such a lengthy trip will, on reading it, become informed of the
> conditions of the places commented upon.[7]

Kanhaiyalal's text was not merely a report, like Aminchand's, but a textual journey
to Kashmir that would offer its readers the pleasures and benefits of travel from
home. *Sair*'s cover page invoked the region's beauty with a Persian-language
invocation of God in bold letters: "In the name of the One who adorns this world
with gardens and commands the color and scent of its flowers." If Aminchand
had hoped to inspire readers to follow his example by embarking on their own
journeys, Kanhaiyalal hinted that reading could itself be a form of travel.

A few years later, the Gujarati traveler Karsandas Mulji, discussed in Chapter 3,
was more explicit. He wrote of his own travelogue, *Sairistan-i Englaind*:
"O fleet-footed ambassador, whose pen sings the sweetest melodies, widely have
you roamed in the land of letters! Tell me: have you yet encountered ... such a
work from the field of travel so excellent that by reading it ... one may perform
the journey all while sitting at home?"[8] The idea that travel writing was "an ideal

medium for those who wish to travel from home" became increasingly prominent in the following decades and remained a common element of travel writing well into the twentieth century.⁹ A verse popular among travel writers mimicked the excited declaration of the student realizing they could travel the world by reading:

> To take a seat and travel the world?
>   I have seen this wonder in a book!¹⁰

One prolific writer, Nawab Muhammad 'Umar 'Ali Khan, ruler of Basoda State, included the idea in his list of the benefits of reading travelogues:

1. You will know the world without ever leaving your home.
2. You will not get lost should you later decide to travel.
3. You will become more familiar with world history.
4. A knowledge of the variability of climates enhances medical knowledge.
5. A knowledge of crops and their regional prices is a boon to the businessman.
6. You will become worthy of respect thanks to your wisdom and knowledge.¹¹

'Umar 'Ali Khan here claimed that reading about travel would give readers nearly all the benefits of travel without ever leaving home.

This section examines two popular and representative travel-from-home accounts intended primarily for children: *Sair-i Maqbul* (Maqbul's tour/The most acclaimed journey, 1872) and *Tarikh-i Badi'* (A wondrous account, 1879). Both offered a mélange of what the latter book called "travels and journeys and experience and knowledge!"¹² Both these travelogues were at least partially fabricated. In every language, and in every era, travel and fiction have had an entangled relationship.¹³ Consider Daniel Defoe's *Robinson Crusoe* or Jonathan Swift's *Gulliver's Travels*. For contemporary American readers, these books are fictional novels. This understanding of genre, though, belongs to just one moment in time.¹⁴ In the eighteenth century, there was often little distinction between the "travelogue" and the "novel."¹⁵ Many English readers of the eighteenth century understood these English novels to be veracious travel accounts.¹⁶ Boundaries of genre are also located in place. In South Asian libraries both these novels are often shelved in the travel section today. In short, travelogues often gain the attention of readers by offering eyewitness accounts of the world, but retain it through the judicious use of embellishment, and sometimes outright fabrication. In some cultural contexts, the discovery of fraud might lead to scandal, but not for colonial-era Urdu readers. As Pasha Khan argues, in this social milieu, the distinction between fact and fiction was opaque; few readers were troubled by selective veracity.¹⁷ Rebecca Jones similarly argues that African travel writing shared "textual conventions and readerly expectations" with literary fiction, and that separating the two ruptures the literature's "textual ecology."[18] True or not, the travel accounts discussed below are not larger than life. They present themselves as travelogues, and generally retain their verisimilitude.[19] Intended primarily for an audience of children, they focus on crafting an ideal but enjoyable textual journey.[20]

The Most Popular Journey

"Oh, good sirs! ... If you listen to my tale, consider it carefully and heed it, then I am certain ... it will astonish and entertain you, and you will also gain much experience from it."[21] Thus began Munshi Sayyid Ghulam Haidar Khan's *Sair-i Maqbul* (1872), one of Urdu's most successful nineteenth-century travelogues.[22] *Sair* is the fictional travel memoir of a seventeenth-century trader, Agha Maqbul Isfahani. The book was one of the first popular travelogues to include foldout maps, introducing readers to rare visual images of the world (and also reflecting its publisher's appraisal of its commercial value). Maqbul, through his first-person narration and his claim to be a self-made man who traveled and prospered through his own ambition and intellect, showed readers just how wide that world was. His journeys, which lasted from 1664 until 1723, took him across virtually the entire world. He introduced readers to names like Irkutsk, Charleston, Salamanca, and Formosa. The book displays intense genre hybridity, encompassing elements of the travelogue, autobiography, history, epic, advice manual, and even commerce guide. It is also a novel of sorts, for a significant portion of the book is an Indianized retelling of *Robinson Crusoe*.

This overlap with a classic of British colonial fantasy is no coincidence. Maqbul's life story broadly delineated an Asian version of the British colonial myth. He used his limited resources to trade. He accumulated wealth and garnered respect around the world. When, like Crusoe, he was shipwrecked, he taught civilization to Africans while performing archaeological studies. In this sense, the text expressed an aspiration—that Indian readers could do what Maqbul and the British had done—and served as a primer on how to do it. The book entertained readers while teaching them about commerce, trade, and travel. It succeeded thanks to its innovative, engaging format. Meanwhile, its easy orality meant it could reach a wide range of Urdu speakers, including those who may not have had access to literacy or formal schooling.

Sair was initially written as a submission to a government contest for educational books in Indian languages. The contest began in 1868 in response to colonial concerns that the preference for poetry, epics, and love stories in India prevented "Oriental people from recognizing the extent to which the evils of their society were valorized in their literature, whose gorgeous texture and rich imagery were a seductive distraction from the plot and theme."[23] In order to promote reading that was wholesome, educational, and moralizing, but also entertaining, the government offered cash prizes for "the production of useful works in the vernacular."[24] As is well known, the winner of the first competition was Nazir Ahmad's *Mir'at al-'Urus*, a moralistic novel that emphasized the traits of the ideal Muslim woman.[25] Among the contest's losers was *Sair-i Maqbul*.

Haidar Khan's pedagogical objectives certainly aligned with those of the contest's sponsors. He agreed that Indians were reading too many love stories, but while he disdained the Urdu romance as vulgar, he also recognized its popularity. His goal was to make the romance compatible with reformist objectives. Combining the romance with the travelogue, Ghulam Haidar took colonialism's most prized genre and reworked it to produce an entertaining text suitable for all religious communities, genders, and ages. The book was original, engaging, and informative to boot. So why did it not win the contest?

Alas, the prize committee detested it. Mathew Kempson, the Director of Public Instruction, called it "useless," a "waste of paper." He found it "dreary reading" with "no general information, no literary skill, no humour, and little power of reflection." He complained that Haidar Khan "has the art of prosing on interminably like a professional story-teller, regardless of inconsistencies and repetitions." Worse, the "commercial gentlemen who do the traveling are not 'characters.' They suffer shipwreck over and over again, and are constantly in trouble, but are rarely equal to the emergency. Their hair stands on end, their liver becomes water, or they become *be hosh* [unconscious]." It was a terrible source of geographic knowledge and unlikely to achieve its stated aim of "encouraging a taste for travel."[26] It lacked a "manly tone." Its information was out of date and vague: "The account of Madagascar ... might refer just as well to the Mauritius or Jamaica.... The author ... might produce something more worthy ... if he treats of matters which fall within his own observation and experience in India, instead of carrying his readers to Konk and Timbuctoo."[27]

Kempson hated it, but much to his chagrin, he also understood that Indian readers would love it. He admitted that its language was "fluent and idiomatic" and that he could "easily imagine that a circle of uncritical native listeners would be highly amused by the narrative."[28] And amused they were. After his book failed to win the colonial prize, Haidar promptly re-submitted it to Urdu's most renowned publisher, the Naval Kishore Press in Lucknow. The press brought out two editions, in 1872 and 1898. This pivot from government patronage to a popular commercial publisher exemplifies the shift in the production of travelogues. Early travelogues were printed by government order because there was not a large enough popular market to turn a profit through sales alone. In the 1870s, though, men like Haidar could expect to find a publisher and reach a readership directly. Official critics like Kempson had little power to control the genre now.

One can see why Kempson would be vexed by this text. From the moment Maqbul begins his narrative, it is clear that space and time will not align. The fictional protagonist was born in the 1600s, but he described the world as it was in the 1860s, with Haidar presumably using information taken from geography textbooks.[29] Many of these sources were clearly out of date. Maqbul's description of the United States, for instance, corresponds to 1836, suggesting that Haidar was not drawing from the most contemporary literature available.[30] By contrast, all the historical events Maqbul described occurred in the seventeenth century. Like a Muslim Forrest Gump, Maqbul was present at every major event of his lifetime, from the eruption of Etna in 1669 to the sacking of Basra in 1685–86. These events anachronistically played out in a nineteenth-century geography in which the British Empire oversaw the world's transportation and trade. *Sair*'s narrative was set in the past, but the book was meant to offer readers and listeners useful and accurate information about the present-day world as imagined in British India. Thus, locations were given their English names, rather than their Arabic, Persian, or other original versions. Dates, too, appear only according to the Gregorian calendar. In Urdu this dissociation of time and space was not unsettling because each aspect played its own independent role, supplying either knowledge or experience. Maqbul himself, meanwhile, was a modern subject. His beliefs, language, and actions can only be described as the embodiment of nineteenth-century ideals, similar to those found in *Mir'at al-'Urus*. Maqbul taught his readers to travel, economize, study hard, respect "civilization," and disdain injustice.

In the book's first lines Agha Maqbul states that he was born into a family of traders in Isfahan. In 1664, he opened a shop and left home to trade across the Middle East, not returning for twenty years. Maqbul's narrative was structured around descriptions of the places he visited: some places received long descriptions, while others merited just a few commercial notes. All destinations were clearly marked and described (and indexed!), much like a geography book or atlas. He enumerated the goods available in various ports, displaying his business savvy and diligence. Maqbul was also fascinated by movement and detailed his journeys in a modern way. Chapter 1 argued that precolonial narratives often elided detailed descriptions of their journeys and instead focused on their destinations. Maqbul, though, embodied the nineteenth-century modern by giving ample attention to the mundane details of his journeys. He made sure to identify the vessels he traveled on and to name and describe their English captains (the total dominance of the English in Indian Ocean travel is another anachronism).

Maqbul also emphasized his businesslike charisma and ability to make friends easily. The people he befriended told him their own stories, which he then recorded. The focus of the narrative shifts between Agha Maqbul and his friends as they endure shipwrecks, highwaymen, and unscrupulous partners and guides, only to be saved by remarkably ubiquitous Englishmen.[31] This layering is typical of the *dastan* genre. In this tradition of epic romances, the story is renewed using an endless cycle of tales that switch from narrator to narrator. The stories of Maqbul's friends take up a significant portion of his book, including some of its most remarkable tales, such as that of his friend Yusuf, who moved to the United States, married a Native American woman, and ran port between Portugal and Charleston.

Ultimately, though, it is Maqbul's own stories that are most astonishing. Roughly a third of the book, and its most engaging portion, describes Maqbul's escape from Berbers and subsequent arrival on a lonely island. This retelling of Robinson Crusoe's journey is remarkable for the way Maqbul's commercial career ultimately led him to fully occupy the role of colonizer and to fantasize about civilizational superiority and domination. Even as he remained faithful to the themes of Defoe's work, Ghulam Haidar Indianized its content. The action is relocated from the Caribbean to the Indian Ocean—Maqbul's island is located in today's Djibouti. Cannibalism, a European obsession and a theme of *Robinson Crusoe*, had no place here.[32] Rather than potential terrors needing to be managed, in *Sair* the natives are docile beings requiring love and care.

More like Crusoe, Maqbul is the monarch of all he surveys as he systematically explores "his" island. In colonial schools, students learned from textbook travel accounts that the British traveled the world, profiting from it and civilizing it. Urdu readers were familiar with images of Europeans as benevolent civilizers abroad. Here they found Maqbul functioning as civilizer to Africa. Maqbul became a benevolent colonizer, helping his subjects and assessing his land's natural and architectural value. The mimicry even led him to measure and map Africa's archaeological ruins. This was an elaborate fantasy of the Indian as African colonist.[33] He was a modern Mungo Park, a hero who acted out "the values that underwrote the greatest non-reciprocal non-exchange of all time: The Civilizing Mission."[34] Urdu speakers, the text implied, could be colonizers, too.

Like Mungo Park, Maqbul spoke and acted with benevolence in Africa; he was pointedly more generous than Crusoe, who did not treat his island's people as entirely human. Although Maqbul considered the Africans frightening, they otherwise bore little similarity to the inhabitants of Defoe's island. Crusoe infamously gave his friend Friday an arbitrary name, but Maqbul named his friends Muhsin and Muhsina, both actual Muslim names, meaning "benefactor."[35] These names acknowledge the pair's role in ensuring his survival on the island. However, they are not identified as Muslim, despite their location in an undeniably Muslim region of Africa (as will be seen in Chapter 5, many Urdu writers failed to acknowledge African and Asian peoples as fellow Muslims). Another twist in the Crusoe story that aligns Maqbul's account with the dastan rather than the English novel is how he made his fortune. Rather than survive by virtue of his own industry, as he had throughout the rest of his narrative, here Maqbul stumbles on a trove of gold in a cave. When he is finally rescued, he sensibly invests it in commercial ventures. In *Sair*, the Urdu romance met colonial pragmatism.

Sair thus took up the pedagogical travelogue, but made it palatable to a wide audience by wedding it to pleasurable forms of Urdu literature without losing sight of the genre's educational bent. While education still lay at the heart of the text, the colonial travel chronotope and the supposedly objective narration of a single male explorer were both abandoned as Ghulam Haidar Khan fashioned a text that entertained readers and offered them the benefits of travel without ever leaving home. He invited his readers to imagine the possibilities of the Indian traveler-trader, one who is intelligent, industrious, and respected at home and abroad. Maqbul lived in a British world, traveling on English ships, interacting with English captains, and following colonial trading routes. He asserted a medial space in a civilizational hierarchy. Maqbul was not shown to be superior to the English, but he was certainly presented as superior to Africans, Asians, Arabs, and Native Americans. Even before Indians began to migrate to eastern Africa in great numbers, Maqbul asked his listeners, children in particular, to imagine what they might do there. Given the tens of thousands of Indians who went to work and visit Africa in the 1890s and 1900s, at least a few of them would have read this book in their childhood.[36] These travelers must have imagined themselves in Africa long before they went themselves.

A Wondrous History

Tarikh-i Badi' (1879) was another entertaining account that taught that travel and intellectual ambition could unlock social and financial success. The book claimed to be the first-person travel narrative of a seven-year-old child named Munshi Muhammad Yaʿqub Khan who wrote to encourage other children to travel. He claimed that he preferred to write in Persian but that he opted for the more demotic Urdu to better reach his target audience and disseminate his newfound knowledge.

The details of Ya'qub's travels are of less importance here than the shape of the text and its framing, which exemplify the play between pleasure and pedagogy that developed in this period.

Addressing the reader, Ya'qub explained that the book would narrate a voyage with his father through Punjab, Delhi, and the Deccan:

> I was studying the seventh chapter [of Sa'di's *Gulistan*] when my dear father occasioned to take a trip to the state of Jind. I went with him.... Then ... my father intended to travel to the Deccan. I decided to join him for, according to the poet Sa'di, gaining the experience of travel is necessary. As he writes in the *Gulistan*: As long as you remain in the house, o unformed one, you will never become human.[37]

On his journeys, he bantered with maharajas, befriended British residents, and endeared himself to all he met through his intelligent conversation and poetic abilities.

While there are several instances of children writing Urdu travel accounts—in 1913 the twelve-year-old Maimuna Sultan (1900–82) published an account of England under the supervision of her mother-in-law Sultan Jahan, the Begum of Bhopal—*Tarikh* was almost surely written by an adult.[38] The device of the child-narrator simply made the text more engaging and accessible. Ya'qub's astonishing success, combined with an eloquent vocabulary and a humble but matter-of-fact tone, made Ya'qub eminently likeable. This precocious child's character engaged the reader and offered an ideal model for children to imagine travel's potential.

For Ya'qub, travel's value came from the experience it provided. Knowledge on its own was not enough to succeed; one must be in the world to understand it. This attitude contrasts with Maqbul, for whom knowledge was superior to experience, for it allowed him to succeed in commerce by knowing where to buy and sell and what prices to pay. Ya'qub insisted that young readers emulate his life and join what he called a "wave of knowledge" enveloping Punjab, an apparent reference to an emergent passion for reading and learning. He offered insight on moral behavior and social etiquette, demonstrating how to interact with social superiors. As with *Sair al-Muhtasham* in Chapter 2, *Tarikh* was didactic, prescriptive, and moralistic, even as it was entertaining. *Tarikh* drew on the popularity of moral (*akhlaq*) guides to provide readers with a full guide to life centered on travel.[39]

Like *Sair-i Maqbul*, *Tarikh* was both pleasurable and informative, wedding colonially inspired travel ideology with the demands of the popular market. Neither was a fantasy of travel to Europe. Some Indian elites were increasingly interested in writing about Europe, but for everyday Urdu speakers, Asia, and particularly

India and its neighboring regions, remained the primary points of interest. *Tarikh* also underlined the extent to which, even within a pedagogical space that emphasized colonial modernity, a connection to precolonial ways persisted. Ya'qub, for instance, continued also to justify his travel with reference to the classical Persian verse of Sa'di. In fact, this classical framing got the first mention, for the cover page bears the Persian hemistich, "Obtain greatness to become beloved to the world," emblazoned in bold letters. The colonial pedagogical lesson was made more palatable by re-casting it with a classical Persian heritage.[40]

Asia, Sexuality, and the Global Imagination

Not all Urdu travel authors wrote didactically. Many instead went all in on pleasure, embracing the bohemian possibilities of travel, particularly for adult male readers. Themes ranged from descriptions of foreign brothels to the comparatively anodyne narrations of music, dances, and parties, as in Miyan Dad Khan "Sayyah's" (1830?–1907) *Sair-i Sayyah* (The tours of the tourist/Sayyah, 1872). Sayyah was a disciple of renowned poet Mirza Asadullah Ghalib (1797–1869), one of Urdu's most famous *bon vivant*s. Ghalib used the mail service to communicate with friends and mentees across India, and Sayyah was one of Ghalib's favorite interlocutors.[41] True to his penname, which means "a great or frequent traveler, an itinerant," Sayyah loved to travel.[42] He related his travels to Ghalib in his letters, who relished these mini-travelogues:

> I expect that you will continue to write to me to tell me about all of your journeys, just as you have described for me your trip from Lucknow to Banaras. I too am an avid traveler:
>> If I cannot see heaven, all is well, for I have seen everything else
>> I have had the good fortune to have spent my life in travel
> If I am not able to travel myself, I will have to content myself according to the phrase, "discussing life is half of life." I will listen to the travel accounts and experiences of Miyan Dad Khan Sayyah, instead.[43]

Sayyah was a poet, a dandy, and a ne'er-do-well who wrote for pleasure.[44] His travelogue comprised two parts. The first related his travel through the North-Western Provinces in rhyming prose. The second portion was a collection of all the verses recited at all the poetry gatherings he attended on his trip. For pleasure-seeking readers, his account did not disappoint. It was filled with dramatic and wry descriptions of parties, delightful conversations, and urban wonders like this:

Smack in the middle of a rainy season the likes of which I had never seen before, in
the midst of a storm beyond even my wildest dreams, a deluge akin to Noah's—nay,
even worse—God not only saved my life, but also granted me a glimpse of Lucknow.
There I was, and with me Munshi sahib [publisher Naval Kishore]. There were
more of those same gatherings, those same spectacles, those wonders of the city,
those same meetings with lively friends. Chaube Ganesh Prasad sahib, the lawyer ...
organized two pleasure parties. The exquisiteness of seeing [the Lucknow courtesan]
Bi Gauhar Jan sing and dance was beyond anything that I had ever heard of before.[45]

The second half of the book, with its collection of verses, was equally pleasurable.
For Ghalib's student, what was most remarkable about the places he visited were
its poets.[46] His travelogue thus participated in genre hybridity by incorporating
the *tazkira,* or a collection of poetry grouped together around a common theme.
In this case the theme was Sayyah's own pleasurable journeys.

***

Sayyah's account serves as a convenient introduction to pleasure in Urdu travel
writing. Unlike the didactic, if entertaining, accounts discussed earlier, *Sair-i
Sayyah* is picaresque. If one major strand of writing argued, as seen in Chapter 3,
that travel makes one a successful and respected member of society, the writing
of men like Sayyah showed that venturing out into the world could also be
about enjoyment. Pleasurable accounts like Sayyah's were not about globalized
intellectuals; the Urdu travelogue also imagined how the world could be engaged
beyond reformist or practical concerns. This section will show how male travelers
imagined newly accessible regions of the world as spaces of pleasure.

The expansion of Urdu travel writing and the cultivation of a new global
imagination was in part fueled by the sexualization of travel and the possibility
of illicit interactions. The sensual side of Urdu travel writing has precolonial
parallels, as in Dargah Quli Khan's (b. 1710) Persian travelogue on the fleshy
aspects of Delhi.[47] Of course, the sexualization or fetishization of men and women
abroad has long been identified as a discursively powerful aspect of South Asian
travel writing.[48] Existing literature has focused particularly on the ways that
this sexualization emerged in travelogues of Europe, and how it was tied to the
cultivation of colonial ideologies.[49] In the late eighteenth and early nineteenth
centuries, Urdu and Persian (male) travel writers described Europe as a land of
erotic fantasy, a place filled with beautiful women who did not mind having direct
interaction and even physical contact with unfamiliar men.[50] This exoticization of
Europe continued into the twentieth century, even as travel to the region became
increasingly common.[51] The sexualization of Europe in South Asian travel writing

developed in the context of an unequal relationship of power wherein colonized visitors to the metropole often felt themselves inferior.[52] It ultimately gave shape to Indian discourses of nationalism by helping to define an Indian self against a colonial other.[53]

Urdu travel writers imagined the opposite situation in Africa and Asia. Here many were certain of their own sense of superiority, a sense sometimes aided by their identification as citizens of the British Empire. That status afforded them certain privileges, particularly in British colonies in Africa and Asia where the British considered them superior to the local populations.[54] Fetishization of women also played a key role in imagining this superiority and in constructing an idea of the world as a pleasurable space for play. In these discourses, Asian and African women were seen as sexually available and morally questionable, in direct contrast to Indian women, who were imagined as chaste and virtuous. Sexualization in these cases was not only titillating, but could also evoke disgust. Whether positive or negative, the physical appearances and sexual traits of women in Africa and Asia (including marginalized regions of India itself) were used metonymically to refer to these societies' supposed backwardness.

Thus, even as, in mainland India, a budding nationalist movement sanctified the Indian female body, Urdu travelers in Indian hinterlands exotified and sexualized the people they met. One instance comes from a short, versified travelogue by Manzur 'Ali (n.d.) called *Safarnama-i Manzur* (The travels of Manzur, 1894). It was published as a pamphlet in 1894 and described the author's experiences in eastern India and Southeast Asia. Manzur claimed that he accepted the idea that travel engendered success, believing that "without travel, one has neither respect nor status."[55] Yet he soon despaired upon realizing travel's true cost. His stanzas are filled with vivid imagery and emotional laments: a cramped train so hot that cheese forms, people who do not bathe, and markets where a chicken costs as much as a cow. He wrote of Assam:

> They all make a pickle using a handkerchief
>   They let fish rot for three or four years;
> When bugs land in it, it acquires its true taste
>   Then these savages eat it up with pleasure;
> They call it *nafti*, in their own language
>   It is sold as a gift in all the stores here[56]

His enthusiasm deflated by all these experiences, he lamented that he had "traveled for too long now, and am distressed."[57]

Manzur was a skilled laborer who had set out to make his future in the East.[58] His attitude there echoed what British soldiers and administrators wrote about their time in India. He imagined Indians as natural leaders in this "godless" region. As Manzur moved away from the familiar spaces of his native north India, he became increasingly derisive. When he described his journey through the United Provinces and Bengal his descriptions were comical, but not exotifying, and certainly not sexual. Women did not attract special attention. As he entered Assam, at the far reaches of the normative north Indian cultural sphere, his narrative radically changed. He focused particularly on women's sexual availability and immorality. Their physical appearance served to condemn these regions irreparably.

> Every woman looked like a witch—God save me!
> > If you even look at them, they may rush forward to eat you.
> Some are very tall, with skin the color of the palmyra palm,
> > Their arms like chinar [plane] trees, heads like bushes, mouths like mountains.
> If they fought demons then they would destroy them;
> > If Rustam[59] dared to challenge them he would be disfigured.
> Shameless, without honor, none of the women are in purdah;
> > If anyone wants to sleep with them, they are ready.
> Charmless, of bad character and filled with bad intent,
> > They are malevolent, faithless, and friends to no one.
> They could teach Satan himself how to cheat and deceive,
> > They have no equal in the realm of sorcery and magic.[60]

Children were "like monkeys with their tails cut off," and women "stand in front of their shops like blackened logs." The men, meanwhile, were diminutive and passive. Women's supposed immorality and appearance stood in for the entire region. Manzur relented only once he was sure his readers were convinced: "My listeners must hate [this place/these people]; let us move on to Penang."[61]

On his arrival in what is today Malaysia, he continued to use women to epitomize his views of place. In Penang, the women were beautiful and, accordingly, the city is described as wonderful:

> I looked closely on arrival at this land
> > At the beauty and eternal spring of the people of Penang;
> My heart was pleased by every green field,
> > And I saw in every flower the beautiful face of a lover.
> By God, that beauty would put the moon to shame
> > Certainly, Joseph himself would hide his own face if he saw it.

In the evening here there is a bazaar of beauty on display,
   A garden filled with adorned and beautified moons on display.
They express a wiliness to give their heart and to take hearts too.
   Their beauty is apocalyptic; it signals the coming of the End Times;
The people of this land are refined, well dressed and beautiful.
   I looked at all of this very closely—I saw they had no equal.[62]

As in Assam, the women of Penang are not in purdah. They, too, are flirtatious
and sexually available. It might seem that these points would earn them censure, as
in Assam. However, because Manzur approved of the city, he described its women
as beautiful and appealing. Thus, women in these two examples became symbols
through which to exoticize and sexualize entire regions. Alternatively, they became
the means through which evaluations of the city were expressed. In both cases,
though, they demonstrate how pleasure (and disgust) shaped the construction
of narratives on eastern Asia. In the case of Penang, Manzur's delight is obvious.
In Assam, while he expressed horror and revulsion, his narrative was laced with
fascination and wonder. He fetishized these regions and dwelled on them, clearly
enjoying the opportunity to demonstrate his superiority.

Other authors were more explicit still. In 1907, Muhammad Husain of Aligarh
boarded a train on the recently opened Trans-Siberian Railway in Vladivostok,
heading for Moscow. With the journey lasting over a week, he had plenty of time to
record his experiences. Over the next several days, Husain wrote a spirited account
of the journey that had brought him to the northeastern-most city of the Asian
continent. He had boarded a steamer in Calcutta for Rangoon and then continued
to Penang, Singapore, and eventually Shanghai, Yokohama, and Tokyo. From Japan,
he made a terrifying sea-voyage to Russia, intending to travel all the way to Europe.
His descriptions of these regions are not exhaustive, nor very informative. But
Husain was unrelenting in offering descriptions of the sexual pleasures available in
East Asia, as in this description of Shanghai: "The guide told us that the 'women's
houses' are also wonderful.... I responded, 'That is excellent, please take us there.'
... Here I saw Chinese beauties [*hur*] who were very beautiful—not just beautiful,
but truly praiseworthy. So beautiful indeed that their six-inch feet did not repel
me." If one wished, Husain wrote, the women would join him: "If you so desire,
you can have one of them seated in the carriage with you. Recalling [the Qur'anic
verse] *man 'ashir al-qaum fa-huwa min-hum* [those who appear to belong to a
community are part of it], I asked one to sit in the carriage with me."[63] As these
women appeared to be as beautiful as heavenly consorts, he implied, they must
in fact be heavenly consorts, and were therefore licit. Husain gave few additional
details on Shanghai beyond these anecdotes. In his narrative, China was largely

reduced to the beauty of its women and the pleasure of their company. Moving on to Japan, he then described the brothels of Tokyo in detail, including their number, their customs, how to comport oneself, and then, how he comported *him*self. Muhammad Husain noticed Japan's economic expansion and its growing military might, but he was more impressed by how large and delightful its red-light districts were. As a popular writer, Husain focused on what he considered the pleasures of the region. For him, East Asia was a sexualized landscape where brothels, rather than bazaars, lay at the heart of the city. Japan was, in his global imagination, a space to exert his masculinity and move about freely and confidently, something many Indian travelers felt unavailable in Europe.[64]

***

Travelogues like the works included in this chapter, from Dr 'Ali Sabzvari to Manzur 'Ali to Muhammad Husain, are not outliers. While not famous or remarkable in their own right, these travelogues are representative of a whole class of writing in Urdu and other South Asian vernaculars. Their interest in writing about Africa and Asia was not to find alternative economic models for a new nation or negotiate a positionality vis-à-vis Europe.[65] Travel writers like Muhammad Husain or Dr Sabzvari instead approached Africa and East and Southeast Asia as tourists, describing foreign places as arenas of pleasure with the potential for dominance. Their dominance was not defined by actual power, but by an expression of an ideology of superiority.[66] Accounts like Manzur 'Ali's were published widely, and to some extent still are today. The notion of a sexualized East Asia continues to inform Indian and Pakistani literature and imagination. These very texts may well have helped shape the representations of East Asia and East Asians in Indian popular cinema.[67] This vision also lives on in the persistent association of Northeast India and Southeast Asia as spaces of sexual access and excess.

Not every Urdu writer who visited Asia or Africa sexualized it. And yet most travel accounts from this period, at least those written by men (women's engagement with Africans and Asians is taken up in the following chapter), participate in this discourse to varying degrees. For instance, the princely ruler of Rampur, Hamid 'Ali, managed to include, within the bounds of decency, suggestive descriptions of mixed-sex nudity in Japan.[68] These texts demonstrate that the sexual objectification of men and women in Indian travel writing was not limited to accounts of Europe. If in Persianate writing on Europe "a woman's body served as an important marker of identity," in the case of East and Southeast Asia, there was no comparison with women back home. Unlike in Europe, many

Urdu travel writers like Husain (as opposed to intellectuals like Ross Masood) felt no sense of cultural or civilizational competition with these countries and instead offered readers the opportunity to imagine the pleasurable possibilities of being culturally superior visitors to Asia.

Conclusion

In an advertisement for his account of Sri Lanka, Kazim Barlas, whose Indian Ocean trilogy introduced this book, played on the dual meaning of the word *sair*, which can mean both "to tour" and "to peruse." He wrote, "Those who nurture a desire to hear or see the conditions of ... Lanka ... must absolutely peruse/tour this wonderful book."[69] Thanks to this semantic quirk, even the most sedentary Urdu readers in nineteenth-century India could tour the world through the travelogue. As printing presses overflowed with fresh accounts of global exploits, travel experience was abundantly available. Urdu authors embraced the possibilities offered by the idea of sair, which allowed readers to gain in knowledge and experience simultaneously. By the end of the century, styling one's travelogue a sair was chic: *Sair-i Rangun, Sair-i Jaipur, Sair-i Panjab.* Titles like these simultaneously invoked both the authors' and the readers' journeys to these enticing destinations. Authors explicitly positioned their texts as viable substitutes for the journey, and sometimes even as better than the real thing. Having found its market, travel writing became detached from government support, allowing authors to integrate entertainment into their writing and speak to a broad readership. References to pedagogy and individual advancement remained, but from the 1870s travel writers freely embellished their accounts with popular literary elements, including devices like dialogue and by drawing on genres like the dastan. Both these elements— pedagogical value and audience appeal—were crucial to travelogues' success. Authors also argued that book learning needed to be complimented by experience. For most travel writing in the latter half of the nineteenth century and beyond, *'ilm* and *tajarba*, knowledge and experience, were two sides of the same coin.[70]

At the same time, pleasurable travelogues offered a place for Urdu writers to reimagine their relationship to the world. Southeast Asia and Africa were peripheral to northern India, but in the late nineteenth century the logic of colonial interconnectivity brought Penang and Rangoon, Mombasa and Cape Town into conversation with Aligarh and Muradabad. Urdu travel writing often imagined a relationship with these regions that was hierarchical, mimicking European colonialism and even fantasizing the possibility of domination. The pleasurable Urdu travelogue portrayed the Indian as a colonizer in Africa and Asia.

This representation was not about physical hegemony, but ideology. This literature was published and sold on the market for readers to consume and, perhaps, to see themselves in it.

The following chapter continues to explore Indians' relationships to their neighboring regions, but with a focus on Islam and the potential for transnational religious unity as imagined in women's writing between 1900 and 1950. Depictions of a world defined by a shared Muslimness began to emerge in the 1890s and grew in importance and influence in the first decades of the twentieth century, coinciding with rising literacy among women and the emergence of literary spaces where women could express their own global imaginations. They did so largely in women's magazines like *Tahzib al-Nisvan*. The following chapter explores how women burst onto the travel writing scene to imagine a worldwide Muslim community. The following passage by Qaisari Begum (1888–1976), which describes her preparations for the hajj in 1936, introduces the excitement and passion for travel to the Middle East felt by many writers of her era. It also demonstrates the substantial difficulties women faced while traveling.

Notes

1. Mas'ud, *Mazamin*, 175–76.
2. Mas'ud, *Mazamin*, 176–77.
3. Orsini, *Print and Pleasure*, 2.
4. Orsini, *Print and Pleasure*, 6.
5. Green, "Forgotten Futures," 611.
6. 'Abd al-Hayy, *Sair*, 2.
7. Pandit Kanhaiyalal, *Sair-i Kashmir*, 2.
8. Mulji, *Sairistan*, 1.
9. For example, in 1935, Khan, *Pa Payada Safar*, c.p.
10. Pyare La'l, *Dunya*, 1; see also Singh, *Bhugol Hastamalika*, c.p.
11. Khan, *Zad-i Safar*.
12. *Sair o safar o tajarba o ma'lumat.* Khan, *Tarikh-i Badi'*, 34.
13. Adams, *Travel Literature*, 8–33.
14. Fowler, *Literature*, 38.
15. Adams, *Travel Literature*, 81–102.
16. Eagleton, *Novel*, 34. It is also suggested that "the modern novel ... arguably came into being as an imitation of contemporary travelogues." Thompson, *Travel Writing*, 51.
17. Khan, "Marvellous Histories," 527–56.

18. Jones, *Crossroads*, 9.
19. Despite its fictionality, generations of catalogers and scholars have catalogued *Sair* as a travelogue. *Sair* has also been anthologized, again as a travelogue: 'Abidi, *Kitabeñ*, 337.
20. On pedagogical children's travelogues in Hindi, see Chandra, "Pedagogic Imperative," 294.
21. Khan, *Maqbul*, 4.
22. I make this assertion based on several factors, including the issuance of two editions and the number and geographical spread of copies today. Copies are today available at libraries and collections in the US, the UK, and Japan, and in at least a dozen South Asian libraries in Lahore, Delhi, Hyderabad, and Patna, among others.
23. Viswanathan, *Masks of Conquest*, 130.
24. Pritchett, *Nets of Awareness*, 185–87.
25. Naim, "Prize-Winning Adab," 300.
26. *Selections*, 3:120–21.
27. *Selections*, 3:123–25.
28. *Selections*, 3:125.
29. Particularly Babu Shiv Prasad, *Chhota Jam*.
30. His enumeration of the states in the union indicate that his source described the country as it existed then.
31. Khan, *Maqbul*, 39.
32. Weaver-Hightower, *Empire Islands*, 91–127.
33. African writers, too, engaged in similar colonizing discourses in their travels, as when Yoruba-speaking writers from Lagos depicted Igbo peoples in southeastern Nigeria as "savages" and cannibals. Jones, *Crossroads*, 75. For similar examples in Swahili, see Geider, "Early Swahili Travelogues."
34. Pratt, *Imperial Eyes*, 83.
35. Khan, *Maqbul*, 91.
36. Green, "Africa in Indian Ink," 131.
37. Khan, *Tarikh-i Badi'*, 2.
38. Maimuna Sultan, *Siyahat-i Sultani*; Maimuna Sultan, "Maimuna Sultan."
39. Comparable texts include Shankar, *A'ina*; Baij Nath, *Englaind aind Indya*.
40. On the retroactive creation of a "Muslim travel canon," see p. 54.
41. For a study of his life and work, see Madni, *Miyan Dad Khan*.
42. Platts, *Dictionary*, sv.
43. Imam and Kanda, *Ghalib*, 14. The verse is Bedil's.
44. Ever the sapeur, "Sayyah was the very embodiment of style and elegance in his city. He kept a passion for beautiful clothing and perfumes until the end of his life.... If he happened to see anyone whose ensemble violated fashion's

tenets then he would gently explain [the error] to them. " Madni, *Miyan Dad Khan*, 24.

45. Sayyah, *Sair-i Sayyah*, 3. On courtesans, literary culture, and the city, see Williams, "Songs," 591–609.

46. Sayyah's innovation was followed by others. See also Jhanjhorvi, *Safarnama-i Bamba'i*.

47. Khan, *Muraqqa'*, 190–203.

48. Tavakoli-Targhi, *Refashioning Iran*, 54; Sharma, "Delight and Disgust," 119; Burton, *Heart of Empire*, 172.

49. Sharma, "Mohan Lal," is a notable exception.

50. Tavakoli-Targhi, *Refashioning Iran*, 54–61.

51. Tagore, *Letters*, 41.

52. Tavakoli-Targhi, *Refashioning Iran*, 76.

53. Chatterjee, *Nation*, 126–27.

54. Low, *Imperial Mecca*, 111–13.

55. Manzur 'Ali, *Safarnama*, 2.

56. Manzur 'Ali, *Safarnama*, 5–6.

57. Manzur 'Ali, *Safarnama*, 10.

58. Manzur 'Ali, *Safarnama*, 2. Perhaps he had read or been inspired by Kazim Barlas's account of the region from two years earlier which had called Indians to go there.

59. A legendary Persian hero described in the *Shahnama*.

60. Manzur 'Ali, *Safarnama*, 6. These lines recall Yusuf Kambalposh's writing on South African women. Kambalposh, *Tarikh*, 59.

61. Manzur 'Ali, *Safarnama*, 8.

62. Manzur 'Ali, *Safarnama*, 9.

63. Husain, "Japan," 6.

64. As expressed, for example, in Tagore, *Letters*, 41.

65. Mukhopadhyay, "Writing Home," 311.

66. On similar positioning by Indians vis-à-vis Africans while in London, see Burton, "Spectacle of Empire," 137.

67. Examples include films like *Howrah Bridge* (1958) and *Love in Tokyo* (1966) as well as more recent efforts like *Bombay to Bangkok* (2008) and *From Chandni Chowk to China* (2009).

68. 'Ali Khan, *Masir-i Hamidi*, 1:112–13.

69. Barlas, *Lanka*, iii.

70. For a comparable discourse in colonial Nigeria, see Jones, *Crossroads*, 88.

The Book of Life

Qaisari Begum

[1936]

The pilgrims returned [to India] during the five months I was away [from Hyderabad] in Delhi. Some of them even asked me what it was that he[1] had gained by preventing me from going [on hajj] myself....

Last year he stopped me from going on hajj by calmly informing me that the two of us would go together the following year, but God knows he fears the ocean and quakes at the very mention of going. And then, in the blink of an eye, a year passed and the time for hajj was near once again. My heart was in such a strange place. I wanted to just fly away. I was so unsettled that no matter what task I took up, my heart was never in it. Sleep was impossible. I couldn't do anything, for what was I to do? The closer the hajj season came, the more the fire of my passion blazed. I lost all control. My goal was to convince him to let me go. His goal was to keep me from going. He said to my brother Ihtisham al-Din sahib, "How can she make such a long journey? Please stop her. Maybe she'll listen to you." In fact, I was willing to accept each and every word my brother said, but when he asked me my true feelings, I told him without hesitation. "Brother, I'll hear out whatever you say, but don't try and stop me. I can't be stopped now." He reported back that I was unstoppable, that he should let me go.

I had already thought about all the preparations that would need to be made. I worried constantly how I would be able to pull this off without anyone else's help. I enlisted [my nephew] Na'im al-Haqq to do a few tasks for me and he reluctantly agreed out of fear that I might become cross with him. Tasks like making visits to the hajj guide, Badr al-Din, or gathering logistical information about the trip, like when the caravan would leave, where it would halt, and so on.

And then, lost in a world of confusion and worry, what did I see in a dream but myself traveling with some eminent personage. Water and sand were commanded by the slightest movement of his finger. I was praising him to the other women, telling them how venerable he was. I couldn't stop thinking about what this dream meant. What trip was this? Who is this great person? It didn't make any sense. How could my feeble intellect make sense of it all? I would have to ask my spiritual guide and leader, Hazrat Pir Jama'at 'Ali Shah,[2] I thought. If one has a spiritual guide, may they be like him.

I am infinitely thankful and grateful to Allah that He always reassures His servants during times of worry. His Word tells us *inna ma' al-'usri yusran*: "Every difficulty is followed by ease."[3] Trust always in His grace and generosity. One of my most basic concerns was how to get the money for the trip. I had a house in Delhi sold for the purpose of funding my hajj. The money was paid in Delhi but there were incessant delays in transferring it to Hyderabad. I feared the caravan would set off before it arrived, leaving me behind, perplexed and distressed. Though I knew in my head and my heart that Allah is the Causer of Causes, my worry increased by the day, until, suddenly, I learned that the caravan would be departing soon. Unknowing human! How can you hope to know the will of the Divine, and who and what He draws toward Himself?

I spent my days thus: in the morning, I would wake up full of hope. I would pass the day waiting. There would be no news of the money. At night, I would go to bed dejected. All my luggage was packed and ready. I had my smallpox and cholera vaccinations. Everything was taken care of. But this one tiny snag threatened to unravel the whole plan. Then the day of hope finally dawned. I was sitting there, lost in worry, when the son of a dear friend, *barkhurdar* [young man] Sayyid Mazhar Husain, arrived. He was elated. "My Aunty is going on hajj!"

When I explained the difficulties I was having in getting the money, he said without a moment's thought, "Aunty, I have some cash laying around unused. Please take it." I declined out of politeness. He refused to take no for an answer and went home to get the money. He soon returned and gave it to me without so much as asking for a promissory note or any kind of receipt. I was in a daze. God! What kind of angel have you sent me, who comes and smilingly hands me the money without even being asked?

It felt as though rain were falling on dried husks of rice. My heart swelled, my body came back to life. My courage returned. I wrote him a receipt and also got out some jewelry to give as collateral. He reluctantly accepted them. I asked my husband to give him the money from Delhi, which would arrive any day now, inshallah. Then another wonderful thing happened. There was a widow in our neighborhood called Husain Bi who wore a lot of gold. She suddenly turned up looking for her hen. I said to her, "Husain Bi, what's the use in wearing all that gold jewelry. Sell it and go on hajj."

She said, "If I go, will you come too?" I told her calmly that I would go whether she came or not. "What I am saying is that you should exchange this jewelry for the hajj." This had a profound effect on her. "Alright, sister. I'll go." She went home and declared her intention. Everyone offered their full support, telling her that such an opportunity was unlikely to come again. It's your good luck, they told her. You must go. Everything was taken care of in a flash, and she soon returned to me with banknotes in hand. "Take it. I'm coming with you."

This is the greatness of God, His divine power. He has bestowed His grace on me again and again; rained down showers of blessings. Even that poor woman will perform the hajj and visit Medina, whose greatness she could never have imagined seeing herself. I thought to myself that if she sold her jewelry, then why shouldn't I sell some of my bangles? Thinking of the merit of such an act, I sold off a few gold ones. In return, I did not receive cash so much as the keys to the kingdom of the seven realms. He has showered me with His blessings.

It is the heart itself that calls you to go on the hajj and to make a pilgrimage to Medina. Once you have this desire, Allah will take care of the rest. There was a woman from Gulbarga Sharif who was going on the hajj. One of her relatives had traveled with her up to Bombay to make sure she boarded the ship without difficulty. But then, his heart would not allow him to disembark and he remained on board until the ship had pulled away from the harbor. When the people on the ship learned of this, they began soliciting donations from the passengers until they were able to cover the cost of his passage. I saw with my own eyes that his hajj and pilgrimage to Medina were completed without him spending a single cent of his own.[4]

Notes

1. The author's husband. As was typical in women's writing and speech of the period, she does not take his name out of respect.
2. Probably Amir-i Millat Jama'at 'Ali Shah (d. 1951), a Naqshbandi Sufi leader and prominent supporter of the Pakistan movement.
3. Qur'an 94:6.
4. Qaisari Begum, *Kitab-i Zindagi*, 451–53.

5

Seeking Sisterhood

In 1936, Qaisari Begum (1888–1976) finally found her chance to go on hajj, but it was not going to be easy (Figures 5.1 and 5.2). The hardest part of the journey was leaving Hyderabad. She had to manage it all herself. Her husband tried to stop her; her family members dissuaded her. She sold some property to fund the trip, but the transfer was delayed. She also lacked an appropriate male companion. But she persevered and, finally, she reached the Holy Cities. She was enraptured: "I was so happy I was barely conscious. What I felt at that time is indescribable.... I leave it to you all, my readers, to imagine it yourselves."[1] Qaisari Begum's exultations extended even to her human encounters. She was elated to meet Muslims from around the world. The Egyptians, the Syrians, the Turks, they all seemed radiant and beautiful to her. The sight of this community—her community—filled her heart and reinvigorated her faith. How do we locate this effusive emotion and intense celebration of the Muslim community historically? Had Indian pilgrims always imagined themselves as part of a global Muslim community in this way, or was it created, in part, through travel writing?

Indian Muslims in the Muslim World

Since the 1890s, Urdu travel writers have lavished more attention on the Middle East than on any other region barring India itself. As European imperialism neared its global crescendo, Urdu authors increasingly grappled with the concept of the "Muslim world," which they often referred to as the *bilad-i Islamiyya* (the Muslim countries).[2] Through their travels, they gave a concrete definition to

Figure 5.1 An advertisement for travel supplies for the hajj

Source: Author.

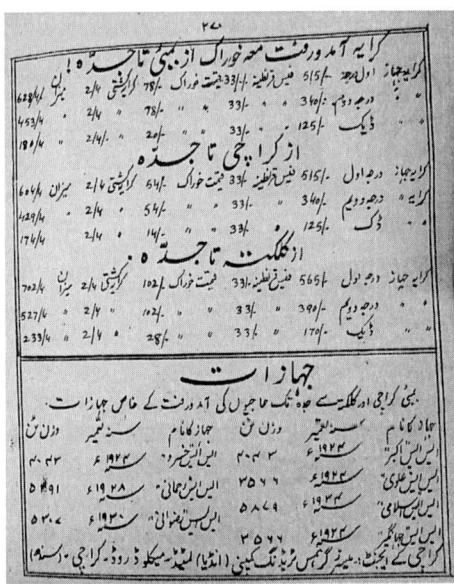

Figure 5.2 A list of prices for travel to Jeddah from South Asia, alongside a list of available ships

Source: Author.

the bilad-i Islamiyya and asked what it might mean to be part of a global community united by creed. This idea reflected a shift in Indian writing about the Middle East (itself a term that only emerged in English in the nineteenth century). For Indians, the lands between Iran and Egypt had once been more of an idea—distant regions where important historical events had occurred—than a geographically known place. By the turn of the twentieth century, though, it had taken on a definite geographical shape, partly because huge numbers of Indians were now visiting the region on increasingly safe and affordable steamships, whether as pilgrims, in transit, or on business.[3] Geopolitics had its own role to play. As Muslim rule fell to colonial empires around the world, Indian Muslims increasingly saw colonialism's conflict with Islam in global terms. These developments pushed the Middle East to center stage just as religion was becoming a primary marker of identity in India. Simultaneously, politicians, theorists, and philosophers imagined new religiopolitical entities and categories like Islamic universalism and fashioned the concept of the "Muslim world."

Travelers played their own role in imagining the Muslim world, making a pan-regional Islamic community tangible through first-person narrative. Women like Qaisari Begum were hugely influential in this process. Their travel accounts imagined the Muslim world for audiences in cities and villages across India. One highly influential author was Nur Begum, the daughter of a minor landowner in rural Punjab who performed the hajj in 1932. A successful writer acclaimed for her mastery of the Qur'an, *hadith*, theology, and Punjabi poetry, she narrated her pilgrimage in real time by mailing home versified letters for public recitation. A year later, she published a full account of her trip in Punjabi verse.[4] The volume was endorsed by religious scholars and, remarkably, was still being printed in large runs two decades later. Through reprints and recitations, Nur Begum's poetic global imagination of the Middle East spread across Punjab. Her vision celebrated global Muslim unity, but also reserved special veneration for the Arabs:

> As soon as we got off the boat [in Jeddah] and set our feet on the dock, God granted us our first sight of the Arabs. There was a stone kiosk beside it with a few Arabs sitting on chairs. God! what a beautiful sight! They were wearing jubbas with wondrous turbans on their heads. "Ya hajji!" they called to us respectfully, "from which country do you hail?" "Ya sheikh! We come from Punjab," and that was all we said. The Hindis [northern Indians], the Sindhis, and the Bengalis answered next, and on and on it went![5]

As a woman of relatively limited means, Nur Begum traveled the region by camel and camped out in the elements. Nevertheless, she found ease in every difficulty on this sacred journey. Even the dreaded medical quarantine was to her a paradise. Here, travelers underwent examination by gruff attendants in hot, crowded facilities. Yet to Nur Begum it was a meeting place for the world's Muslims:

> The women went into a separate room to have their bath, standing in line one after the other.... Standing under these showers, all the women washed themselves; just turn a knob and water falls like rain! From all directions came the sound of "*Allah hu!*"[6] so loudly nothing else could be heard. *Subhan Allah*! We were surrounded by such energy, the splendor of God's blessings on full display! Mothers and sisters have come together from across the world, and now they are playing, laughing, and bathing together.[7]

Here the quarantine becomes a utopic space of shared worship and community. Despite their many differences, Nur Begum is united with a global community of "mothers and sisters." Earlier Indian travelers had not felt the affinity she and Qaisari Begum did. Mid-nineteenth-century travelers like Yusuf Kambalposh,[8] Sayyid Ahmad Khan,[9] and Sikandar Begum[10] show little sense of a global Muslim fraternity. Their reactions to Arab Muslims ranged from distaste to disgust. The idea of an affective Muslim world had not yet been imagined.[11]

The emotional and affective nature of Urdu travel writing about this region that emerged in the later nineteenth century played an important role in creating an imagination of a united Muslim community in Urdu. Scholarship on transnational Muslim solidarity, though, typically focuses on its political implications, and particularly on the overwhelming Indian Muslim support for the Ottoman Caliphate. Ayesha Jalal, for instance, writes that "there was more logic than romance in Indian Muslim support" for the caliphate.[12] By contrast, this chapter shows that, unlike political leaders, everyday travelers were not so baldly strategic. They were motivated primarily by the romantic idea of a united ummah, or Muslim community. Urdu authors strove to find meaningful, affective religious community across borders in their personal interactions, and to reify it in writing. This affective connection was facilitated by a broad shift in the way emotions were expressed in early-twentieth-century Urdu literature. As Margrit Pernau argues, Urdu authors in this period moved away from the careful management of emotion to embrace passion, or *josh*, as an ideal. This dynamic perfectly fit Urdu travel authors' efforts to evoke in meaningful, vivid ways the connections they felt to their imagined Muslim community.[13]

But this was not a total lovefest; this novel connection was fraught and unequal. Yes, Urdu's travel authors imagined Muslims as a united, world-wide community, but even in their wildest imaginations they were unable to escape the logic of race and class. A travel literature that imagined Indians as colonizers in Africa and Central and Southeast Asia (see Chapter 4) could not easily also extend unity to these very same regions. How Urdu travelers imagined their connections to certain Muslims, but not others, shaped a critical chapter in South Asian history and still informs South Asian Muslims' view of their "Muslim world" today.

Women's Autobiography and India's "Muslim World"

In Urdu, the "Muslim world" did not simply mean the Muslims of the world, at least not in practice. When travelers went to Malaysia or Tanzania, most authors did not frame these places as constituting part of the bilad-i Islamiyya. Instead, Urdu writers seeking Muslim unity focused on the Ottoman Empire, which then included Turkey, Mecca, Medina, and the Levant, or its successor states and territories. Interest in the Ottomans partly reflected domestic Indian politics. The nineteenth century saw many of India's most prominent Muslim rulers, from the Mughals on down, deposed, and their kingdoms dissolved (see Chapter 2). Colonial prejudice against Muslims (who were sometimes viewed as disloyal or potentially so) meant that they often felt leaderless. Many looked to the Ottoman ruler as the ultimate representative of Muslim preeminence. They did not claim political allegiance to him, but they did express deep sympathy for him, and sacrificed significant financial sums for his cause.[14] This sympathy was manifest in every genre of Urdu literature. Urdu journalists breathlessly covered Middle Eastern affairs.[15] Novelists dispatched characters from India to Turkey to fight the Russians.[16] In poetry, the Arabs and the Ottomans were extolled in grandiloquent verse.[17] Philosopher-poets like Muhammad Iqbal penned lofty invocations of historic Muslim greatness.[18] Meanwhile, travelogues quenched the thirst for eyewitness accounts. Arabic scholar Shibli Nu'mani recalled that when he returned from Constantinople, "everyone I met insisted I write a travel account.... I too remembered my own condition before I made this journey. Whenever I met a traveler who had been to Constantinople, etc., I would ask after the state of things there for hours on end."[19]

Actors like Shibli Nu'mani and Qaisari Begum constantly produced fresh accounts of the Middle East and Turkey. Academic focus on the political aspects of this engagement, though, means that personal, affective perspectives are overlooked. As Seema Alavi notes, those "who did not participate in the overdetermined clash [between nationalism and pan-Islamism] ... fell off the pages of history."[20] While Alavi's work recuperates the trajectories of influential Muslim men who traversed the old imperial networks of the Ottoman Empire, Urdu travel writing offers the opportunity to move beyond the male political elite.

For travelers like Nur Begum, ardor for Arab Muslims transcended politics. These women travel writers, who have until now fallen off the pages of history, have an important story to tell about their role in fashioning an aspirational, transregional Muslim community.

Women's travel writing in Urdu is copious but almost unstudied.[21] What scholarship does exist largely focuses on accounts of Europe. Studies of travel writing on the Muslim world draw almost exclusively from male accounts. Decades ago, Gail Minault argued that "women were a powerful opinion group within the Khilafat movement," suggesting a fruitful line of inquiry for future scholars.[22] Yet only recently have scholars pursued this thread further by taking up South Asian women's autobiography and its relationship to Indian political and social history.[23] This writing offers a critical perspective on how Indians imagined these regions, particularly since women travelers were privy to—sometimes forced into—spaces unavailable to men, giving them absolute power to narrate women's social spaces.[24]

Women's Travel Writing in Urdu

In the acclaimed Urdu novel *Umra'o Jan "Ada"* (1899), the eponymous protagonist, a courtesan, mentions in passing having once made the pilgrimage to Karbala from her home in Lucknow.[25] She does not elaborate, and her interlocutor does not ask. The statement demanded no further clarification because it was not particularly remarkable: Indian women of all classes have always traveled. However, before the twentieth century, they only wrote about it on the rarest occasions.[26] While some elite women may have previously written accounts for private circulation, women did not begin to publish travel writing in Urdu until 1906.[27] From then on, it remained an almost exclusively Muslim phenomenon.[28] Although Urdu was a "transregional, transnational language community," it was also an ecumene structured by gender.[29] Urdu was the dominant language of the north Indian literary public sphere, but that sphere excluded many women. Women were expected to bear the markers of "their" religious communities. Muslim women's travel writing thus emerged in Urdu. Sikh women wrote in Punjabi, and Hindu women in Hindi and other regional languages.[30] Non-Muslim women only rarely wrote in Urdu and did not write travel writing in Urdu at all.[31]

Women's travel writing in Urdu first appeared in Muslim women's journals from the turn of the twentieth century. *'Ismat, Tahzib al-Nisvan*, and *Khatun* were among the most prominent, but "more than a hundred distinct women's magazines in Urdu existed between 1900 and 1947, published from across the subcontinent."[32] Though the readership for these magazines was neither exclusively female nor Muslim, their content was designed for this demographic. In the early years, women's journals focused on the needs of secluded women, but "once print had brought the outside world into the *zenana*, women could express views about the world and make their influence felt upon it, also via print."[33] Articles featured content about household tasks and family issues, but also introduced readers to the lives and practices of women abroad. Soon a literary culture emerged in which readers wrote to the magazine to respond, ask questions, and discuss issues collectively. Through it, a "sense of extended family was fostered within the journal itself ... in which women could write to the editor and other readers, as well as receive replies."[34] Readers even referred to each other as sisters: " *'Ismati* sisters," " *Tahzibi* sisters." When one of the magazine's readers traveled, she might submit an article to inform her sisters of her experiences and insights.

Although men regularly published travel accounts in women's journals, the reverse was rarely true. Women nearly always published in journals "for women." Women also circulated their travel accounts in private family newspapers, diaries, semi-public letters, and published books. Whether or not "women's writing" constitutes a meaningful conceptual category, it was largely treated as distinct from men's writing, a fact that has had profound consequences for its accessibility and preservation, and thus for our ability to rewrite women into South Asian history.[35] On a research visit to the private Jhandir Library near Bahawalpur, I saw hundreds of rare Urdu travel accounts but not a single work by a woman. When I remarked on this, I was told the library had a separate section, in a different building, for "women's travel writing." I was immediately whisked there by the librarian and one of the collection's owners, where they enthusiastically read aloud from Nur Begum's travelogue, which they considered the crown jewel of that section. The physical copy was filled with tick marks next to verses the owner particularly appreciated. Had I not asked for women's travel writing specifically, though, I would have never known this section existed. At this library, and for its catalogers, women's travel writing was a separate category entirely.

"Everyone's Naked in the Bathhouse": Meeting Muslim Women Abroad

The first woman known to write a travel account in Urdu was the ruler of Bhopal, Nawab Sikandar Begum, in 1867. Remarkably, she was also one of India's few women monarchs and the first sitting Indian ruler to perform the hajj. Sikandar Begum's good relations with the British allowed her to travel abroad secure in the knowledge that her throne would be waiting for her on her return. Before she departed, the resident and his wife asked her to record a narrative of her journey. Sikandar Begum's manuscript account, *Tarikh-i Safar-i Makka* (Chronicle of a journey to Mecca, 1867), was written before the appearance of India's fascination with the "Muslim countries," and it suggests little affinity for Arabs. At one point she even commanded that no woman be given entry to her quarters who did not speak Urdu.[36] Her dislike appeared to be total:

> No one [in Mecca] knows how to sing or to dance. The women clap, snap, and whistle quite a bit. When there is a wedding, amusing dances are performed at home, that is, they dance themselves. But the dancing and singing are not good. Seeing it, one cannot help but feel disgusted and devoid of all interest. The women here are more violent and outspoken than the men.... In conversation there is always a great amount of deception and lying.... The children of Mecca are very spoiled and disorderly and always cause a great racket.[37]

For Sikandar Begum, even elite Meccan women were disagreeable. She was equally unimpressed with Mecca's men. The "Muslim world" was still decades away.

By the twentieth century, though, the zeitgeist had shifted. An early indication of this change appears in an important travel account, Begum Sarbuland Jang's *Dunya 'Aurat ki Nazar Meñ* (The world in the eyes of a woman, 1910/1936). Begun in 1909 as a semi-private travel diary of the Middle East and Europe, it was only published after the death of her husband, probably because the liminality of widowhood made this public visibility more socially acceptable.[38] The journal was likely published in 1936, probably with minimal edits. Born Akhtar Hamid Sultan, she was descended from the Mughal court, but her father had moved to Hyderabad in the aftermath of the violence and disruption of 1857.[39] In 1894 she married Hamidullah Khan Sarbuland Jang (1864–1930), one of India's most prominent Muslim intellectuals and reformers.[40] Begum Sarbuland observed purdah in India and conscientiously avoided public attention, but was active in women's social reform movements.[41] Her travelogue was similarly committed to the exploration of Islam and womanhood. Begum Sarbuland primarily addressed her female readers, calling on them to become ideal women who were educated, pious, and free of wasteful or frivolous habits. She encouraged them to study the women she introduced in her travelogue and to adopt the practices they found beneficial. She clearly embraced the idea of a united Muslim womanhood, but struggled to overcome cultural and class divides.

Before her journey, Begum Sarbuland hired a female Arab servant to be her Arabic tutor. She had surely had some limited knowledge of a formal version of the language from her childhood—there was no dearth of classical Arabic instructors in Hyderabad. But because she sought meaningful interaction with the region's women, she presciently focused on the colloquial language of the Arab zenana. Erudite Indian travelers constantly found the classical form of the language almost useless for travel and conversation. Shibli Nu'mani lamented that "contemporary Arabic is so completely different from classical Arabic that should an accomplished scholar from our country travel to Egypt or Syria, he will be no faster in acquiring the local idiom than even the commonest man."[42] Another traveler kvetched, "The language of the common Arabs is not pronounced correctly. Travelers must learn to understand this pronunciation to avoid difficulties."[43] Perhaps taking advice like this to heart, Begum Sarbuland preemptively acquired a knowledge of vernacular Arabic. She then set out to meet the women of the Ottoman world.

Begum Sarbuland met her would-be sisters in homes, mosques, bathhouses, bazaars, and palaces. At a dinner party in Constantinople—the name she knew the city by—she met a group of Ottoman noble women. Since Begum Sarbuland was the descendent of Turkic migrants to India, she shared with these women both a religion and an ethnicity. What they did not share was a language. They did the best they could:

> Two or three extremely beautiful Turkish *bibi*s took my arm and led me upstairs.... There were five or six bibis there, all of whose hair and dress were just like those of *mem*s [European women]. These were all Muslim women Turks. They are called *khanam* [lady]; no one knows the word begum [lady].[44] I asked the khanams their names and they asked me mine. Because I am, in fact, a khanam too, I told them my name was Akhtar Hamid Sultan khanam. Their ears perked up at this.... All this conversation was conducted partly through gestures, and partly through one bibi who knew some Arabic. The rest just stared, for they only know Turkish. After an hour, we called for a translator.... They summoned a mem who knew both English and Turkish.... The moment she arrived she said, "I am very happy to have been called in your honor."[45]

The mem, it turned out, did not know Turkish, but was fluent in Arabic. The women set up a language chain by which Begum Sarbuland's English was translated into Arabic, and then to Turkish. The system was not particularly effective, but the women spent several hours conversing in this way. By Begum Sarbuland's account, it seems that while she was interested in their shared Muslimness, the women themselves were far more interested in their shared ethnic background. "They asked me, 'How is it that your name is Sultan?' I explained my family's history to them, and they were delighted. 'She is a Turk!' they said." At the end of the evening Begum Sarbuland Jang thanked them and declared: "I lament that I do not speak Turkish for, otherwise, on the occasion of this gathering, I should have liked to give each of my Muslim sisters a speech."[46]

This interaction reveals both the aspirations and the limitations of Begum Sarbuland's global imagination. She identified with the khanams in terms of class and stature: "I am, in fact, a khanam, too." Both she and the Turkish women were members of a ruling elite. In addition, they shared a bond of sisterhood based on ethnicity and religion. The Ottoman women were thrilled to learn that Begum Sarbuland was an ethnic Turk—ethnic Turkish nationalism was burgeoning at precisely this time. In India, though, religious nationalism was on the rise. Begum Sarbuland framed her fascination not in terms of ethnicity, but in terms of religious affiliation, as "Muslim sisters." Begum Sarbuland's aspirations were thus not entirely shared by these Ottoman women.

There is a third presence in this interaction. The women converse through the "mem." While Persian and Arabic were still potential bridge languages between Indian and Ottoman elites, among these women, interaction was only possible through a non-Muslim intermediary. Although they spent several hours together, the translator is only mentioned on one more occasion, when she is quoted as saying, "Until today, I have never seen a khanam before. This is the first time I have been in a Turkish home. It is very rare for a Turkish bibi to associate with a European [*angrez*] mem."[47] If this event had taken place in India, it is far less likely that this unnamed "European" would have been sidelined and shown to be an inferior servant in this way. But here, the woman was peripheral to the project of Muslim unity. Meeting in the heart of the world's largest Muslim empire, Begum Sarbuland inverted India's colonial power dynamic, pressing this woman of evidently remarkable talent into the role of an unnamed Christian "angrez." Begum Sarbuland reveled in a setting where this woman was not just superfluous, but perhaps even jealous of the gathering of Muslim women. The mem, despite her critical role in facilitating this conversation, was a mere accessory to Muslim sisterhood.[48] Of course, this image was ultimately illusory. Europe dominated the world, while the Ottoman Empire was about to collapse. In this passage, though, Begum Sarbuland conjured a shared Muslim imaginary with a subordinate Christian Europe looking on. She did not hide the fact that this was an aspiration, but rather revealed both her linguistic difficulties and the mismatch between religious and ethnic conceptions of community.

On the other hand, Begum Sarbuland's husband, Hamidullah Sarbuland Jang, was less willing to reveal the limits of transnational unity. In his travel account,

Safarnama-i Qustuntuniya (Travelogue to Constantinople, 1912), he represented the same event differently:

> Begum sahiba was invited to the women's dinner, and she left. Because Begum sahiba (Mrs. Sarbuland Jang) descends from the [Turkic] Mughal family, the Turkish women considered her one of their own and treated her with the greatest love and affection.... The Turkish women chatted with Begum sahiba in Arabic, but one of the guests was a Christian mem sahiba who was able to speak English and Arabic well. But since Begum sahiba already knows Arabic, and also speaks English, the mem sahiba was not much help. Everyone got by simply by speaking Arabic.[49]

In Hamidullah's version, the Turkish women's attraction to Begum sahiba again appears to be shaped more by ethnicity than religion. In his telling, though, Muslim unity was already accomplished: the women chatted with one another in Arabic, rendering the mem "not much help." The discrepancy with his wife's account may not have been intentional, but it was not coincidental. The picture of a multi-national group of Muslim women chatting together projected an image of Islamic unity rooted in politics. Hamidullah's account was itself explicitly invested in an idealized, politicized Muslim unity. His book was even dedicated to the Ottoman "martyrs" of the Balkan wars, "for whom the world's Muslims feel great sorrow due to their shared Islamic brotherhood."[50] While the nawab connected his travelogue and his passions to contemporary politics and the defense of an imagined Muslim ummah, his wife's account reflected a more personal and improvisatory formation of this utopian imaginary, one rooted in everyday experience.

This was not Begum Sarbuland's only effort to make this imagined unity real. Earlier, upon arrival in Damascus, she intended to stop at the hotel, wash up, and head to the city's sacred sites. Until then, she and her husband had only stayed in the finest European hotels, but at the train station she was convinced by a local tout that, as a Muslim, she should stay in a "Muslim hotel." She agreed, but instantly regretted her decision. The hotel was not clean, and worse, there were no bathing facilities. They had to visit the hammam. Her travelogue dedicated an entire section to the experience, titled "Everyone's Naked in the Bathhouse," a proverb akin to "we're all in the same boat." This was a deeply intimate space in which she was undressed and bathed by the hammam attendants and local women. Begum Sarbuland, at least initially, felt out of her depth.

> Inside [the hammam], I saw thirty or forty women gathered.... Light-skinned, rosy women who had finished their baths were busy getting dressed. Others were taking off their clothes and heading into the hammam to bathe. All the men and women

in Damascus are very light-skinned, Africans excluded. I paused, thinking to myself that I was in quite the dilemma. I'll wait to begin my bath, I thought, until everyone else has finished. This being my intention, I was standing there when a woman came up to me, took the bag from my hand and began to remove my clothes. I said, "Wait, wait!" and she retorted, "No, let's go!" and God knows what else in Arabic. I fell silent when I saw she had no intention of listening. She took off all my clothes. I wrapped myself up in a towel and she took me by the hand and led me away.... We passed through three different levels of the hammam and entered the fourth, where I saw all the women seated barefooted before water taps, washing themselves.... The woman began to rub my body, washing me. In fact, three or four of the women stopped bathing themselves and, coming over to me, began to scrub me as well. In Arabic, they asked, "Who are you? Where are you from?" I said to them: "I am Indian. In India, hammam at home. In town, no hammam, but here I see hammam in town, none in home. I am surprised." With great effort, I managed to answer a few of their questions.... I moved to leave, but they took hold of me, saying, "Don't go, sit down for just a while more."[51]

Begum Sarbuland was confused and discomforted by the hammam's social order. Though ill at ease, she and the women endeavored to know one another. In the Urdu text, Begum Sarbuland recreated this dialogue in broken, colloquial Arabic without translation. While the meaning is generally clear, it is hard to follow, and reveals her limitations in speaking the language. Nevertheless, it illustrates Begum Sarbuland's great effort to connect.

Later, on cool-headed reflection, Begum Sarbuland decided that she liked the hammam and decided to return the following morning, "in part because it gave relief to my body, but also because it was one of the more memorable experiences of our trip." The nearest hammam was not yet open, but the hotel owner's wife, "an Arab woman, wearing a beautiful Turkish skirt and a veil over her face," agreed to show her another one:

This woman first took me to her house.... There were attractive sofas and chairs. The hotel owner's mother was seated on a raised platform upon which a soft mattress had been placed. The poor woman was very weak. When she saw me enter, she raised herself up with the greatest difficulty, saying, "Please, come in." I took her by the hand and helped her to sit down again, saying that she should not go to such trouble. Then the hotel owner's sister and daughter came in. All these women were dressed in English clothes. The girl was wearing a frock. They were very beautiful, and their complexion was extremely fair.... I went and sat near the hotel owner's mother. All these women spoke Arabic. It was unfortunate that I could only understand them with difficulty. They were very hospitable towards me.[52]

Once again, Begum Sarbuland strove to acquaint herself with the lives of the women she met, and remarked on their beauty, especially their fair skin. And once again, she lamented her inability to communicate. Still, she took stock of their lives by describing their homes, clothes, and food, thus offering a picture of Muslim life beyond the gaze of male Urdu travel writers.

Taken together, these interactions—home, khanam, and hammam—gesture to the aspirations of Urdu's global imagination, but also to its limitations. These passages make clear Begum Sarbuland's desire to create tangible bonds between Indian and Middle Eastern Muslim women. They demonstrate the possibilities for cross-cultural interaction, and the desire to overcome linguistic and cultural challenges. Begum Sarbuland entered elite spaces more easily than the everyday world of the bathhouse. For all her eagerness to meet ordinary women in Damascus, her experiences in the hammam were discomforting. And yet she was eager to forge bonds across cultures and considered all these women her Muslim sisters.

At various moments in her trip, Begum Sarbuland projected this Muslim unity for European audiences, presenting it as an eternal bond. In Aden, Begum Sarbuland's ship was visited by Somalis who performed aquatic feats in exchange for money:

> All the ship's passengers began to throw coins to them. I threw some as well. I had heard that these savages [*wahshi*] speak Arabic.... When I spoke a few words to the performers, my English lady friends were shocked. "Oh! *Tum kya bolta hai*?" [What are you say?!] I replied, "This is our pure Arabic language. I speak a bit of it."[53]

While the English women are lightly mocked for their broken Urdu, the reader already knows that Begum Sarbuland's Arabic is equally imperfect. She does not reveal to them her efforts to learn Arabic, nor her struggles to communicate, suggesting instead that her ability to speak to the performers stemmed from their shared religion—"our"—language of Islam. Similarly, of Port Said she wrote: "Many poor Arabs come to sell trinkets here. Today I spoke to them in Arabic for quite a while. All the ladies were shocked. I replied, 'We are Muslims. Our pure Qur'an is in Arabic. We know Arabic well.'"[54] Muslims, she explained, shared a book in a single, pure language, which functioned as a universal medium among its members. On another occasion, she assured an English friend that it would be safe for them to visit an Egyptian bazaar together because no one would harm a fellow Muslim.[55] She projected Muslim unity before these English women, refusing to let them in on the secret her Urdu readers knew: that Begum Sarbuland struggled to interact with Middle Eastern Muslims throughout her trip, and that she only felt kinship with some of them. Her account thus displayed two opposing representations of Muslim unity. The narrative of the cohesiveness of the ummah shifted based on context. It was only for Urdu readers that she revealed that this transnational Muslim becoming was an unfinished project.

The desire for transnational Muslim solidarity, first visible among women's writing in Begum Sarbuland Jang's account, soon became a standard element of the Urdu travel account; the desire for global Muslim sisterhood only increased in the following decades. A comparable set of exchanges was narrated by Fatima Begum (1890–1958), an activist, reformist, and editor of women's magazine *Khatun*, in which she regularly published her travel writing.[56] She traveled to Mecca in 1934. "In the place where I said my prayers [in Mecca]," she wrote,

> there were several young Egyptian ladies also praying. I tried to communicate in halting Arabic. When they heard Arabic coming from the mouth of an Indian, they were astonished. When I asked if any of them spoke English, they pointed to a young Egyptian lady in the row behind them and said, "Munira Khanam knows English." Another young woman was with them, Hussain Khatun, who could also understand a little English. I spoke with Munira Khanam, and we talked about every subject. Mashallah, she is a very intelligent lady. We spoke for a long time about Egyptian women's schools and the state of their education, about purdah, and about domestic arrangements. As our exchange of ideas went on, it became clear that Egyptian women are progressing in every aspect of life.... Afterward, it became the routine that when I saw her in the Haram Sharif, either I'd call her over and talk to her or she'd call me over. On this occasion, I very much regretted being so ignorant of Arabic that I couldn't exchange ideas with my sisters.[57]

Like Begum Sarbuland, Fatima Begum was eager to speak with women from other parts of the Muslim world, particularly these Egyptians, largely by relying on colonial languages.

The expression of Muslim sisterhood in Urdu travel writing reached a zenith in the writings of the reformist author Sughra Humayun Mirza "Haya" (1884–1958).[58] In *Safarnama-i Yurap* (Travels to Europe, 1926) an especially poignant moment occurred in Switzerland, where she and her husband were invited to visit the deposed Ottoman caliph, Abdülmecid II (1868–1944), and his wife, Şehsuvar Khanam (1881–1945). Mirza imagined a special bond between Indian Muslims and the Caliph's family:

> Her Highness, Queen Şehsuvar[59] Khanam—may God grant her prosperity—entered the room.... Not a single hair on her head could be seen; only her face remained uncovered. She respects and keeps the true Islamic purdah. I had brought a few gifts with me, among which was a copy of one of my own books. Her Highness asked me to dedicate the book to her in my own hand. It was only when I asked the

private secretary for Her Highness's name that I came to know that she was Queen Şehsuvar Khanam.[60]

The two women established an immediate rapport:

> The Queen's blessed eyes welled up with tears when she told me that I was the first Muslim woman since the time of their exile to have traveled so far just to visit her and her husband and to express sympathy for their plight. A little while later both the Caliph and Her Highness expressed a desire that we stay to dine with them as their guests. We thanked them and accepted their invitation. She then said to me: "You, an Indian Muslim, will be the first woman to dine with me since I left Turkey. I will never forget this kindness of yours for as long as I live." The Queen then said: "You look very similar to Turkish women. Do all women in Hyderabad look this way, or is it that you have Turkish roots?" I was astonished to hear this and replied that my grandfather was from Turkey and the family on my maternal side was from Iran, but that now we are Hyderabadi.[61]

As the evening wore on, the two found themselves drawing ever closer together:

> While we were eating dinner Her Highness took my hand over and over to tell me that this meeting and our kindness and affection would remain a cherished memory forever. "You are my Islamic sister," she would say. Her Highness's deeply sorrowful words tore my heart to pieces.... As I was leaving Her Highness the Queen embraced me and said many prayers and wishes for my well-being. As she was doing this, the embroidered lining of my sari got caught on Her Highness's clothes. Seeing this, she said: "Now the love between us has become permanent. Inshallah, it will never wane. Even our clothing has joined together."[62]

As with Begum Sarbuland Jang, these women shared a religion and an ethnicity. Here, though, both women prioritized Muslimness. Exiled from Turkey along with her husband by the secularizing, Turkish nationalist government, Şehsuvar Khanam was, in this telling, invested in Islamic universalism. According to Mirza's account, both women imagined that Indian and Turkish Muslim women had become bound together. If the project of Muslim sisterhood was aspirational for Begum Sarbuland, for Mirza it became tangible, as the women's garments were literally intertwined. Mirza never revealed how she communicated with Şehsuvar Khanam. Did they speak in French, in Persian, or, most likely, through the private secretary? The passage elides linguistic and cultural difference to conjure the impression of a meeting of two lost sisters consoling one another over a tragedy beyond the barriers of language, class, and culture.

The Borders of the "Muslim World"

The above passages do not just reveal the expression of Muslim sisterhood, but also its limits. As Adhira Mangalagiri's work demonstrates in the case of Cold War Hindi travelogues, ellipses are often the most revealing aspect of a travel account. Attention to "silences, tensions and omissions" counterbalances explicit intentions and desires.[63] The ellipses in Muslim women's aspirational travel writing on the "Muslim world" speak loudly, collapsing at key moments and drawing sharp frontiers across this global imagination. In the passages above, Begum Sarbuland sought out friendship and exchange with Ottomans and Levantines of all classes, but simultaneously withheld concern for Somali Muslims, to whom she threw small change for sport. She called them savage (*wahshi*), and was dubious that they spoke a language as "pure" as Arabic. Ironically, she nevertheless found them useful, instrumentalizing them to perform Muslim unity for her English friends. In her quest to know her ummah, then, she excluded a fair bit of it. As much as women writing in Urdu typically felt an affinity for their "Muslim sisters," these sisters tended to be light-skinned (a descriptor that appears repeatedly in this literature). Muslim women from Africa or Asia[64] were rarely called "sister," and these places were rarely, if ever, included in the bilad-i Islamiyya. Often, they were not mentioned at all.

Begum Sarbuland's interaction with the Somali performers in Aden was not unique. Nearly everyone traveling on a British ship towards the Middle East or Europe stopped in this extraterritorial outpost of British India, providing a single reference point to trace the possibility of a bond between Indian and African Muslims. Twenty years earlier, Shibli Nu'mani had revealed a similar outlook:

> One very interesting thing about Aden is that members of the Somali community come out to the ship on little boats and perform strange and debasing actions for rewards. Some sing and dance, some join together and speak meaningless words and strike their sides. The most amazing thing is that anyone who wants to give a few annas' reward throws it into the water so that they dive down and retrieve it. Most of the Englishmen were involved in [enjoying] this activity ... but my state was altogether different. I mistakenly thought that this place was mostly populated by Arabs, so it was only natural that I held a deep respect and love for the [performers]; seeing them perform such degrading, belittling, and inappropriate acts for the sake of a prize was completely repugnant to me. It was a warning to see that the Arabs have reached such a place that they could perform actions like these in front of strangers without any sense of shame. These thoughts made my heart suddenly swell with sadness, to such an extent that my eyes began to well up with tears and, without any warning, my tongue spoke *Qumm ya 'Umar!*[65]

He was not sad for long. "I went into the city and investigated. Once I had ascertained fully that these Somalis are not Arabs, I felt much consolation. My anger over this [conduct] inspired me to write an intense satire of this worthless community in my travel poem, and truly, they deserve it."[66] Shibli Nuʿmani here used racist tropes to describe Muslim Somalis even as he evinced "respect and love" for the Arabs and connected this feeling to their shared faith (as indicated in his invocation of the Caliph ʿUmar).

To be sure, views like these are complicated by the fact that Sub-Saharan Africans, and many Asians, were unfamiliar to some Indian travelers. Nevertheless, this unfamiliarity was also the result of Urdu writers' failure to engage with these parts of the world meaningfully. Figure like Manzur ʿAli or Dr Sabzvari in Chapter 4, who traveled to Africa and Asia, generally did not describe them as being populated by Muslims, even when they were. Thus, even travelogues that did acknowledge the presence of Muslims foreclosed the possibility of imagining Africa and Asia as a part of the Muslim world. Ummat al-Hafiz, whose travels to Madagascar were published in ʿIsmat between 1939 and 1941 (see Figure 5.3), is typical:

> The original inhabitants of this place, the Malagasy, have made much progress in the last fifty years, though they were once as savage as the Africans.... The Muslim women take a large cloth and wrap it around their entire bodies.... The people do not observe purdah in the slightest, although some women do apply thick layers of a type of tree bark, soaked in water, which obscures the general features of one's face. They say that this makes them more beautiful and is far better than creams, rouges, or powders. They also call this "purdah." It is often applied by brides. It is only natural that even the ugliest and blackest woman would want to try to make herself beautiful.[67]

This passage is remarkable both for what it says and what it does not. First, it turns a less-than-charitable eye to the local Muslim community and its practices, which are found to be un-Islamic. Physical appearances are singled out as unattractive and improperly concealed. At the same time, there are no evocations of unity or sorority. Ummat al-Hafiz's account replaces all attempts to celebrate sisterhood with jaundiced anthropological description joined with religious critique. She described the Malagasy Muslims not to learn or associate, but to criticize.

Fatima Begum took a similar approach to Sudanese women in Mecca:

> Today I saw a group of Sudanese women. There are huge scars from wounds on their faces. Each face bears three scars, an inch apart and about three or four inches long. They're very conspicuous. I stopped short when I saw these scars. These women are of a black color. They have thick lips that stick out noticeably, and efforts have been

Figure 5.3   Sample cover of *'Ismat* magazine from 1955
Source: Author.

made to turn these lips blue by tattooing them with black collyrium. Some have
turned purple and some greenish black. When I asked why these wounds have been
made, I learned that they are there to adorn the women with beauty and splendor.[68]

Still curious, she continued her research:

> After further inquiry, it also turned out that at some time in the past, there was great
> violence, together with the slave trade, and the aristocrats marked their children with
> wounds. This scar was to show that these people are from high families and they
> should remain protected from the slavers' plundering. Now most people must have
> forgotten the reason for these scars. They just make the wounds out of respect for
> custom and tradition. During the hajj I saw hundreds of men and women adorned
> with these scars.[69]

Fatima Begum encountered "hundreds of men and women" from Sudan, a region
that, like Egypt, was an Arabic-speaking British colony. Though she might have also
attempted to speak English with these Sudanese women ("women," not "sisters"),
she does not. With the Egyptians, she "very much regretted being so ignorant of
Arabic that I couldn't exchange ideas with my sisters." There are no such laments
here. Even if she had spoken with these women (who, like the Egyptian "sisters"
she eagerly befriended, presumably also spoke Arabic), she believed they would
not have been able to provide the "correct" answers, an attitude that echoes
Agha Maqbul's colonial-scientific explorations of Djibouti, discussed in the
previous chapter.

Writing on Africa in Urdu more generally was often coolly ethnographic at
best, and more often overtly dismissive. One text, *Sair-i Afriqa* (A tour of Africa,
1930s), began thus: "While Europe and Asia can offer up a good number of
civilized peoples, Africa has only two peoples of which it can be proud: the people
of Egypt, and those of Carthage.... Aside from Egypt, which is a fertile valley and
delta, the rest is nothing but wilderness."[70] This disparaging attitude appears
widely in South Asian travel writing, even where the question of religion is not in
play. Particularly prominent in this textual tradition is Yusuf Khan Kambalposh's
1838 *Tarikh-i Yusufi* (which, as noted in Chapter 3, once served as a textbook
at Delhi University). Kambalposh seems at pains to include negative and comic
descriptions of Black South Africans, including sexualized descriptions of Black
women. He contrasts their supposed lack of humanity with the splendor of the
White South Africans.[71] This discourse remained so deeply embedded in Urdu's
global imagination that well over a century later, little had changed. Even the desire
of Begum Sarbuland and Fatima Begum to fashion an image of a global Muslim
community could not overcome it.

East, Southeast, and Central Asian Muslims fared only slightly better. They
were largely unremarked. Kambalposh noticed the Malay community at Cape
Town and even hired a Malay servant, but aside from noting their religion and
their steadfast adherence to it, he had little to say.[72] Among Muslim women writers

of the twentieth century, Muslims from these regions were again either ignored or pitied. Fatima Begum, for instance, criticized the clothing and veiling of Uyghur women:

> They are very tall women, who wear coarse, mud-colored tunics reaching down to their feet, and their faces and heads are wrapped up with muslin scarves. A place is left open for their eyes and a smallish hat is perched on top of their heads, over the scarf. It's amazing that so much care has been taken to cover the head and face, while the chest is completely open, which is shameful to see. Each of these women was given a scarf for wearing with their pilgrimage robes, but not another tunic for them to put on instead. Clothes were requested from the ship, and a charitable and generous gentleman of Bombay donated two new tunics and two women's pajamas. As Mirza Zafar said, we'll make this army of indigents shine.[73]

Again, pity rather than compassion; a desire for change, not exchange. Why did Fatima Begum not record any conversations with the Uyghurs? Why does she call them women and not sisters? The passage contrasts remarkably with her encounter with the Egyptian women. When it comes to these Muslim women, she seems entirely disinclined to seek solidarity and community.

The limits of India's imagined Muslim world also appear in physical descriptions of Muslim women. Passages on Africans are not complimentary, whether in terms of dress or physical attributes. They are neutral at best, as when Begum Sarbuland noted simply that the Africans of Damascus are not light-skinned. This contrasts with her constant celebration of Turkish and Arab women as "extremely beautiful," "light-skinned [and] rosy," and so on. Other authors also remarked on the beauty and grace of Turkish, Levantine, Egyptian, and Iranian women. As she elaborated on her joy at seeing the prosperity of Middle Eastern Muslims, Ummat al-Ghani (1885–1915) compared Damascene and Lebanese women to *hurs*, or heavenly consorts: "The beautiful women who visit the gardens present an absolutely stunning sight. It would be no exaggeration if I were to explain these gardens to you by comparing them to the gardens of heaven, or if I were to compare these women to the houris of Paradise."[74]

Qaisari Begum was similarly rapturous. Egyptian women had "fair complexions and uncovered faces. It was as though the very nymphs of heaven had descended to earth. I was completely astounded. I was so struck with wonder that I was frozen to the spot, unable to move. I stood there taking in every detail like a woman mad with love." Syrian women were "healthy and fair-skinned." Palestinian women "had their own unique grandeur." Bedouin women, she wrote, "wore black-colored, blanket-like burqas" so enveloping that "you couldn't see so much as their fingernails." These they wore at all times, "even while circling the Kaaba...; their beautiful faces, their moon-like visages, remained covered."[75] Like the infatuated lover of classical Urdu poetry, Qaisari Begum was convinced of the Bedouin women's beauty, sight unseen. She simply imagined it. The only women in her catalog of women in Mecca to be denied such praise were the Yemenis. She briefly described their method of veiling but expressed no emotion, nor any description of their beauty.[76] Sub-Saharan African women did not enter her catalog at all. She certainly encountered African women in Mecca and Medina, for she noted their presence elsewhere in passing.[77] Yet they were never described beyond a single uncomplimentary observation, nor were they acknowledged as Muslim. Mecca and Medina were the gathering places of the Muslim world, but the parade of Muslim beauties described by Qaisari Begum did not include everyone.[78]

Southeast Asian Muslims were similarly absent. Indian pilgrims undoubtedly encountered them, for they comprised a huge proportion of the annual pilgrims, and in fact once more than doubled the number of Indian visitors.[79] One author who did mention them was Nawab Sikandar Begum, who simply wrote that "there is a race of people called 'Java' who live in a place beyond Calcutta; they believe gold can be extracted from the [colorful] stones [found at Jabl al-Nur]."[80] Mentions of Chinese and Turkistani Muslims were also rare in women's Urdu travel accounts, though they too were easily encountered. Many travelers from Central Asia went on hajj via India, and the number of pilgrims from this region in Mecca easily surpassed fifty thousand a year.[81] It is striking that these communities were so little remarked at precisely the moment when Indian Muslims authors were at such pains to celebrate the size and diversity of the Muslim community and to fashion a global imagination centered on the ummah. Certainly, African and Asian Muslims were a key part of Muslim India's response to Europe and useful as proof of Islam's reach, as seen in Ummat al-Ghani's description of the diversity and unity of the hajj in 1909:

> There are Arabs, Turks, Egyptians, Iranians, Hindustanis, Levantines, Bukharis [Central Asians], Chinese, and Afghans. In short, people from every country and region of the world.... The people of Europe go on and on raising cries of "Unity!" Can they present any sight such as this? Any instance where so many different people have come together as one? In fact, unity is the very inheritance of the Muslim.[82]

Yet beyond these broad, instrumentalizing claims, Urdu authors largely ignored or marginalized African and many Asian Muslims in their efforts to fashion a Muslim community. As with Begum Sarbuland's account of the Somalis, they might be useful for demonstrating Muslim unity, but they were not truly imagined as fellow sisters and full members of the Muslim world.

There are, of course, exceptions to the sense of sorority that many Muslim women travelers felt for Arabs while in the Middle East. One of the most remarkable examples comes from the irascible and ever-cantankerous Rahil Begum's (1894–1983) account of her 1923 hajj, *Zad-i Sabil* (Provisions for the path, 1929). She approached the Bahraini Arabs on her ship with a cold anthropological eye: "They seem to have some sort of hatred for Hindustanis. What's more, they don't speak Urdu, so I haven't gone to meet their women. I pass in front of their cabins often enough, but aside from finding that they are avid eaters, I haven't been able to learn much else about them. The women are somewhat ahead of the men in terms of cigarette smoking."[83] She was also contrarian in forcefully rebuking her fellow Indian passengers for what she saw as their racist mistreatment of the ship's "Chinese" stewards and sailors.[84] Rahil Begum is unique in this view, though, and in seemingly denying unity to nearly everyone.

Conclusion

By the early twentieth century, travel writing was among the most popular genres in Urdu. This flood coincided with a pervasive interest in the lives of Muslims abroad and the imagined possibility of reuniting the world's Muslims. This imagined Muslim community was shaped in part by the emotive and personal connections made by Muslim women through travel, and through travel writing. In 1934, Qaisari Begum's daughter Muhammadi Begum (1911–90) found herself moved to spiritual heights simply by overhearing two Egyptians converse in a London train on Eid:

> We found a place to sit in one of the carriages. Two Egyptians were already sitting there. They were speaking to one another in Arabic. I tried to follow their conversation, but they were too far away, and speaking so fast I couldn't catch a word. Still, it gave me a sort of happiness to hear the Arabic language after so long. I was even happier to think that, although we come from places thousands of miles apart and are completely different from one another in terms of traditions and in other aspects, the very fact that we were co-religionists joined in the same purpose made these men seem a little less like strangers to me. In fact, I watched them with interest. After a while they began to make the *takbir* and to read prayers and Qur'anic verses out loud. Their prayers inspired me, and I too began to recite the *kalima* and who knows what under my breath.[85]

Muslim unity could be found in unexpected moments.

And yet unity had its limits. Pan-Islamic ideals were bound by racial and class hierarchies. Even as Muslim authors underlined the global nature of Islam, their writing was never fully inclusive. They seemingly favored Muslims who were seen as cultural or civilizational equals, or superiors, with a strong emphasis on race and skin color. As a result, Urdu women's travel writing focused on the Middle East, which became synonymous with the "bilad-i Islamiyya." Because race and class defined the terms of engagement, European Muslims appear in this literature to be more readily accepted than African and Asian Muslims. This is witnessed, too, in what Aamir Mufti calls the longstanding "attachment of Indian Muslims to Arab Spain," and Roanne Kantor calls the creation of "a kind of 'psychic connection' between Spain and India."[86] This fascination produced a separate flood of travel writing that sought to reclaim European history for the Muslim world; these travelogues were the precursors to Muhammad Iqbal's famous 1935 travel poems on "Qurtuba" (Córdoba).[87] Earlier generations of Indian travelers to Spain too had sought the same psychic connection to this lost Muslim land. Fascination with Europe's Muslims was also reflected in the attention lavished on converts. When the British convert Evelyn Zainab Cobbold (1867–1963) published a hajj account in English in 1934, it was quickly translated into Urdu, apparently to offer wayward Indian Muslims "a guiding light."[88] Cobbold was not only rapidly welcomed, but made a hero and an exemplar. Other authors eagerly embraced European converts (or potential converts), but neglected wide swaths of Muslims whose racial backgrounds seem to have made them ineligible for sisterhood.[89]

Cemil Aydin argues that Muslims' experience of discriminatory racialization under European colonialism inspired them to see themselves as a coherent group with shared interests; the ideal of the "Muslim world" was thus itself forged in response to racism.[90] And yet, as this chapter has shown, Muslims' own racial attitudes shaped their imagined ummah. Unlike Turkish women and British converts, Muslim women from Africa and most of Asia were excluded or described as Others, or as not fully Muslim, in Urdu travel writing. This may have been the product of precolonial ideas, but these exclusions were reinforced by the colonial education system, which introduced civilizational hierarchies and encouraged the idea that Indians were superior to Africans. When Indian Muslims re-imagined the world as one defined in part by a single, knowable Muslim ummah, this unity rarely included regions like Zanzibar or Malaysia (except perhaps by reformist movements as targets of proselytization). There were exceptions; Muhammadi Begum, for instance, wrote that "there is more in common between the Asian and African peoples than is accepted."[91] On the whole, though, travel writing was complicit in Indian Muslims' racialization of Islam, a view that continues to inform the politics of South Asian Muslim sympathies today.[92]

The following chapter extends this focus on the impact of exclusionary politics. In India, Muslims were themselves being racialized and shaped into a single community as anticolonial nationalism was increasingly expressed in terms of religious affiliations. Religious nationalism in South Asia ultimately culminated, in 1947, in the division of India into two separate countries, Pakistan and India, both of which were largely defined, whether explicitly or implicitly, by their Muslim and Hindu religious majorities. The border's sudden appearance introduced an entirely new set of ideas around community which were defined not just by religious identity, but by national belonging. The border meant that even one's own family members might suddenly become "other." What did it mean to be Indian or Pakistani? As the border solidified, this question became ever more important. Travel writing offered the opportunity to reflect on this question and to imagine new futures at odds with political reality.

One such vision came from 'Abd al-Majid Daryabadi, an influential religious leader from India. He had once been deeply opposed to the creation of Pakistan, but he later discovered through his travels that perhaps Pakistan was his homeland, too. The passages translated in the next section, originally published in Lucknow in the newspaper *Sidq-i Jadid*, discuss the poisonous past of Partition, before moving beyond it to seek out a better future. As the following chapter will show, travel writing between India and Pakistan was, and is, above all about aspiration. Through it, writers imagined a kinder world where citizens of these two nations could co-exist, and even reunite.

Notes

1. Qaisari Begum, *Kitab-i Zindagi*, 483.
2. It was also referred to, though less often in travel writing, as the *Islami dunya*, literally, the Islamic world.
3. White, "Hajj," 145, 148; Bose, *Hundred Horizons*, 204. For a comparison with early modern pilgrimage from India, see Das Gupta and Pearson, *Indian Ocean*; Pearson, *Pilgrimage*; Choudhury, "The Hajj from India."
4. It is important to include Punjabi verse here, since linguistic usage in the Urdu world was shaped by gender. While many Punjabi men published in Urdu, Punjabi women had far less access to this language of the public sphere. Nur Begum also shows that the experiences of women travel writers who spoke Urdu—as represented by the ten authors cited and translated from Urdu in this chapter—extended into other languages and regions as well.
5. Nur Begum, *Mazahir*, 16. Here and later, I have rendered her verse in prose to facilitate reading. For a further study of Nur Begum, see Nur Begum,

"Nur Begum." In this passage, the pointed lack of a dominant Indian identity, even as late as the 1930s, is strikingly clear.

6. A ritualistic phrase invoking God's oneness.
7. Nur Begum, *Mazahir*, 14.
8. Kambalposh, *Tarikh*, 111–36.
9. Khan, *Musafiran* (1961), 111.
10. Sikandar Begum, "Tarikh," 45–49.
11. Aydin, "Paradoxes," 179; Aydin, *Muslim World*, 10–11.
12. Jalal, *Self and Sovereignty*, 198.
13. Pernau, *Emotions and Modernity*, 8.
14. Minault, *Khilafat*, 5. See also Schimmel, *Islam*, 219; Jalal, *Self and Sovereignty*, 191.
15. Minault, *Khilafat*, 35–6; Robb, *Print*, 127–53.
16. Dubrow, *Cosmopolitan Dreams*, 36.
17. Shackle and Majeed, *Hali's Musaddas*, 130–31.
18. Majeed, "Geographies," 148–51.
19. Shibli Nu'mani, *Safarnama*, 6. Constantinople (Qustuntuniya) was still the standard name for Istanbul in this period.
20. Minault, *Khilafat*, 4; Alavi, *Muslim Cosmopolitanism*, xi.
21. Majchrowicz, "Malika Begum's Mehfil," 862. More broadly, see Grewal, *Home and Harem*; Burton, *Heart of the Empire*; Fisher, *Counterflows*; Fyzee-Rahamin, *Atiya's Journeys*. And in a similar context, Ramabai Sarasvati, *Pandita Ramabai's America*.
22. Minault, *Khilafat*, 149.
23. Malhotra and Lambert-Hurley, *Speaking*, 1–23. Andrew Amstutz, for instance, argues that journalist Mahmuda Rizvi's travelogue to Iraq used geographical, historical, and religious connections to posit "imagined connections between the territories that would become Pakistan and the Middle East." Amstutz, "New Shahrazad," 382.
24. In a similar vein, Sunil Sharma argues that British women travelers' accounts of the Middle East were different from those of men in part because of their authors' exclusive access to women's spaces. Sharma, "Speaking Without Language," 99.
25. Ruswa, *Umra'o Jan "Ada,"* 92.
26. Fisher, *Counterflows*, 222. The primary exception, discussed later, is an 1867 hajj account that the ruler of Bhopal State, Nawab Sikandar Begum, wrote at the behest of a British official. Sikandar Begum, "Tarikh," 2.
27. Fyzee-Rahamin, *Atiya's Journeys*, 2.
28. For a detailed examination of travel writing by Muslim women in South Asia, see Lambert-Hurley, Majchrowicz, and Sharma, *Three Centuries*.

29. Dubrow, *Cosmopolitan Dreams*, 1–2.

30. On women and cultural representation, see Chatterjee, *Nation*, 116–57. See also Amstutz, "New Shahrazad," 376–77.

31. The sole exception I have found is 'Ali, "Dihli se Landan."

32. Alam, *Familial Intimacy*, 22. For a detailed study of pre-Partition women's magazines, see Akhtar, *Jara'id-i Nisvan*.

33. Minault, *Secluded Scholars*, 119.

34. Fyzee-Rahamin, *Atiya's Journeys*, 9.

35. This question was widely debated by feminist scholars of travel writing in the 1980s and '90s wishing to reclaim Victorian history for women. For an influential treatment, see Mills, *Discourses*, 28–46.

36. Sikandar Begum, "Tarikh," 56. My analysis and translations of Sikandar Begum's writing in this section are based on the original Urdu manuscript.

37. Sikandar Begum, "Tarikh," 47.

38. Unfortunately, Begum Sarbuland Jang's book has not been well preserved. Only two copies exist today, in Delhi and in Austin.

39. Server-ul-Mulk, *My Life*, viii. See also Khwaja, "Jamal Khwaja."

40. Robinson, *Separatism*, 406.

41. Lambert-Hurley, "Fostering Sisterhood," 46.

42. Shibli Nu'mani, *Safarnama*, 193.

43. 'Ali, *Mah-i Maghrib*, 124–25.

44. Both words have equivalent meanings in Turkish and Urdu. The word "begum" (properly *begam*) was itself the feminine form of *beg*, an old Turkish word for a nobleman. The masculine form existed in contemporary Turkish as *beğ*, but clearly the feminine form was unfamiliar to the Ottomans, who referred to Turkish noblewomen as *hanım* in Turkish (khanam in Urdu).

45. Begum Sarbuland Jang, *Dunya*, 138.

46. Begum Sarbuland Jang, *Dunya*, 140.

47. Begum Sarbuland Jang, *Dunya*, 139. The exact identity of this woman is unclear. She may have been a Coptic Christian from Egypt, but the question is complicated by Begum Sarbuland's tendency to racialize religion. Christians are thus termed "angrez" or "mem," while "Arab" is in her account synonymous with "Muslim."

48. Sunil Sharma explores how women's encounters abroad were shaped by the political dynamics of colonialism. Sharma, "Speaking Without Language," 108.

49. Khan, *Safarnama*, 53–54.

50. Khan, *Safarnama*, dedication.

51. Begum Sarbuland Jang, *Dunya*, 66–68.

52. Begum Sarbuland Jang, *Dunya*, 72.

53. Begum Sarbuland Jang, *Dunya*, 20.

54. Begum Sarbuland Jang, *Dunya*, 178.

55. Begum Sarbuland Jang, *Dunya*, 28.

56. Fatima Begum's account is among those that I found in the women's section of Jhandir Library. Coincidentally, she traveled on the same ship as Begum Sarbuland Jang on the latter's second hajj pilgrimage.

57. Fatima Begum, *Hajj-i Baitullah*, 83–84. Translation by David Boyk. See Fatima Begum, "Fatima Begum," 164. For a similar instance of exchange with Egyptian women in English, see pp. 99–100 of the Urdu original.

58. Begum Humayun Mirza was a frequent travel writer with at least six travel books to her name. She also published smaller accounts constantly in journals. As founder and editor of the monthly *Zeb al-Nisa*, she featured her own travel writing prominently. For example, Mirza, "Siyahat-i Nanda'ir."

59. The text erroneously gives Şehvar for all occurrences of her name in this passage.

60. Mirza, *Safarnama-i Yurap*, 2:152–53.

61. Mirza, *Safarnama-i Yurap*, 2:153.

62. Mirza, *Safarnama-i Yurap*, 2:153.

63. Mangalagiri, "Ellipses," 510.

64. As used in this chapter, the term "Asian" denotes people from Central, East, and Southeast Asia.

65. "Rise up, O 'Umar!" A reference to the second Caliph, who greatly expanded the power and territorial range of the Islamic empire.

66. Shibli Nu'mani, *Safarnama*, 16–17.

67. Ummat al-Hafiz, "Madagascar ka Safar," 29.

68. Fatima Begum, *Hajj-i Baitullah*, 101. Translation by David Boyk. See Fatima Begum, "Fatima Begum," 166.

69. Fatima Begum, *Hajj-i Baitullah*, 101–02. Translation by David Boyk.

70. *Sair-i Afriqa*, 1. This sweeping dismissal of Africa as a vast wilderness was clearly common. In a travel letter from 1878, written in Bengali, a teenage Rabindranath Tagore expressed surprise at Egypt's lushness: "I had previously imagined Africa to be from top to toe an arid desert wasteland, but looking around me, it in no way resembled that. On the other hand ... [it] seemed to me marvelous indeed." Tagore, *Letters*, 30.

71. Kambalposh, *Tarikh*, 56–60.

72. Kambalposh, *Tarikh*, 60.

73. Fatima Begum, *Hajj-i Baitullah*, 53. Translation by David Boyk. Fatima Begum, "Fatima Begum," 163.

74. Ummat al-Ghani, *Safarnama*, 67.

75. Qaisari Begum, *Kitab-i Zindagi*, 474.

76. Qaisari Begum, *Kitab-i Zindagi*, 474–75.

77. Qaisari Begum, *Kitab-i Zindagi*, 484.

78. Remarkably, though, none of the authors studied here commented on the presence of Balkan, Chechen, or other "White" Muslims, as Malcolm X famously did on his pilgrimage in 1964. *The Autobiography of Malcolm X*, 340. This may have been due to their small numbers at the time.

79. Tagliacozzo, *The Longest Journey*, 5; McDonnell, "Muslim Pilgrimage from Malaysia," 205; Bose, *Hundred Horizons*, 204.

80. Sikandar Begum, "Tarikh," 51.

81. Can, *Spiritual Subjects*, 17, 27, 38; Lally, *Silk Roads*, 194; Kane, *Russian Hajj*, 72–83.

82. Ummat al-Ghani, *Safarnama*, 34.

83. Shervaniya, *Zad al-Sabil*, 25.

84. Shervaniya, *Zad al-Sabil*, 18.

85. Muhammadi Begum, "Diary," 4.

86. Mufti, *Enlightenment*, 44; Kantor, *Global English*, 94. Kantor explores the postcolonial manifestations of this engagement with Andalusia in postcolonial South Asian literature. Kantor, *Global English*, 88–112.

87. Prominent works include Khan, *Qand-i Maghribi*; Mir, *Safarnama-i Undulus*. The later was even used as a textbook in some Urdu-language schools.

88. Nizamat Jang, "Muqaddama," alif.

89. Rahil Shervania, on hajj in the 1920s, showed deep interest in supporting a potential English convert. Shervaniya, *Zad al-Sabil*, 27–28. Begum Sarbuland seems to have personally escorted a British convert to Mecca in 1937. Bidwell, *Foreign Affairs*, 12:282.

90. Aydin, "Paradoxes," 182–86; Aydin, *Muslim World*, 3–4.

91. Muhammadi Begum, "Diary," n.p.

92. Visible, for instance, in the enduring concern in South Asia for Palestinians, but comparatively little agitation in favor of the Rohingya in Myanmar, or persecuted Muslim communities in Xinjiang or the Central African Republic.

Two and a Half Weeks in Pakistan: A Blessed Journey

by Maulana 'Abd al-Majid Daryabadi
Publisher: Maulana 'Abd al-Majid Daryabadi Academy, Lucknow [1952]

Pakistan is a foreign country now. This is no ordinary foreignness, but one riddled with distrust and wrapped in layer after layer of obscuring cloth. How could a trip there be as simple as buying a bus ticket and setting off? Acquiring the necessary permissions and permits itself involves so many stages and steps that even the most courageous and daring will have their patience tested to the limit. A few moments ago, Lahore and Karachi were our own, just like Bombay or Calcutta. But now there are so many veils [between us] that from this perspective going to London or New York would be far easier....

On the first of April, the seventh of Sha'ban, after saying the Friday prayer, we departed on the late afternoon train from Lucknow to Amritsar. Before Partition, this train went straight to Lahore. It used to be called the Calcutta–Punjab Mail. On the train platform such a crowd of relatives, friends, supporters, and others had gathered to see me off that it felt as though I were not going to Pakistan, but rather going on hajj and to visit [the Prophet's grave in Medina]. It felt as though I were going on a trip that would last years, not just two and a half weeks! Among the crowd were pure-hearted old men who had full faith in their supposition that I was on a political mission, as a Governor-General, or to serve as a constitutional advisor. They were sure that I could assist their [relatives] in securing jobs and promotions for bureaucrats and office workers at every rank. "Listen, please find a job for my dear So-and-So. The poor boy has yet to find a position." Innocent people piled filing cabinets' worth of requests and petitions onto these weak shoulders with complete faith. The scene of my departure was emotional, and anyone with a feeling heart would have been overcome with melancholic sorrow and pain. It was just like the soul's journey at the end of life. You are surrounded by your friends, and [after you die] they carry your corpse to the grave, and then you are on your own!

The train began to move, and my mind was filled with images of Pakistan. The Spokesman of Truth, [Muhammad] Iqbal, had worked tirelessly to find a firm mooring in people's hearts for the movement for this "Islamic" country. Thousands of sincere, fearless supporters responded by passionately crying out "labbaik."[1] There were so many desires; so many grand plans were made. But what did all those sweet and pleasant dreams actually mean? How much has the ummah lost in its pursuit, how much has been stolen away in its name? After achieving it, what has been gained? How do you measure profit and loss, or calculate inflation or deflation in this economy? I continued to think in this way as evening fell. Soon it was night. Half-awake, half-asleep, the night passed and the train crossed out of Uttar Pradesh and into Punjab. Soon, it was morning.

This stop is Ambala, a town that had once been made into a rose garden by the presence of the Sheikh of *Tabligh* [proselytization], Mir Nairang. And this, this is Ludhiana. And here is Sirhind, home to the tomb of the Renewer of the Age [Ahmad Sirhindi], which even today bears the appellation "noble." And there, that is Rajpura. And so on, until, by dusk, we had reached Jalandhar. How many [Muslim] scholars and experts had lived here until so recently! Day and night, the sound of testimony to the unity of God had resounded from the minarets of countless mosques [here]. But now, instead of happiness and joy, my heart was overtaken by melancholy and sorrow. Look. We were now traveling between Jalandhar and Amritsar! Do not ask me to explain how my heart sighed. My mind's camera was filled with image after image, images filled with sorrow and dripping with blood. This land is surely seeped in the blood of countless innocent children, boys and girls. How many elderly men and women writhed to death on this land? How many innocent women were mercilessly raped here?[2]

***

[Two and a half weeks later]

And then, finally, it was time for me to leave [Karachi], whose people are so filled with love. Our party arrived at the station before eight. This time we used City Station, the last stop in Karachi. As I had expected, there was a substantial crowd of people waiting to see me off. I no longer remember all their names, nor is there any need to list them. All I can remember now is that among my dear ones, my friends, and my acquaintances there were several strangers, too. A few of them, whose faces revealed their religious piety, came to request spiritual advice. Their devotion left a deep impression on me. Just as the train began to pull away, one man gifted me a nice fountain pen. I no longer remember his name nor his face, and I cannot recompense him for his sincerity. Many well-wishers ... saw me off in such a way that it felt as though I were not a foreigner returning to my homeland, but as though I were leaving my own homeland. Perhaps the word "homeland" does not refer to particles of soil or the mortar in our houses, but rather to those who love....

The night passed and day dawned. All the station views repeated themselves just as they had when I first saw them on my way [to Karachi]. Bahawalpur, Multan, Montgomery [Faisalabad]. The scent of love wafted in from so many places! But it is not man's fate for his every desire to be fulfilled. In each of life's journeys, we must accept that we will encounter so many destinations that we may only gaze on longingly as we quickly pass them by.[3]

Notes

1. "I am here," a religious phrase used by pilgrims to announce their arrival in Mecca.
2. Daryabadi, *Dha'i Hafte*, 12–16.
3. Daryabadi, *Dha'i Hafte*, 106–07.

6

Border Crossings

When colonial India was partitioned into the two sovereign nations of India and Pakistan in 1947, it occasioned the greatest mass migration in human history. The violence precipitated a refugee crisis of unimaginable proportions. Some ten million people were uprooted. Hundreds of thousands were killed, raped, or abducted.[1] By 1948 about 50 percent of Lahore's population consisted of refugees. In Delhi, it was 30 percent.[2] This was only the beginning of a calamity whose consequences still reverberate. The upheaval was followed by confusion as states, societies, and individuals considered who and what would belong where. For those who stayed as well as those who left, Partition inaugurated a generations-long struggle to reconcile and rebuild. Society underwent profound changes, while an increasingly rigid barrier restricted the ability of people and ideas to flow between the two new countries. For Pakistani novelist Intizar Husain (1925–2016), the challenge of crossing this border was emotional as much as logistical:

> The other countries of the world are one thing, and India is another. Trips abroad usually go something like this: *tuk dekh liya, dil shad kiya, aur chal nikle* [I looked around a bit, enjoyed myself, and went on my way]. A straightforward journey, a straightforward discussion. But for us [Pakistanis], a trip to India is a complex experience. On this journey, how many opposing emotions battle one another? We abhor India, and we are drawn to it. Just as [political] relations between India and Pakistan have their ups and downs, so too do our own contradictory emotional states oscillate in the same measure.[3]

For those who experienced Partition, or who live in its aftermath, this is a journey unlike any other.

Urdu writers have long used the power of narrative and language to represent the complexities of Partition. Alongside oral histories, this literature has become an alternative archive for historians to access Partition's emotional violence, implicitly suggesting that literature is perhaps "better able to cope with the challenges of writing about Partition than history [itself]."[4] Historiographic engagement with this literature gave rise to what I call a historian's "Partition canon," which consists primarily of short stories and other fiction, typically by well-known authors, read in English translation from Urdu and Hindi.[5] This canon centers on works dating to the first years after 1947 and typically foregrounds violence, particularly in Punjab.[6] The dominance of these themes limits the Partition canon's ability to capture the full range of Partition's experiences and emotions and its persistent, everyday violence.[7] Similarly, the historian's Partition canon does not fully account for Urdu literature's engagement with Partition. Not all Partition literature in Urdu is fiction, nor is it necessarily historical or focused on violence. Every literary genre engages with Partition differently, and the omission of contemporary and non-fiction writing like the travelogue limits our understanding of Partition, its literature, and its ongoing reality.[8] Urdu travel writing is a site of aspiration, a space not just to reimagine past events, but also to imagine alternative futures, including ones where Partition is overcome. If the historian's Partition canon is about looking back, the travelogue is about imagining the future.

Cross-border travel writing emerged rapidly after 1947, contemporaneously with seminal Partition stories like Sa'adat Hasan Manto's "Thanda Gosht" (Cold meat, 1950) or "Toba Tek Singh" (1955). The Indo-Pak or cross-border travel account has thus always been a prominent space in contemporary Urdu literature for engagement with Partition. It is distinct among Partition literatures for its autobiographical engagement with the unfinished nature of Partition. At the same time, it stands out from other travel writing in its approach to its subject and as a bearer of affect. Travel writing is usually outward-looking, but this literature is unabashedly introspective. Cross-border accounts nominally describe international journeys, but, as 'Abd al-Majid Daryabadi suggests in the passage that introduces this chapter, these accounts are typically "journeys home." In Urdu, cross-border travel is not simple tourism. It is, as the Urdu journalist Santosh Kumar argued, a "spiritual exigency."[9]

While the Indo-Pak travel account details an intimately personal journey, writers must simultaneously navigate readers' expectations and sensitivities in both countries. Readers demand more than introspection: they want accurate information on conditions "over there." With mail service frequently blocked and news sources biased or unreliable, the Indo-Pak travelogue offers an essential conduit for firsthand reports. Even today, in the censorship-subverting age of the

internet, the specific, intimate insights of travel writing make it a prized source
of information. Newspapers and magazines still publish written accounts, while
visual narratives proliferate online. Digital media (whether via Youtube, Instagram,
or Tiktok) garner a wide viewership, facilitating debate and reconciliation in
previously unimaginable ways. Digital media are new, but travel writing has always
been published primarily in similar spaces that facilitate simultaneous public
consumption. Whatever the format, generations of Urdu readers have vicariously
traversed the border through travel accounts. As one critic put it, cross-border
accounts are "not the travelogue of one person but the journey of lakhs of people,
of generations of people."[10]

These generations of people do not always appear in Partition historiography.
Earlier scholarship focused on either colonial-era party politics or the violence of
1947, though this approach has since been replaced by perspectives that reconsiders
Partition's timescale.[11] Vazira Zamindar proposes the term "long Partition" to
suggest we "stretch our very understanding of 'Partition violence' to include the
bureaucratic violence of drawing political boundaries and nationalizing identities
that became, in some lives, interminable."[12] Amber Abbas argues for thinking
of Partition as a process, "partitioning," in order to create "space to examine ...
communities" and give attention to "continuities and not just cleavages."[13]
"Partitioning" captures how communities and individuals continuously negotiate
Partition in the present. Many who left India for Pakistan initially believed the
situation was temporary, or that they would be easily able to return for visits. Even
high-ranking officials assumed migration would be impermanent.[14] "Partitioning"
allows us to read Partition's indeterminacy and subsequent developments in
postcolonial South Asia (like the creation of Bangladesh in 1971) as part of a larger
process. This approach undoes the tendency of moment-centric historiography to
"deny [Partition] historical continuity, to place it outside the pale of South Asian
history, and to deny communities of survivors the possibility of a future," and
instead attends to ongoing "changes in perception between communities, within
neighborhoods and across borders."[15]

In Indo-Pak travel writing, partitioning is ever-present. Just as both personal
and collective memory shift over time, so does the meaning of the past respond to
the present.[16] Cross-border travel writing, typically written as first-person memoir,
reveals how "shifting boundaries of memory" interact with the politics of everyday
life in post-independence South Asia.[17] The Indo-Pak travelogue creates a space
through which to imagine and enact visions for the future informed by the past.
As a genre, it is unambiguous in its recognition that Partition is a continuing
process rather than a completed event. It is unique in offering a critique of Partition
and nationalism that neither relegates Partition violence to the past, nor absolves
inhabitants of the present—including the self—of complicity.

This chapter examines two distinct phases of Indo-Pak travel writing. The first dates to before 1965, when the long-term implications of Partition were still murky. Governments and citizens alike struggled to determine how the nascent states would relate. In this period, travel writing sought to make sense of Partition and to explore concrete solutions to it. The second phase was inaugurated by the war of 1965. That war, and another in 1971, cemented political animosities and foreclosed lingering hopes of reunification. In their aftermath, the 1970s and '80s witnessed a surge in travel writing by members of an aging generation who had lived through Partition and were returning to their ancestral homes for the first time. Authors of this pre-Partition generation, Hindu, Muslim, and Sikh, turned to Urdu literature to come to terms with their experiences, imagining their work as a "bridge," a unifying force for a binational readership.[18] These authors sought a personal rather than political solution to Partition. Not included in this chapter is the current, third phase. This began in the 1990s, when cross-border travel writing became dominated by writers born into a divided subcontinent, the grudging inheritors of a half-century of rancor. These accounts continue to be written today. Despite their calendrical distance from 1948, they are no less emotional, probing, or cathartic, for partitioning continues to shape lives in tangible and intangible ways.

The Indo-Pak Travel Account

Cross-border travel writing often employs narrative arcs drawn from fiction. Protagonists overcome obstacles and traverse emotional minefields to achieve their goals before returning home enriched and at peace. Commonly invoked themes include the overwhelming desire for return (see Ram La'l later in this chapter), fear of return (Mumtaz Mufti), reconciling the past with the present (Santosh Kumar, Iffat Ilahi 'Alavi), seeking closure (Intizar Husain), reuniting with friends, family, or beloved places (Saliha 'Abid Husain), and reestablishing links with communities of shared interest, language, or ethnicity (Khwaja Hasan Nizami, 'Abd al-Majid Daryabadi). The Indo-Pak travel account is typically marked by activist language and intent. Drawing on Urdu's close affiliation with resistance politics in South Asia, cross-border authors typically combat communalist or nationalist sentiment through their writing. "Mutual understanding" is a primary concern, and the word *samjhauta* (negotiation or compromise, a word etymologically suggesting understanding) is ubiquitous. Some accounts also seek to maintain subnational links with cultural and social affinities (Kumar) or religious groups (Nizami, Daryabadi). As both countries drew further apart, travel writers worked, through texts, to slow or reverse that trajectory.

Crossing the Border

Cross-border travel writers were painfully aware of the privilege of their journey. One might spend a lifetime pursuing a visa and never succeed. After Daryabadi's journey, things only grew worse. By 1965, border closures were constant. Mail delivery became unreliable.[19] Families and friends fell out of touch.[20] Magazines and newspapers failed to appear.[21] In 1976, Indian author Ismat Chughtai (1915–91) noted with surprise in her cross-border travelogue that newly printed copies of her writing were available in Lahore: "I had no idea how those stories made it there. There were even stories which had been published during the worst times, when all [cross-border movement] was totally suspended. It turns out that magazines and books go to Europe first, from where they reach Pakistan."[22]

Intizar Husain lamented in 1989 that "the nature of travel to India ... constantly changes." For travelers,

> the path is sometimes open, sometimes half open, sometimes completely closed. No one from there can come here, and no one from here can go there. It is as though it were a city located across the seven seas. Then the path opens in such a way that it is open and closed at once. Traveling to Delhi [from Pakistan] is like managing to complete the *Haft Khvan*.[23]

Travelers did what they could. Daryabadi acquired a visa to Pakistan through high-ranking contacts—and then struggled to leave India, where officials were suspicious of those very contacts, "as though the high ranking do not understand the meaning of personal affection, friendship, and shared interest!"[24] The Indian writer Khwaja Hasan Nizami (1878–1955) also relied on personal contacts. Having been denied permission to visit Pakistan, he wrote an angry letter to Governor-General Liaquat Ali Khan, demanding to know why an old friend of Muhammad Ali Jinnah's, the founder of Pakistan, was being denied entry. Khan capitulated.[25] Indian Santosh Kumar took another tack, asking his old contacts in the Lahore press to help.[26] Visitors could also acquire a pilgrimage visa. Intizar Husain first returned to India as a pilgrim to the shrine of Nizamuddin Auliya in Delhi.[27] Pakistani author and columnist Ata ul Haq Qasmi (1943–) went to Sirhind for the *'urs* (death commemoration) of Ahmad Sirhindi, though in truth he only wished to visit Amritsar, his birthplace.[28] Mumtaz Mufti (1905–95) was interested in *yunani tibb*, or Greco-Islamic medicine. Unlikely to get a visa for homeopathic research, he too became a pilgrim:

> [A friend] told me: My dear! Why get caught up chasing after a No Objection Certificate? Why go sifting the soil from door to door? Just join a group of pilgrims. One bird, two stones. Give your greeting to the saint. Attend the 'urs. Bring back

homeopathy books. Amir Khusrau's 'urs is happening in August. Shoot off an application. If your name is drawn, great. If not, write another application, and another, and another.[29]

Mufti dedicated his book to Amir Khusrau, whose supernatural intervention he credits for his successful border crossing.[30] For every trip across the border there is another visa story.

Traversing the border brought travelers under suspicion, particularly if they were public figures or intellectuals. Newspapers fanned the flames: "A feature item in the newspaper was published with the sensationalized headline that in one year so many writers and artists have come [to Pakistan] from India.... If the person crossing the border is one of those sinful writers [as opposed to cricket players], then their going is suspicious, their coming is suspicious."[31] But once they had crossed, travelers became an unrivaled source of information. Every installment of Santosh Kumar's serialized newspaper account "began to attract scores of letters, some of which were filled with praise, and others which drew my attention to the minutest offense in colorful terms."[32] His work apparently made "such an impact" on then-Prime Minister Indira Gandhi that she had it translated into English.[33]

With cross-border travel so difficult, the traveler was a rare source of firsthand knowledge. One day Intizar Husain fell into conversation with a Hindu rickshaw driver in Banaras:

After driving only a few feet, he said: "How's Pakistan doing nowadays?"
"It's doing well."
"Are people happy?"
"Very happy."
He paused. Then he said: "Look, don't be suspicious of me. We all used to be together. Now we've been separated. So when someone comes from Pakistan the heart yearns to ask how the people over there are doing."[34]

Husain similarly remarked that "there are certain questions that are always asked of travelers to India":

For example, "What is the state of Urdu in India?" "How are Indian Muslims being treated?" "How is inflation there?" I must be able to provide answers to these questions. If I fall short in providing answers then my friends are entirely justified in saying to me: "Well, then why did you even bother to go to India in the first place?"[35]

The creation of Pakistan and establishment of independent India touched everyone in north India. Friends, relatives, and neighbors migrated, and communities transformed, sometimes even beyond recognition.[36] Those who lived through the tumultuous 1940s had participated in years of debate on the subject and perhaps seriously considered migrating themselves. There remained a strong interest in seeing how things were, how they might have been. As Daryabadi wrote: "Is there any Muslim whose heart does not yearn to make a pilgrimage [*ziyarat*] to Pakistan?"[37]

Negotiating Partition: The Early Years

Sa'adat Hasan Manto's (1912–55) short story "Toba Tek Singh" (1955) tells the tale of Hindu, Muslim, and Sikh inmates at an insane asylum who cannot comprehend the division of the country. Where were these new places, and who belonged to which? The inmates spend their days elaborating business plans and romantic interests with no certainty as to where they truly belonged. In her reading of the story, Frances Pritchett points to the surprising fact that, even several years after Partition, the inmates are still unaware which country their homes are in.[38] The satirical uncertainty of the inmates mirrored the confusion of countless people across South Asia who, even in 1950, did not know where they belonged. Once the conflict was over, would they be able to return home? Would they regain the property they had left behind? Would India and Pakistan be reunited?

Amid the confusion, many sought guidance from community leaders, some of whom, like Khwaja Hasan Nizami and 'Abd al-Majid Daryabadi, commanded extensive networks organized around the press. Nizami was a journalist and Sufi reformer from Delhi. He visited Pakistan twice, in May and November 1950. Accounts of his journeys were published in installments in *Roznamcha*, the journal he founded to inform followers about his activities. He later combined the installments together into a standalone publication, *Safarnama-i Pakistan* (Travelogue of Pakistan, 1952).[39] Nizami was a prolific travel writer, but unlike in earlier works, here he did not describe his surroundings. Instead, he limited himself to reporting on meetings with community members, evaluating Pakistan's administration and commitment to Islamic principles, and chronicling his daily activities. Nizami was perhaps the most prominent Sufi of his day. He was born into the family of the hereditary keepers of Nizamuddin Auliya's shrine in Delhi. As an adult, he supervised hundreds of thousands of disciples through the press.[40] Over the course of fifty years he founded several newspapers, wrote at least seven book-length travelogues, and authored books on a range of other subjects.[41] A reformist saint in an era of mass media, his influence was immense.[42] His stature earned him the ear of politicians and intellectuals from Shibli Nu'mani and Abul Kalam Azad to Muhammad Ali Jinnah. One of his stated goals in writing a travel account of Pakistan was to facilitate a political reconciliation of the two states.[43]

'Abd al-Majid Daryabadi (1892–1977) traveled to Pakistan in 1955, three years after Nizami. He was affiliated with the major intellectual centers of Muslim north India. A prolific writer focused on journalism and religious reform, his travelogue to Mecca has never gone out of print and is perhaps the single most influential pilgrimage account in Urdu literature.[44] Like Nizami, he used periodicals to spread his global imagination. His readership experienced his impressions of Pakistan through ten articles published in his newspaper, *Sidq-i Jadid*.[45] These articles were widely republished in both countries. Daryabadi received a "constant flow of letters ... sent by readers of almost every class."[46] This inspired him to republish the articles as a book titled *Dha'i Hafte Pakistan Meñ: Mubarak Safar* (Two and a half weeks in Pakistan: A blessed journey, 1955). It retains a niche readership in India even today.

Of the two men, Nizami was the more forceful in denouncing Partition: he simply refused to accept it. Nizami began his travel account by rejecting the very idea of two nations and by claiming Pakistani territory as his birthright. Nizami was born in Delhi, but this was a journey *home*.[47] On the very first page he baldly stated: "[I], Hasan Nizami Dihlavi, submit that my *Safarnama-i Pakistan* is not a travelogue about a foreign or unknown place, for this book discusses my travel in regions whence my forefathers hailed."[48] This claim is reinforced by the phrase "apna ghar" (my home), which variously refers to Karachi, Lahore, and Delhi. From the outset, Nizami looked beyond the new international border drawn by Cyril Radcliffe and instead described a spiritual geography in which the subcontinent was divided into Sufi *vilayat*s, or territories.

To explain his claim, Nizami recounted the story of a fourteenth-century ancestor who traveled to Delhi from Ghazna (in modern Afghanistan) to find the solution to an intractable religious dilemma. Unsuccessful, he turned homeward. On the way, he met Baba Farid al-Din in Ajodhan, now in Pakistan, who solved his issue, inducted him into the Chishti order, and married him into his family. Thus, despite being born in Delhi, Nizami's spiritual ancestry tied him to a geographical space now in Pakistan. On this basis he proclaimed that "the areas on which Pakistan has been constructed are my ancient homeland. For this reason, my trip through this region was a **JOURNEY THROUGH THE HOMELAND**," a fact he underlined by putting these final words in a triple-sized, bold font.[49] The book rejected nationalism in favor of an older understanding of territory, one that Nizami hoped would inform the future. It was an unexpected temporal shift for a book about a new state. Nizami proposed a political imagination for the present inspired by the memory of a better past.

Nizami began his trip in Lahore by praying at the grave of his daughter, Hur Bano, who died shortly after migrating. The magnanimity of the caretaker at the Miyan Mir shrine where she was buried contrasted starkly with Nizami's most recent interlocutors: cruel Indian customs agents. Nizami then began a hectic schedule of meetings with disciples around Pakistan. He also visited businessmen, toured factories, and investigated potential publishing ventures. He chatted with high-ranking politicians. When he attended a grand night of *qawwali* music on Nizamuddin's birthday he was joined by twenty-five thousand devotees. Nizami told them that Nizamuddin himself had been a *muhajir*, or migrant, just as they were. Nizamuddin thus remained relevant to their lives, even from a distance. Throughout his trip, Nizami sent dispatches to Indian newspapers so that readers there could follow along.

Daryabadi, on the other hand, acknowledged the creation of Pakistan, but still expressed a desire for Partition to be reversed. His writing, like Nizami's, kept a partitioned community informed. He had been deeply critical of Partition and the "un-Islamic" state of Pakistan, as he liked to call it. Yet his aversion metamorphosed into reverence during his trip, and his account was accordingly laden with religious symbolism. The journey was *mubarak*, blessed. He felt as though he were "going on hajj."[50] His re-entry process into India reminded him of the old hajj quarantine station at Kamran. If the journey to Mecca was a hajj, Daryabadi explained that the journey to Pakistan was a ziyarat, a pilgrimage to a sacred site.[51] After all, Pakistan was a Muslim country composed of people of "the very same flesh and blood, heart and soul." His desire to see it mirrored the passion of the lover in Sufi imagery. Daryabadi indicated this mystical dimension by quoting two Persian hemistiches from Hafiz:

> [*nazir-i ru-i to sahib-nazaran-and are*]
>> *Sirr-i gesu-i to dar hich sari nist ki nist*
> [Those who have caught sight of your face possess insight, indeed!]
>> There is no head in which the secret of your dark locks is not [found]
> [*na man-i dilshuda az dast-i to khunin jigaram*]
>> *Az gham-i 'ishq-i to pur-khun jigari nist ki nist*
> [I am not the only one inflamed in this love for you]
>> There is none who is not inflamed from the sorrow of your love[52]

Pakistan took on the role of the beloved, longed for by the suffering lover. Indian Muslims had heard much about this beloved, but never seen its face. Misinformation was rife; the truth was a secret for the few. The first verse may be read in two ways: that only those who see Pakistan for themselves know its reality, or else that there is no other whose locks contain such mystique—there is no other country whose mystery so entices. The second verse, of course, suggested that this relationship caused the suffering of Muslims across India. Linking Pakistan to the holy cities and to Islamic mysticism revealed the depth of Daryabadi's "spiritual endeavor."

Ultimately, Daryabadi came to terms with Pakistan, calling it his "homeland" (*vatan*). While less insistently than Nizami, Daryabadi invoked the term vatan with increasing frequency as his trip, and his newspaper articles, progressed. In India, customs officers gave this superstar maulana no special treatment, but in Pakistan he received a hero's welcome. When he left Karachi he "was seen off as though I were not a foreigner returning to his homeland, but rather as though I were leaving my homeland. Perhaps the word 'homeland' does not refer to particles of dust or the soil at our thresholds, but rather to those who love."[53] He said the same of Lahore: "So many well-wishers, dear ones and friends were present that it seemed that this was my own homeland."[54] Almost despite himself, Daryabadi enjoyed life in this "un-Islamic country." Of course, Pakistan was not his homeland in any literal sense. This was an aspiration, a way of reimagining the world, of effecting a personal peace in a conflicted space. This cathartic ending was meant to be shared by readers.

Nizami and Daryabadi's travel accounts were prominent early attempts to negotiate Partition through travel writing. Despite their distinct viewpoints, each inhabited a similar social position that allowed them to put their global imaginations before legions of readers. Both fought the centrifugal forces of Partition. For Nizami, this meant keeping his community informed through print. Nizami never intended for his account to be a lament. Nevertheless, he did fall into moments of despair. Seeing Delhi's hereditary merchants in Karachi, he wrote, "[M]y heart wept bitterly at this blighted freedom that has torn all of us from one another."[55] Daryabadi, too, declined to accept the finality of Partition, expressing an eagerness for reintegration in his conclusion.[56] As the first major cross-border accounts, *Dha'i Hafte Pakistan Meñ* and *Safarnama-i Pakistan* mark the shift from a genre focused on "going abroad" to "coming home." Cross-border accounts spent little time describing this "foreign" land. Their authors were more interested in unity than in difference. They proposed solutions to the conflict and imagined a shared future for readers on both sides, and even a borderless future.

Lesser-known Urdu writers also had their say. Among this group was a Lakhnavi-turned-Lahori named 'Iffat Ilahi 'Alavi, who visited India in 1957. She described the emotional journey from Lahore with a mix of depression, loss, and fascination. 'Alavi published "1957 ka Hindustan" (India in 1957, 1959) in the women's magazine *'Ismat*. She opened with a rumination on the tragic sense of rupture she felt. And yet, like Daryabadi, she too found spiritual and aspirational dimensions in the journey. For her this was not a pilgrimage but a religious migration, or *hijrat*. Even after leaving Lucknow for Lahore, she wrote, "love and respect for [India's] greatness remain in our hearts. This love and respect call out to us, asking us to return. A Muslim's hijrat is not complete until they reacquire the country they left behind."[57] This was a reference to the Prophet's own hijrat in 622 CE, when he and his followers fled from Mecca to Yathrib, or Medina, to escape persecution. Eight years later, they returned to Mecca victorious. While it is unclear whether 'Alavi meant to suggest that migrants to Pakistan would "reacquire" India metaphorically or literally, her account drew on the ideal of return, suggesting that Pakistan itself was a shelter, but not a permanent home, for a persecuted Muslim minority.

'Alavi's account expressed surprise and disappointment in the many ways Lucknow had changed since 1947. There were now more Hindus and fewer upper-class Muslims. For her, India was a land marked by Muslim presence, and she painted a picture of devastation she defined in religious and class-based terms.

> And what did I see in India of 1957? Men and women wearing *dhoti*s on the street wherever you look; there were plenty of *shalvar*s, long beards and turbans, but only a few pajamas and hardly any burqas. The shops are filled with *lala-ji*s reclining on throw-pillows, while Muslims are afraid to go to restaurants because they serve non-halal meat and sometimes even pork.[58]

Business was down, she reported, and customers were few. "Anyone who makes a larger purchase is understood to be a Pakistani [buying gifts and favorite items]. Nevertheless, they are welcomed." Muslim merchants were devastated by the lack of customers who appreciated fine wares. Some former clients had moved to Pakistan, and the ruling families in the former princely states could barely afford to feed themselves. Muslims could not get jobs; the ban on cow slaughter had decimated butcheries. In the villages, Muslims were being "purified," or converted to Hinduism. She lamented the dissolution of communal and family ties and the obliteration of Islamicate culture as India's Muslims found it "fashionable" to adopt "Hindu" styles of dress and conversation. More positively, she noted that Indian Muslims were reformed, their mosques packed. Education had improved. Many new schools had opened, though they only taught in Hindi using a Hindu-centric curriculum that "indoctrinated" Muslim children. Muslims, 'Alavi reported, found solace in the fact that Hindus too found the new, Sanskritized schooling inscrutable.[59] Like Nizami, she was eager to imagine these changes as temporary.

Travel and Reconciliation: Cross-Border Travel Writing in the 1970s and '80s

Lingering hopes for reunification shattered with the war of 1965. The war also had consequences for Urdu literature. The Urdu literary community had always been diverse, and though it had survived 1947, Partition introduced new pressures.[60] After 1965, the dominance of ecumenical, left-leaning sentiment among this community was further diminished in 1971 by the bloody war over Bangladesh's independence, which India supported. Urdu's ability to encompass authors from a variety of backgrounds was being eroded as identity became increasingly tied to nationalism and religion. The second period of Indo-Pak travel writing emerged in this context, fueled by the generation that experienced Partition as adults. An aging cohort of writers felt they could wait no longer for an impossible détente to finally visit the other side. Nearly all major accounts from this period chronicle visits to the author's birthplace for the first time since 1947, often on the assumption that this was their last chance. The writing is contemplative, relatively free of jingoism, and marked by a desire for closure and a yearning to visit cherished places and beloved individuals. These accounts were the closing chapters in the process of personal reconciliation for the generation that felt the rupture most keenly. Yet they were not purely retrospective; they were blueprints for a future, postwar South Asia based on the model of a kinder past.

These changes were accompanied by major stylistic shifts in travel literature that reflected global literary trends. Travel writers of the 1970s and '80s, like Intizar Husain (discussed later), borrowed literary devices and techniques from modernist fiction. At the same time, cross-border travel writers increasingly opted for emotional or sentimental titles, like Mahmud Sham's *Kitna Qarib Kitna Dur* (So close, so far, 1972) or Zafar al-Hasan's *Vo Qurbaten Si, Vo Fasle Se* (These seeming proximities, those seeming distances, 1985). These titles call readers to inquire further: who, or what, is so close and yet so far? Only on further inspection do we learn that these are cross-border travelogues, not tragic romance novels.

A Spring of Autumn Leaves

Among the most widely read and critically acclaimed cross-border accounts is Ram La'l's *Zard Patton ki Bahar* (A spring of autumn leaves, 1982). It first appeared as a series of installments in Lucknow's *Qaumi Awaz* newspaper. It was then republished as a book in both Urdu and Hindi (with some vocabulary edited in Hindi) in India, and in Urdu in Pakistan.[61] It has been reprinted many times and remains widely popular. A respected short story writer, Ram La'l (1923–96) was born into a Hindu family in Mianwali in today's Pakistan. He later moved to Lahore to work for the railroad and pursue a career in writing. He was an admirer of Muhammad Ali Jinnah and declared in 1947 that he would proudly remain in Pakistan:

> After the fourteenth of August, 1947, I truly wished to remain as a citizen, but in the aftermath of the bloody events occurring on both sides that neither country was able to control, doing so proved impossible. For the last thirty-five years, I have not been able for even a moment to forget that I was forced from my homeland and pushed across the border against my will. And I have never managed to get that part of this subcontinent out of my dreams.[62]

In 1980, he returned. *Zard* detailed his time in Pakistan, juxtaposing memories of his youth with descriptions of contemporary Lahore and Mianwali, while commenting on the state of Pakistan's literary community. These emotionally charged pages represent thirty-five years of longing and hope.

While his journey was undoubtedly a personal one, Ram La'l aimed to speak on behalf on both countries. Ram La'l invited both peoples to understand one another through his writing. Ignoring formal political discourse, *Zard* envisioned an activist travel literature that undermined the state's divisive power, so much so that the border itself passed by entirely unremarked as La'l reflected on his arrival in Pakistan.

> I came of age in Lahore. And I left there and came [to India] as a young man. Now, at the age of fifty-six, I am going back. How great has been the distance between my youth and my old age, a distance that now shrinks with every passing moment as the train charges forward. It shrinks and shrinks. I have leapt in an instant across this great distance countless times in my dreams, for, in the face of dreams, borders and distance have no meaning. I remain connected to my past because it has remained intact in my dreams. For so long now, I have learned to live in my dreams. If ever I did try to forget my past, it would rear its head in one of my stories. Man's identity is in his past. If this is lost, he himself is lost.[63]

Few could make the journey that Ram La'l did, yet others could share the experience through his travelogue. For La'l, Urdu literature was a shared treasure with the power to form a bridge of understanding. But there were practical limits. Texts, like people, struggled to traverse the border. As a privileged visitor to Pakistan, La'l felt it his responsibility to introduce recent Pakistani literature to an Indian audience, and believed that literature itself could provide a humanistic solution to the countries' political tension.[64]

For a long time now, our authors and yours have established a bridge of love through Urdu literature that should be maintained as it is forever. There is an acute need for books, magazines and newspapers to be exchanged between our countries so that we may know each other's emotions and remain informed about our intellectual trends.... [Literature] is the one thing that cannot be partitioned.... In fact, this is a bridge of love that begins in the heart of one and leads straight to the heart of another.[65]

La'l spoke particularly to those in the younger generation, asking them to know one another, whether through travel, reading, or film. Only they could forge a new era, with help from their elders—scarred though they were—who were the last group to remember South Asia in harmony. But person-to-person contact was impossible. In his preface to the book Agha Suhail suggested that

Ram La'l has extended the hand of friendship to the new generation of Pakistanis, saying, "Oh young children of Pakistan's new generation! This is my hand—that is, not Ram La'l's hand but the hand of the new India.... Take hold, I want to have you know one another, because once I am gone, there will be no one left to introduce you.... Weak bridge that I am, as I depart this world, you must build a firm bridge between both countries."[66]

The youth, La'l suggested, were waiting for the opportunity to know one another. He urged them to travel: "I told them they were welcome, and advised them to visit India in small groups, and to knock at the doors of the government." The youth of Pakistan, he found, were "extremely eager to know about India. They have not been overly affected by either nation's politics or propaganda. To remove their suspicions, it seems necessary for them to see India with their own eyes and to meet as many Indians as possible. And to be able to read Indian literature."[67]

La'l's most moving passages relate to his birthplace, Mianwali. There he told a large audience about the neighborhoods in Delhi named after the city, the places where Mianwali's dialect of Punjabi was spoken in India, and about the community's newspapers and social events. He shared stories of Hindus who had fled. His words moved the audience to tears.

When I spoke about the bitter pain of abandoning my homeland that had become a part of my dreams, of my unconscious, tears began to well in the eyes of the new generation who were sitting in the front rows. I was myself compelled to fall silent for a moment or two.

As he spoke, he shifted from Urdu to the local dialect: "I could not find the proper words in Urdu," he explained, "to accurately express the emotions I felt."[68] *Zard Pattoñ ki Bahar* (A spring of autumn leaves) described these moments as a burst of yellow leaves, a new generation promising new growth in a harshening climate. Ram Laʻl was unequivocal: change is possible through travel, literature, and a love rekindled.

Another Land, Another Sky

Laʻl arrived in Pakistan just after Intizar Husain had published his landmark modernist novel, *Basti* (The settlement, 1979), which explored the social and psychological effects of the long Partition. A conference on the book had brought together the stars of Lahore's literary firmament. The presentations were already underway when Ram Laʻl entered the auditorium. He was not on the program, but the proceedings were paused as he was formally welcomed by poet Kishwar Naheed and offered a seat on the dais alongside Husain. The two authors nodded to each other as a graduate student from the University of Chicago, Frances Pritchett, prepared to speak on Husain's reception in American academia. When she concluded, Nahid invited Laʻl to the microphone to deliver impromptu remarks. The crowd roared. Despite having not yet read the new novel, Laʻl agreed to speak:

> I was aware that some of the literary critics present felt that [Husain's] nostalgia for the past was associated with an affection for India that undermined the two-nation theory ... and so, in Husain's defense, I said: "I too know the anguish that Intizar Husain has made a part of his own consciousness. I am returning to Lahore after thirty-five years. This city is awakening inside me, though it was never really asleep, either.... Intizar Husain has taught us how to present the past through our art. He leads the way for us all."[69]

His words rang true. Thirty years on, *Basti* remains a pillar of the Partition canon and a model for writing South Asia's past. The novel follows the convoluted reflections of a Partition refugee, Zakir, as he confronts life in Pakistan. The crisis of the Bangladesh war in 1971 weaves in and out of focus as Zakir—a history professor whose name translates as "one who remembers, commemorates, or recounts"—is drawn repeatedly into his past. He constantly relives the experiences of his childhood in the fictional northern Indian town of Rupnagar. The past and the present increasingly blur together, blending the strife of the present with nostalgic longing in Zakir's inner consciousness. The natural world plays a prominent role in recalling and symbolizing life before Partition, as when the young Zakir would enjoy the shade of the neem tree or wonder at the birds and monkeys in his hometown.

The natural world and the past are similarly intertwined in Husain's intimate and enigmatic cross-border travel account, *Zamin Aur, Falak Aur* (Another land, another sky, 1984). Time proves slippery as the text vacillates between Delhi-present and Delhi-past. It is difficult to disentangle the two, leaving the reader with an eerie palimpsest in which both coexist but neither is definitive. Chockablock modern Delhi abuts a foggy, forested land speckled with tombs. As Husain walks through crowded, contemporary Nizamuddin, he glides ineluctably into the refuges of his memory. The buildings give way to flat ground. We hear the sorrowful cry of a peacock ring out from the dark scrub. Husain first heard this peacock when he was last here, decades ago. Husain had come from Pakistan to search for this peacock, and with it, Delhi's soul: "Was that a peacock, or was it Delhi's soul [*atma*] wandering about in the scrub around The Beloved of God's [*Hazrat Mahbub-i Ilahi*] tomb, calling out to its lost ones? ... I search everywhere in Nizamuddin for the scrub from which that peacock called to me. I find it nowhere."[70] Still, he presses on. Husain searches tirelessly for India's soul.

Zamin is a collection of three travel pieces ranging from forty to eighty pages each, their length corresponding to the duration of Husain's three trips to India. The titles reflect Husain's interest in the natural world: "Mor ki Talash" (Searching for the peacock), "Bandar ki Dum" (The monkey's tail), and "Zamin Aur, Falak Aur" (Another land, another sky). That these are travel accounts dawns on the reader slowly, and it is only near the conclusion of "Mor ki Talash" that we learn that Husain is on a tour organized for the 'urs of Nizamuddin Auliya. His opening lines do not invoke preparations for the journey, but rather interrogate the space between dream and reality:

I heard the sound of my own footsteps and was astounded. What is this land I walk on? I took each foot and pressed it carefully to the ground, straining my ear to capture every bit of the sound it produced. I then reached out to examine the low wall that ran alongside the path. Then I went and stood beneath a tamarind tree that was some distance away from the wall, broke off a leaf, and pressed it to my tongue. I felt a new taste on my tongue. A fresh breeze blew and a new sort of coolness coursed through my body. So I have really come to Delhi, then?[71]

The next passages move backward in time. Husain is on the outskirts of the city. His train has stopped just short of the Yamuna River, and he wonders nervously if he tried to come to Delhi too soon. Perhaps he ought to have waited longer to visit. The train shudders into motion and he sighs in relief.

He has come to Delhi with just one phone number. As he dials, he is overcome by fear: "What if it happens again? What if my eyes suddenly open?" This would not be the first time he has found himself in Delhi, only to awaken and realize he is still in Lahore. "Is it different this time?" He replaces the receiver. "Really? The ground I walk on belongs to Delhi, then? I was perplexed."[72] He turns toward Jamia Millia Islamia University to meet with Urdu scholar and literary critic Gopi Chand Narang, but instead runs into professor Shamim Hanafi. This personal interaction helps Husain gain certainty that this time, at last, he is not dreaming. As with La'l, the pain, rupture, and confusion of Partition is mediated and lessened through the shared space of Urdu literature:

> Narang sahib's office is full of friends, friends I am meeting for the very first time. Here, in this gathering of friends, I departed from the station [*manzil*] of doubt and arrived at the station of certainty. "I am in Delhi," I whisper to myself. "I can now call [my friend] Revati sahib and tell him that I have arrived. I am in Delhi. I am wandering in Nizamuddin Basti. I am looking for the peacock that cried out to me ... at the time when the two ages were coming together [*us same ki donoṅ vaqt mil rahe the*]."[73]

Only now, finding himself at last at the station of certainty, does he explain his earlier doubts:

> This is my first time to come to Delhi since leaving for Pakistan. In going *there*, I never managed to forget all that happened *here*. That is why the tomb of the Sultan of Saints [Nizamuddin] and of Amir Khusrau appear desolate, why Ghalib's tomb itself appears desolate. Now the two ages are coming together.[74]

As his account progresses, his certainty grows. Spaces that recalled his Partition experience initially awaken fear, but these emotions gradually recede. His consciousness moves ever more firmly into the present as his mind brings the past and the present together. Still, he never manages to find the soul of Delhi that cried out to him in 1947 as he trudged through the desolation of Nizamuddin, for the city had already slain its peacock. "The *dargah* [shrine] of the Beloved of God lies next to the Intercontinental [Hotel]—this is yet another of Amir Khusrau's absurd juxtapositions [*anmil*]. Basti Nizamuddin was built up by sacrificing its peacock. And this is not just Nizamuddin—this description fits all of Delhi."[75]

The search is critical—the future of India, Pakistan, and their literatures hangs on finally finding this elusive bird:

> "At the moment, no great poet or writer can be born in India," I announced.
> "Why not?" Mohan glared at me.
> "The thing is that India's soul is its *devmala* [mythology and customs]. A writer cannot become great until he recognizes his own soul." ... In the old stories,

a demon's life force was hidden in a parrot, and how difficult it was to reach that parrot! Fearless princes would have to cross the seven seas, placing their lives in mortal danger to reach it. In the same way, the soul of a nation is also [hidden] in a parrot. Every nation has its own parrot. The Hindu nation's parrot is its devmala. Muslims don't have a devmala, only history. It is this very history that is their parrot. But just like in Pakistan, I saw Indian writers fleeing from their parrots. The business of reaching the parrot is perilous.[76]

Contemporary India, Husain finds, has turned its back on its old customs and beliefs, and thus lost its soul. This, in turn, prevents the country from producing great writers and artists. Pakistan is no better. In "Mor ki Talash," Husain searches tirelessly for Delhi's peacock and India's parrot, but "the present imposes itself everywhere on the past."[77] Husain finds the peacock only in his memories.

Even as India rejects its soul, Husain finds satisfaction in touring all that Delhi has abandoned. He visits as many of the city's historical sites as possible. On his return to Lahore, he carries with him only two objects: a copy of Mirabai's (1498–1547) mystical poetry and two small clay parrots, symbolizing India's elusive devmala, in which its soul resides. The trauma of loss is negotiated by holding on to these physical reminders of that essence which is ephemeral in contemporary India. The two ages remain separated.

As he becomes a regular visitor to India, though, Husain turns inward less frequently. Unlike *Basti*'s Zakir, for whom the past and the present blur, for Husain the distinction between past and present becomes increasingly distinct, though increasingly focused. In his later visits he is more confident of his ability to return to India, though he rebukes himself when he realizes he has taken this access for granted. Yet his comfortable place in Delhi's social and literary scene does not displace the India of his dreams. He refuses to allow the "two ages" to merge. These two temporalities coexist side-by-side in "Bandar ki Dum," the book's second section. The title refers to an incident in the *Mahabharata* when Bhima's path is blocked by a great monkey who suggests Bhima simply walk around his tail. Bhima tries, but the tail is so long he can never get around it. Husain's own monkey is stretched across the road between Aligarh and Dibai, his hometown, which he intended to visit for the first time in decades. He first encounters an actual monkey that will not make way for his car. The driver goes around it, but Husain is unable to pass its metaphorical tail. This once-familiar road is now paved. He gets lost looking for the turnoff and asks a stranger for directions, before abandoning his search: "The better part of the day had already been spent on this trip when I slowly began to understand. The monkey never moved from the road, and I was unable to leap over its tail."[78] He will not go to Dibai. He will not revisit the place of his birth. The changes there would be overwhelming.

For the previous thirty-three years, Husain had dreamt of this town incessantly. In each of these dreams, he wandered from lane to lane, trying to reach home, only to get lost or wake up suddenly. He would not go there now with the help of a stranger. The town will only receive him in his dreams. It is better, Husain resolves, to leave the town as it was in 1947. The India of the past and the India of the present will henceforth inhabit two different worlds. "Goodbye and farewell! I am returning to my homeland." Back in Pakistan, Husain reflects. Is India what exists in his mind, or what exists across the border? He wonders,

> Did I even go on a trip to India at all? I was beginning to doubt myself when I suddenly recalled the monkey with its tail blocking the road between Aligarh and Dibai. Did its tail let me pass or didn't it? In fact, India begins on the other side of that tail![79]

No matter how often Husain visits India, he will neither get beyond the tail nor find India's soul, which now only exists in his dreams. He is at peace. He accepts that the past is a living memory. Unlike Ram La'l, Husain offers only an individual resolution to Partition. His insistence on keeping the two worlds apart is his own negotiated response to the disrupted coexistence of partitioning.

By the final chapter, Husain has become a regular visitor to India. He visits Delhi, Lucknow, Patna, and Hyderabad. The past, he feels, has been abandoned with little to replace it. "Which Lucknow did I go to see, and which Lucknow did I end up seeing? I was reminded of a line from [the Lakhnavi poet Mir] Anis: "Ab yahañ ki zamiñ aur, falak aur hu'a" (This now is another land, another sky).[80] Nevertheless, he is certain of himself, free of confusion and fear: "What have I gained from this trip? So much. So much that I could not quantify it if I wished to. And a little bit of sadness as well. And pain, too. The plane soared higher. Delhi was left far behind. Oh, desolate streets of Hapur! Go back now. I will meet you some other time, in my dreams."[81]

Hapur here symbolizes the permanent and stable separation of the two ages. Husain had passed through Hapur, a town 50 miles to the northwest of Delhi, on his second trip. He saw it only from the train platform. From that vantage, Hapur appeared precisely as he remembered it, a place of happy memories and day trips from Dibai. Thus, only in Hapur do the two ages coexist with no tension or contradiction. "I go to the gate and look with concern. Perhaps this place has changed, too? No, nothing has changed."[82] He does not enter the city, leaving this delicate conjunction intact. Of course, Husain knows that Hapur has changed. By declining to investigate further, he fulfils a desire to have someplace he can imagine to be congruent in both memory and recent experience.

Despite the introspective nature of his account, Husain still engages with broader political and social issues. He reflects in particular on the place of Urdu literature in post-Partition politics, considering not just its restorative potential (as expressed in his encounter with "friends" he had never met before), but also its potential divisiveness. These reflections emerge from a conversation with Urdu author Qurratulain Hyder, who asks:

> "Well, tell me this: when you go back, will you write?"
> "I'll write something when I go back. As for what I will write, I haven't decided yet."
> But Qurratulain Hyder is true to herself: one burned by hot milk will even blow on buttermilk.
> "A poet came from your place once. Forgive me, Intizar sahib, she was a very shallow girl.... When she went back, the things she wrote! ... What I want to ask is, why do you all look down your noses at Indian Muslims so much?"[83]

Everyone in India, he realizes, wants to know whether he will write, and if so, then what he will write. In Banaras, a friend asks him why Pakistani travelers mock India's Muslims so mercilessly. Hearing this,

> Qurratulain Hyder's words again came to mind.... [They] were a warning. These people must be reading all those essays by travelers to India that are published in Pakistan's newspapers and are brimming with pity. Compassion is a pure human emotion, but pity—that's an ugly thing.
> "Intizar sahib, tell me, will you write when you go back?"
> Slowly, I was beginning to understand. Really, what these Indian Muslims are asking me is this: You, who come here with a sense of superiority, what will you say about us when you go back? ... I was taken aback; they had gotten to my core.[84]

Husain vows to root out his misplaced sense of superiority over the people "left behind." These dynamics reveal the difficulty of seeking solutions to an intractable problem through literature. La'l considered Urdu a bridge of love between India and Pakistan, but as Qurratulain Hyder points out, it was a perilous bridge. This realization had a deep effect on Husain. Several years later, he wrote that in the cross-border account "we [Pakistanis] have thrown Indian Muslims into the kiln to preserve our own [sense of] well-being."[85]

A similar view can emanate from India, too, as indicated by a short piece by the Indian writer Saliha 'Abid Husain. Her global travelogue, *Safar Zindagi ke li'e Soz o Saz* (Travel, life's joy and sorrow, 1982), included a chapter on Pakistan. Echoing Intizar Husain, but in reverse, Saliha lamented the penury of the muhajirs (Partition migrants) she encountered on her second trip to Karachi in the 1960s.

"I was in a constant state of sorrow as I saw all of the poor neighborhoods populated by muhajirs, including even some of the people that I had specifically come to visit."[86] Unlike Intizar Husain and Ram La'l, Saliha never migrated. Nevertheless, she too grappled with the trauma of Partition, her identity, and the meaning of the past. She reflected on the emotional impact of Partition during her brief visit across the border:

> Writing on Pakistan separately [from India] still feels strange to me, but it is nevertheless now an independent country. I had gone there several times before Partition, but it was only after Partition that it came to feel like another country, although its western wing is filled with so many dear ones, so many friends, so many acquaintances that my heart simply refuses to consider it a "foreign land." I have been there so many times, and I always return with the sense that "love has no borders." This is despite the fact that, for the Muslims of India, the creation of Pakistan was like a fingernail being torn from the flesh. And it still is. But we have now swallowed this bitter pill. Hundreds of thousands of individuals even now remain closely connected to one another on either side, but the younger generation does not know of the love, sincerity, friendship, and intimacy of these two nations in the way that the older generation does.[87]

Saliha came to terms with the enormity of change in post-Partition South Asia, but her account also revealed the continued ambivalence of reconciliation. The creation of Pakistan might be incontrovertible, but the pain was still excruciating. It was not just a thorn in her side or a bone in her kebab, but a fingernail torn from the flesh. Not all writers were, like La'l, hopeful for the future. She had little hope the younger generation would ever understand. "It is only natural that those who were born or raised in Pakistan, and who have seen two or three wars between these two nations, cannot feel the love and devotion that we do."[88] The process of partitioning continues on.

Conclusion

Partition was not a discrete event that happened at midnight on August 14th/15th, 1947, even if from that date we speak of two independent nations. The transition was, and remains, fitful at the level of administrative policy and of individual relationships. Even as governments set to working out their own identities, communities and individuals were forced to do the same, Muslims particularly.[89] Urdu is the only vernacular language in which cross-border travel writing is consistently written. This literature almost always engages travel across the western border; travel writing between West Bengal and East Pakistan was largely nonexistent in both Urdu and Bengali, perhaps because there had been less violence there, and the border was less tightly closed. A cross-border travel literature only developed in Bengali after Bangladeshi independence. Even as publishing in Hindi surged after independence, cross-border accounts remained rare in that language. More accounts were written in Punjabi, but since 1947 cross-border travelogues have been primarily produced in Urdu by writers of all religious backgrounds.

Against this cross-border tradition, which was largely conciliatory, a parallel category of nationalist travel writing also emerged in Urdu as Pakistanis explored their new country, engaging a nationalist project of uniting people from Karachi to Kohistan. Tellingly, travel writers almost never traveled from Karachi to Chittagong; the eastern wing of Pakistan, which became Bangladesh, was of little interest to travelers from the western wing.[90] There was instead a strong (and often paternalistic) interest in discovering the cultural essence of a yet-unknown (West) Pakistan. Women's magazines of the 1960s, for instance, encouraged readers "to discover the beauty within Pakistan's diverse regions."[91] Book titles gesture directly toward this sense of a country "out there," waiting to be discovered: for instance, *Ajnabi Apne Des Meñ* (A stranger in my own country, 1984) was the narrative of a Punjabi traveler in Balochistan, a land he considered his "own." Meanwhile, in postcolonial India, the task of narrating the nation shifted from Urdu to Hindi, which developed its own nationalist travelogue industry. In the domestic accounts of both India and Pakistan, each nation's physical geography looms large, unlike the people-centric "homecoming" of the Indo-Pak account. The cross-border account, however, is far more compelling, probing, and critically acclaimed. This may suggest that for Urdu writers and readers, the need to resolve the trauma of Partition has been a more urgent and emotionally fraught project than that of nation-building.

Yet both cross-border and domestic travelogues are ultimately about the creation of new global imaginations, new possibilities for the future. They do not simply present things as they are, but instead propose how they ought to be. Nationalist travel writing insists that these "imagined communities" are real, and seeks to reify them, typically by overlooking the faults of their nationalist projects and asserting the existence of a timeless home encompassed by contemporary borders. Cross-border travel writing is equally aspirational, but has its own ideas of what constitutes home, ideas that are not limited to contemporary political borders. It probes division and conflict for the purpose of finding a solution, either individual or societal. As the texts examined in this chapter show, cross-border travel writers typically negotiate and memorialize the trauma of Partition to produce a catharsis in reader and writer alike. The term "partitioning" suggests a process of gradual separation, but it need not be so: successful or not, cross-border accounts work against the movement emanating from 1947 to reunite the region through samjhauta, or compromise. Literature is shown to push against the logic of borders and permits by providing conceptual solutions to intractable problems. This is evinced as much in Ram La'l's call for a literary bridge of peace as it is in Intizar Husain's ability to nurture India's pre-Partition past in his heart as he navigates a new world. The Indo-Pak travel account never forgets the horrors of 1947, but it almost always ends with an aspirational resolution.

Travel remains a fertile space for producing new global imaginations that engage with the past of Partition and its ongoing effects today. In fiction, authors continue to explore and negotiate the legacy of partition through the theme of cross-border travel, as with Geetanjali Shree's acclaimed 2018 Hindi novel *Ret Samadhi*.[92] Meanwhile, the tradition of conciliatory cross-border travel writing in Urdu and other languages continues today in its third phase. Emotional and moving accounts from La'l's "younger generation" continue to appear on social media apps like Instagram as often as in newspaper columns. New monographs arrive frequently, like Raza Rumi's *Delhi by Heart*, an English-language travelogue on India, and Samir Khatlani's *The Other Side of the Divide*, on Pakistan.[93] Rumi was born and raised in Pakistan, but felt intimately connected with Delhi nonetheless. When he finally reached it in the flesh, he felt he could navigate it as though by heart. And thus, even against the backdrop of unflagging political tensions, the process of partioning continues. Saliha 'Abid Husain ended her account by asking, "Will a day ever come—if not in my lifetime, at least some day—when we, despite being two nations, will completely remove this hatred from our hearts? When affection and trust will take the place of prejudice?"[94] In response, travel writers from Nizami to Rumi continue to imagine humanistic, individual, and community-based resolutions for a better tomorrow.

Notes

1. Brass, "The Partition of India," 75.
2. Khan, *Partition*, 186.
3. Husain, "Pesh Lafz," 9. The poem is an abridgement of a verse by Nazir Akbarabadi.
4. Rockwell, "Myth."
5. Hasan, *India Partitioned*, is indicative. On the use of fiction to negotiate Partition, see Abbas, *First Generation*, 7.
6. Abbas, *First Generation*, 1, 3.
7. The film *Garam Hawa* (1973), with its screenplay written by Ismat Chughtai, is an important exception.
8. On the ways that genre affects how Partition is represented, see Mufti, *Enlightenment*, 177–243.

9.   Kumar, *Lahaurnama*, 8.

10. Agha Suhail, "Dibacha," 9. A lakh is a hundred thousand.

11. See Khan, *Partition*, 188–204.

12. Zamindar, *The Long Partition*, 2.

13. Abbas, *First Generation*, 1.

14. Pandey, "Partition," 9–10.

15. Abbas, "Narratives," 2.

16. Trouillot, *Silencing the Past*, 1–26.

17. Abbas, "Narratives," 4.

18. Agha Suhail, "Dibacha," 20.

19. When crossing the border, I myself have been asked to carry across letters, books, and papers for those who have found the mail unreliable.

20. La'l, *Zard*, 250. Blocked mail is a prominent theme in Intizar Husain's novel *Basti*: "Ammi, between India and Pakistan the mails are very much disrupted. Some letters arrive, some don't arrive." Husain, *Basti*, 173.

21. La'l, *Zard*, 211.

22. Chughta'i, *Bari Sharam*, 39.

23. These were the seven tasks required to be completed by Isfandiyar in the *Shahnama*. Husain and Rizvi, "Pesh Lafz," 9.

24. Daryabadi, *Dha'i Hafte*, 10.

25. Nizami, *Safarnama*, 107.

26. Kumar, *Lahaurnama*, 18.

27. Husain, *Zamin*, 27.

28. Qasmi, *Dilli Dur Ast*, 13.

29. Mufti, *Hind Yatra*, 18–19.

30. In recent years, a unique cross-border pilgrimage has elicited significant excitement in both countries. In 2019, the Pakistani government inaugurated a special "corridor" that would allow Indian pilgrimages to access a prominent Sikh religious site in Kartarpur located on its side of the border visa-free. Here Indian and Pakistani visitors to the gurudwara can interact and even share meals in the langar hall. The site thus presents a significantly different perspective from the more traditional "meeting point" at Wagah, where Indian and Pakistani crowds gather on either side of the border to chant nationalist slogans and watch bellicose border-closing ceremonies. Wagah is a symbol of conflict, but Kartarpur represents cooperation and coexistence. Since its opening, several digital accounts of crossing the border at Kartarpur have gone viral, raking in millions of views. One such Hindi/Urdu travel video (vlog) on Youtube by "Guy Who Travels" had over ten million views within ten months of being uploaded. It had attracted some 10,000 comments, almost all expressing love between the two countries, and hope for a conflict-free future. Guy Who Travels, "Kartarpur Corridor."

31. Husain, "Pesh Lafz," 10.
32. Kumar, *Lahaurnama*, 7.
33. Kumar, *Lahore Nama*, xix. Additionally, the 1983 preface to the Urdu version was written by Inder Kumar Gujral, who would himself later become prime minister.
34. Husain, *Zamin Aur*, 77.
35. Husain, *Zamin Aur*, 174.
36. 'Alavi, "57 ka Hindustan," 257.
37. Daryabadi, *Dha'i Hafte*, 7.
38. Pritchett, "Story Notes."
39. I have not been able to locate these original entries. I thus rely here on the book version, which compiles accounts from both trips, along with a reflective preface.
40. Hermansen, "Common Themes," 339.
41. Beg, *Urdu Afsane*, 329–39.
42. Ernst and Lawrence, *Sufi Martyrs*, 113.
43. Nizami, *Safarnama*, 107.
44. Ziad, "Return of Gog," 227–48. For a contextual analysis and translated excerpts from this work, see also Majchrowicz, "Early Indian Muslim Responses."
45. In this chapter I rely solely on the book version of this account, which was compiled from these serialized accounts. I have been unable to locate original copies of these entries as they appeared in the magazine, surely alongside the many reader letters that would have been published concurrently. This loss points to the fragility of Urdu print history, but also to the ways that popular demand—which was what reportedly compelled Daryabadi to bring out a new edition—might save a work from oblivion. Remarkably, in this print edition, the book has continued to retain a niche popularity. Despite its rarity, while on an archival visit to Rampur this work in particular was recommended to me, suggesting that it remains relevant to Indian Muslim readers today.
46. Daryabadi, *Dha'i Hafte*, 5.
47. Nizami, *Safarnama*, 1–4.
48. Nizami, *Safarnama*, 1.
49. Nizami, *Safarnama*, 4. Emphasis in original.
50. Daryabadi, *Dha'i Hafte*, 14.
51. Daryabadi, *Dha'i Hafte*, 7.
52. Daryabadi, *Dha'i Hafte*, 8. The lines in brackets are not cited, but would be familiar to many readers.
53. Daryabadi, *Dha'i Hafte*, 106.
54. Daryabadi, *Dha'i Hafte*, 111.
55. Nizami, *Safarnama*, 50.
56. Daryabadi, *Dha'i Hafte*, 118.
57. 'Alavi, "57 ka Hindustan," 257. "Lala-jis" refers, derisively, to Hindu merchants.

58. ʿAlavi, "57 ka Hindustan," 257.
59. ʿAlavi, "57 ka Hindustan," 257.
60. Ahmad, *The Mirror of Urdu*, 110. See also Laʿl, *Zard*, 21–25.
61. Chhabra, "Meri Bhi Yadeṅ," 3–4.
62. Laʿl, *Zard*, 47.
63. Laʿl, *Zard*, 26–27.
64. The idea that literature is a means to unity and mutual understanding was also raised by renowned author ʿIsmat Chughtai in her "reportage" account of a 1976 journey to Pakistan. Chughtaʾi, *Bari Sharam*, 26.
65. Laʿl, *Zard*, 248–49.
66. Laʿl, *Zard*, 19–20.
67. Laʿl, *Zard*, 64.
68. Laʿl, *Zard*, 118–19.
69. Laʿl, *Zard*, 53.
70. Husain, *Zamin Aur*, 10.
71. Husain, *Zamin Aur*, 5.
72. Husain, *Zamin Aur*, 6.
73. Husain, *Zamin Aur*, 9. The meaning of the "two ages" is not immediately clear. It is only as the travelogue progresses that the reader fully understands that these two ages are the past, as lived by Husain in India, and the present.
74. Husain, *Zamin Aur*, 9–10.
75. Husain, *Zamin Aur*, 11.
76. Husain, *Zamin Aur*, 13.
77. Husain, *Zamin Aur*, 26.
78. Husain, *Zamin Aur*, 38–39.
79. Husain, *Zamin Aur*, 88.
80. Husain, *Zamin Aur*, 121.
81. Husain, *Zamin Aur*, 168–69.
82. Husain, *Zamin Aur*, 83.
83. Husain, *Zamin Aur*, 50.
84. Husain, *Zamin Aur*, 79–80.
85. Husain, "Pesh Lafz," 11.
86. ʿAbid Husain, *Safar*, 82.
87. ʿAbid Husain, *Safar*, 80.
88. ʿAbid Husain, *Safar*, 80–81.
89. Pandey, "Muslim," 608.
90. A rare but important exception is Raziq al-Khairi, *Do Hafte*.
91. Robb, "Gendered Nationalism," 290.
92. Shri, *Ret Samadhi*. It was translated in 2021 by Daisy Rockwell as Shree, *Tomb of Sand*.
93. Rumi, *Delhi*; Khatlani, *Other Side*.
94. ʿAbid Husain, *Safar*, 90.

Conclusion

In the winter of 2017, I traveled by road and rail up the Indus River from Karachi to Lahore, following the thin strip of agricultural land that runs between the river and the edge of the vast Thar Desert. This entire region is renowned for its shrines, monuments, and ruins, but it is also rich in libraries and private collections of books and manuscripts. On this journey I was particularly eager to pass through the city of Bahawalpur. Once the capital of a princely state, I hoped it might hold unique literary collections like those I had found in other former capital cities like Rampur, Hyderabad, and Tonk. I was especially hoping to find a copy of a rare 1854 travelogue of England by a British-backed "native agent" to the princely state.[1]

I was initially disappointed. The city is an active military cantonment near the Indian border and largely off-limits to foreigners. As an American, I only had access to the town's main public library. This century-old institution is split across two buildings, a smaller one for "women and children," and a grander edifice for men and, presumably, for more serious (and salacious?) literature. The library was open, but the older books were under lock and key, and they key-master had not been seen for a week.[2] I spent several ineffectual days poking around town, waiting for him to reappear. On my final visit to the library, probably as a consolation prize, one of the librarians offered to show me a storeroom piled high with uncatalogued Urdu books. As we poked around, I described my research objectives to him. Suddenly, a cleaner working at the back of the storeroom who had been listening in interjected in Siraiki-accented Urdu: "Did you try Jhandir?" Jhandir? None of the librarians had mentioned this place, and it was not even on the map. I wrote down his directions anyhow; it was worth a shot.

Jhandir, it turned out, was a private estate a two-hour drive away, accessible by dirt roads winding through lush, irrigated fields. I doubted I would find anything in such a remote place, but I could not have been more wrong. Here was a rich collection housed in a sprawling compound open to the public. After nearly a decade of research I was suddenly face to face with a private collection so large it put national institutions to shame. The library belonged to three brothers, all in their nineties. This labor of love, started by their father, had grown so large that the family had constructed two enormous buildings to house it. There was also a guest room, offered to researchers free of charge. The library was temporarily closed due to some grave but enigmatic matter, but the collection's owners agreed to make an exception for me for one day. Any work I wished to do must be completed by morning. For twenty hours, I photographed frantically. Among the books I accessed were a trove of travel accounts by women, many of which are discussed in Chapter 5. I never found the native agent's travelogue of England, but I found plenty of other treasures.

It was in Jhandir Library that I encountered Nur Begum's *Safarnama*, which had imagined a world-encompassing Muslim collectivity of "mothers and sisters" praising God together. The book was filled with pencil marks—someone had read it with particular interest. Nur Begum's imagination of a Muslim community united not by politics, but by love and shared devotion, had spread deep into the countryside. I also found the work of Fatima Begum, who imagined the Muslim world as united, but was patently unwilling to fully acknowledge all Muslims as a equal members. Today these books, located in a library open to the public, can be read by anyone. Indeed, it was a member of the local community, the cleaner, who suggested that I visit it in the first place.

This archival vignette suggests the historical and ongoing social diversity of Urdu literature and its consumers. My visit to this library was made possible by men, all Punjabi, from two very different classes. The first was the cleaner at the public library. He had a deep appreciation for literature and knew the literary geography of his region well. In many ways, he represents the producers and consumers of literature that I have focused on in this book. Vernacular literatures have always had a broad reach. Access to Urdu literature did not even require literacy, as many people did, and still do, access literature through oral recitation. Literacy in rural Pakistan remains low, but many people have a sophisticated understanding of literature. The composition and consumption of Urdu travel writing was not the exclusive domain of elites. Instead, it was produced and consumed by a diverse group of Urdu speakers and readers whose accounts appear throughout this book. They were, for the most part, ordinary individuals.

The second group to make my research at Jhandir possible were the three brothers who owned the collection. They were hereditary landlords (*zamindar*s), the richest men in their area, who had spent huge sums acquiring manuscripts and books, and then more to properly house and maintain the collection, building a library adorned with art and antique artifacts. Rather than hoard their holdings, they made them available to the public. Community libraries like Jhandir in Punjab and Saulat Library in Rampur, discussed at the beginning of this book, are common in the Urdu-speaking world. Across South Asia—particularly in the *qasba*s, but even in remote places like Jhandir—literature, and thus travel writing, remains readily available. Jhandir's owners are neither English speakers nor urban elites, but they play a critical role in the preservation and circulation of Urdu's global imagination. Because of people like them, the best record of South Asia's global pasts is often on display deep in the country, and far from the big cities and national libraries.

This regional grounding means that these libraries afford access to local perspectives. In this book I pay comparatively little attention to the biggest names in Indian history, figures whose travel accounts have been celebrated and widely studied, from Sir Sayyid Ahmad Khan to Jawaharlal Nehru. Instead, I have tried to compose a history of overlooked texts by forgotten men and women, as well as lesser-known texts by more famous writers. They have much to tell us about the everyday life of literature and the circulation of ideas in the subcontinent. Figures like Qaisari Begum, or Aminchand, or Nawab Ghaus Muhammad Khan reveal a fascinating history of Urdu literature, and of the traveling lifeworlds of colonial India. The afterlives of their texts tell us how, and where, their legacy survives.

Stories like that of Nur Begum can only be told by visiting the libraries where local histories are preserved. Her books are now available nowhere else. Her story also underlines the importance of paying attention to the material history of the research materials we use—where they were produced, where they were printed, and where they are now. Nur Begum was childless, but she believed her immortality would be ensured by her books, which would long outlive her.[3] This aspiration is as much a part of the story as her initial journey to Medina. To Nur Begum, the physical copies of her book were her offspring. It would not be enough to simply read and analyze her words; the material aspects of her work are just as much a part of her story, as she herself insisted. It is the state and location of where I found her writing that raises some of the most fascinating questions here: how is it that the work of such a popular writer (as indicated by the fact that her travelogue was published at least three times, in large runs) could now only exist in a single archive located hours away from the nearest large town?

What were the politics that led to the erasure of so many copies of her "offspring," and how did two of her surviving "children" come to find a home here in Jhandir?[4] It was texts like hers, and the questions they raised, that led me to the unconventional research methodology of bumbling across South Asia in dusty buses with my camera in my backpack.[5] The subcontinent is strewn with unknown stories in all its languages. I only read accounts in Urdu and Persian, and to a lesser extent in Punjabi and Hindi. Despite my best efforts, I only visited a fraction of the local libraries where works of this kind await their readers. Together, these institutions form part of a larger history of the ways South Asians knew and belonged to the world, and how they filled it with their hopes.

This book explores just a few episodes in the history of India's and Pakistan's global imaginations. The journey of South Asian travel writing is a history of South Asia itself: it reveals what it meant to belong in the world as a South Asian. One of the most profound changes in nineteenth-century South Asia was the ascendancy and dominance of vernacular languages like Urdu over imperial or elite languages like Persian, Sanskrit, and even English. At the same time, India's links to the world were undergoing a massive transition as long-distance travel became more convenient and common and as access to cheap print revolutionized how knowledge circulated. In this new world, travel writing both defined the world and encoded aspiration. Vernacular travel writing was one of the first "new" genres of the nineteenth century, predating other colonial genres like the novel by several decades. These works initiated a dialogue with unfamiliar places and negotiated new connections with an old world. To read the corpus of travel writing is to watch these developments take shape.

Chapter 2 showed how rival princely states cultivated unique forms of Urdu and travel writing to propose their own visions for rulers and courtiers to retain influence in a colonial world. The princes engaged with preexisting literary categories, adapting them to the demands of a new age. Motivated by competing goals and conflicting aesthetics, Indore and Jaora fashioned respected court literatures into something new. While we often speak of the mid-nineteenth century as a moment of rupture, the more gradual development of travel writing shows just how much continuity there was. Vernacular travel writing in South Asia is, in many ways, a colonial genre. But it was constructed from the building blocks of India's literary past. Its gradual development only appears when we look at a range of sources diachronically, including those by unknown or fleeting historical figures like the nawabs of Jaora or Khilchipur or the many Hindus and Jains, like Aminchand and both Bhavani Singhs, who have been expunged from the literary record. It does not appear from reading the accounts of well-known figures alone.

The extent and reach of South Asian travel writing also only appears when it is read according to its literary conventions, in its own literary context, and with proper attention to its materiality and to the details of its production and circulation. Travel writing is not simply a mine for useful facts. Even if it were, mining can only be truly effective if we are familiar with the terrain. As the preceding pages have shown, Urdu travelogues cannot be separated from their literary context. Intertextuality and genre hybridity are rife. This book opened with the suggestion that if travel writing in Urdu is "raffish" in its affiliations, it is also strategic. Form and linguistic style are consciously chosen based on the author's ethos, emotion, or argument. Genre encodes meaning.

Reading travelogues in light of this literary and cultural history allows a reassessment of India's historical engagement with the world. While scholars have long rejected the colonial assumption that India was insular and introspective, a land of people averse to travel and change, we still lack a full understanding of the extent to which a sense of global belonging pervaded India in the colonial period, particularly beyond urban elites. Indeed, this book shows that it was in the agricultural *mufassal* regions that these links were most cultivated. The staggering range of material available in local publications is enough to force a reconsideration of India as inward-looking, or as only concerned with Europe and the Middle East. In the 1940s, women in Raebareli read about Madagascar. Magazine subscribers in Bhopal learned about Malacca in one issue and the Congo in the next. Kings in Punjab wrote accounts of Buenos Aires and Yogyakarta. Their colleagues in Rampur reflected on the Inuit. These residents of rural, landlocked regions of South Asia cultivated an emotive and intellectual relationship to these distant places, as we saw in the case of Kazim Barlas in the Indian Ocean. His musings were part of a network of texts that painted a picture of the globe in familiar terms, in a well-known idiom. These ideas about Africa or Asia were not reflected through the prism of translation from English, but were created by and for South Asians, in a South Asian language.

Crucially, Urdu travel writing was experiential. The idea of "traveling from home" invited individuals from every possible social background to vicariously experience visiting a foreign land, to become fellow travelers, and to share in the process of encountering the world and benefiting from it. An entire genre committed to the vivid description of the world contributed to the development of a sense of place and belonging. To speak of a global imagination is not to suggest that the entire country, or even the entire Urdu-reading public, formulated a uniform sense of their relationship to the world through this literature. There were many overlapping micro-cultures that contributed to this broader intellectual culture. Some travel writing circulated widely in India, up and down the length of the subcontinent.

But some texts remained only in local circulation, speaking directly to the concerns of the author's own community. Kazim Barlas, for instance, was explicit that he was writing for the people of northern India. Thus, even as the world of Urdu travel writing constitutes one whole, it is composed of small spheres of production and circulation. I do not use the word "cosmopolitan" to describe this writing, for much of it was in fact very parochial, such as the writing about African women discussed in Chapter 5. Still, no matter the attitude adopted toward foreign cultures, Urdu's travel literature attempted to carve out a place for its readers in the world.

Later, it also helped reimagine homes torn asunder. Travel writing helped a traumatized community come to terms with Partition, to offer new ways of imagining how the border might look, and how India and Pakistan might relate to one another in the future. The new border created spaces that were intimately familiar, yet also beguiling and unknown. At the same time, the genre was pressed into the service of giving shape to the new states, especially to Pakistan. The space of domestic travel writing became particularly active in the 1970s and '80s as writers from the major cities of the young nation set forth to discover the dimensions of this immense territory and to ask what it meant to be Pakistani. This literature itself is fascinating and complex, particularly for the way typically urban authors from dominant ethnic or linguistic groups (almost always Punjabi or *muhajir*) have sought to celebrate "the nation" and its diversity while fashioning a paternalistic attitude toward Pakistanis that have been marked out as backward, exotic, and in need of reform.[6]

The Next Journey

I encountered thousands of travel accounts while researching this book. While I could only include a small number in my textual analysis, all the titles I found informed my conclusions or became the basis for the graphs and figures included in this book. Even after visiting dozens of archives and libraries, each new research site almost always divulged new material. Later scholars will visit regional libraries I could not reach and will continue to make new discoveries. I was not, for instance, able to visit Karnataka or Gujarat, where more of Urdu's global imaginations await. Studies building on this one might be more precise in their temporal or geographical scale than I have been, perhaps even taking up single texts for close reading within a specific social or literary context. For example, Brannon Ingram has argued that the travel and writing of individual scholars was critical to the global expansion of the Islamic reformist movement with its heart in Deoband.[7] Its advocates, known as *tablighi*s, or proselytizers, frequently wrote Urdu travelogues on regions from South Africa to Japan. How did this literature influence these movements and facilitate their spread?

Another study might look at the engagement between travel writers and their readers in letters to the editors of periodicals. Such a study promises to reveal new perspectives on how Urdu contributed to developing new ideas of local and global across South Asia. A number of studies have looked at shifting conceptions of England or Europe, exploring how India's relationship to the region shifted during the colonial period. Later studies will ask how writing about other regions changed over time, perhaps on Burma, Andalusia, or China. Travel writing was also extremely popular in Gujarati and Bengali, among other vernacular languages. How closely did the history of these literatures track with that of Urdu? How did they influence one another? While few readers in Delhi read Gujarati, more than a few in Ahmedabad read Urdu. But even then, translations between Indian languages were common, and a popular text might appear in several languages. Did the genre develop independently in each of these languages or in response to one another? As the study of travel writing grows, the possibility for cross-linguistic or cross-regional comparative projects does as well.

Contemporary travel writing is equally promising. The genre continues to be exceptionally popular, particularly in Pakistan. Newspapers and magazines constantly serialize accounts. Travelogues fill bookshop shelves and travel writers remain widely recognized. What motivates this fascination, and how does this genre now inform how Pakistani readers see and speak about the world? During my research, I regularly met readers browsing new travelogues in bookstores. Some appreciated the literary merit of this writing, while others felt that reading travel writing in their own language was the best way to know the world. In an intensely unequal global system where even those with the financial resources to travel are restricted from doing so by visa regimes, this literature continues to allow Urdu readers to "travel from home," as it has for well over a century.[8] Whether sociological or literary, a study of contemporary travel writing would be both an insightful and enjoyable project: one of the most joyous facets of contemporary travel writing is its commitment to humor. Writers like Ibn-i Insha (1927–78) and Mujtaba Husain (1936–2020), in the 1960s and 2000s respectively, took the travelogue to new heights by writing comical and often searingly satirical accounts of their travels abroad. Their books and articles were wildly popular and offered unique and often critical insights on the modern world.

With so many unexplored texts, narratives, and itineraries, the journey toward a full understanding of travel's place in the history of modern South Asia is only in its first stages. In this book, I have attempted to reconstitute this neglected literary corpus. The material record of the history of the Urdu travelogue is scattered across South Asia, sometimes in archives that are slowly falling apart. But, as research on this genre grows, these stories will continue to inform and expand our knowledge of South Asia's global past. Urdu's travel writers and their travelogues still have more stories to tell, even as many of them slowly succumb to the elements in underfunded spaces like Saulat Library's three-walled reading room. If we could listen to disintegrating books themselves, perhaps they would say, as the Urdu poet Mirza Rafi' "Sauda" (1713–81) once did:

> *Avaragi se khush huñ maiñ itna ki ba'd az marg*
> *Har zarra meri khak ka hoga hava-parast*
> I delight so much in wandering that even after my death
> Every speck of my remains will ride the wind like dust

Notes

1. Khan, *Sairistan*.
2. This is a common occurrence. Despite months of trying, I never managed to read any books at the library at Delhi's historic Fatehpuri Mosque for this very reason.
3. Nur Begum, *Mazahir*, 72.
4. Similar questions can and should be raised in the opposite direction: why is it that the story of Urdu literature as told in this book required me to spend so much time *outside* of South Asia? So many works cited here are now only available at academic institutions in the United States or in the United Kingdom. The migration of texts from India to the West took place throughout the years of British colonial rule. Just as that movement began to slow after 1947, a new set of legal mechanisms meant that the flow of books was redirected towards the United States, the new world power. American financial resources mean that this flow continues today. The vast majority of these books are not digitized (many are not even catalogued!), making them unavailable to scholars unable to obtain travel visas or access to the elite institutions, whether Harvard or McGill, that control them. The immense collections at the British Library remain similarly inaccessible, though a project begun in 2015 called Two Centuries of Indian Print (1713–1914) aims to address this injustice.
5. While the methodology of "investigative itineracy" was fruitful for me, I would be remiss not to acknowledge the inherent privilege involved. My easy access to multi-entry visas to both India and Pakistan was a product of my identity as an American of non-South Asian descent. My gender allowed me to more safely and comfortably navigate South Asian libraries and other social spaces,

which are overwhelmingly male-dominated. My affiliation with an elite American institution likewise opened up access to texts and privileges like photography that might not be extended to all scholars. A similar set of concerns shaped my investigations in the West, where I was able to enter European countries for research freely, and with institutionally provided funding to support me. All these elements shaped my access to and understanding of Urdu's materiality, and must be acknowledged here.

6. For a similar argument in the context of Yoruba travel writing, see Jones, "Hinterland," 1.

7. Ingram, *Revival*, 160.

8. Travel writing has played a similar role as a site of education, fascination, and social prestige in postcolonial Nigeria, a nation bound by similar restrictions. Jones, *Crossroads*, 55. On the increasing imposition of movement controls in the Indian context, and particularly the evolution of the modern passport in British India, see Mongia, *Migration*, 112–40.

Bibliography

Abbas, Amber. "Narratives of Belonging: Aligarh Muslim University and the Partitioning of South Asia." PhD diss., University of Texas, 2012.

———. *Partition's First Generation: Space, Place, and Identity in Muslim South Asia*. London: I. B. Tauris, 2022.

'Abd al-Hayy, Sayyid. *Sair-i Hindustan ba Tasvir*. Lahore: Punjab Religious Book Society, n.d.

'Abd al-Karim [Abdulkurreem]. *The Memoirs of Khojeh Abdulkurreem*. Translated by Francis Gladwin. Calcutta: William Mackay, 1788.

'Abd al-Qadir. *Maqam-i Khilafat*. Delhi: Makhzan Press, n.d.

'Abd al-Rasul. *Nairang-i Zamana*. Lahore: Punjabi Adabi Academy, 1960.

'Abdullah. *Kisah Pelayaran 'Abdullah ke Kelantan dan ke Juda*. Singapore: Matba' Government, 1886.

'Abid Husain, Saliha. *Safar Zindagi ke liye Soz o Saz*. New Delhi: Maktaba-i Jami'a Limited, 1982.

'Abidi, Raza 'Ali. *Kitabeñ Apne Aba Ki*. Lahore: Sang-e-Meel Publications, 2012.

Abu Talib Khan. *Masir i Talibi*. Calcutta: Hindoostance Press, 1812.

———. *Masir-i Talibi: Mushtamal bar Ahval-i Sair-i Mirza Abu Talib Khan*. Calcutta: Schoolbok Society Press, 1827.

———. *The Travels of Mirza Aboo Talib Khan in the Persian Language*. Edited by David Macfarlane. Calcutta: Baptist Mission Press, 1836.

———. *Travels of Mirza Abu Taleb Khan in Asia, Africa, and Europe, during the Years 1799, 1800, 1801, 1802, and 1803*. Translated by Charles Stewart. Peterborough, Ont.: Broadview Press, 2009.

Accounts and Papers of the House of Commons. Vol. 24, 1. London: House of Commons, 1859.

Adams, Percy G. *Travel Literature and the Evolution of the Novel*. Lexington: University Press of Kentucky, 1983.

Agha Suhail. "Dibacha." In *Zard Patton ki Bahar,* by Ram La'l. Lucknow: Uttar Pradesh Urdu Academy, 1982.

Ahamed, Muzafer. *Camels in the Sky: Travels in Arabia*. Edited by Mini Krishnan. Translated by P.J. Mathew. New Delhi: Oxford University Press, 2019.

Ahmad, Qazi Mushtaq. *Urdu Nasr: Ek Mutala'a*. New Delhi: Modern Publishing House, 2005.

Ahmad, Rizwan. "Urdu in Devanagari: Shifting Orthographic Practices and Muslim Identity in Delhi." *Language in Society* 40, no. 3 (2011): 259–84.

Ahmad, Sa'id. *Azadi ke Ba'd Urdu Safarnama*. Delhi: 'Arshiya, 2012.

Ahmad, Aijaz. *In the Mirror of Urdu: Recompositions of Nation and Community, 1947–65*. Shimla: Indian Institute of Advanced Study, 1993.

———. *Social Ideas and Social Change in Bengal, 1818–1835*. Leiden: Brill, 1965.

Ahmed, Shahab. *What Is Islam? The Importance of Being Islamic*. Princeton: Princeton University Press, 2017.

Aiyar, Sana. *Indians in Kenya: The Politics of Diaspora*. Cambridge, Mass.: Harvard University Press, 2015.

Akhtar, Jamil. *Urdu meñ Jara'id-i Nisvan ki Tarikh*. Vol. 1. Delhi: Kitabi Dunya, 2016.

Alam, Asiya. *Women, Islam and Familial Intimacy in Colonial South Asia*. Leiden: Brill, 2021.

Alam, Muzaffar, and Sanjay Subrahmanyam. "Discovering the Familiar: Notes on the Travel-Account of Anand Ram Mukhlis, 1745." *South Asia Research* 16, no. 2 (1996): 131–54.

———. *Indo-Persian Travels in the Age of Discoveries, 1400–1800*. Cambridge: Cambridge University Press, 2007.

'Alavi, 'Iffat Ilahi. "57 ka Hindustan." *'Ismat* 202, no. 5 (1959): 257–58.

'Alavi, Khalid. *Angare*. Delhi: Educational Publishing House, 2013.

'Alavi, Muhammad Masih al-Din. *Safir-i Avadh*. Lucknow: Al-Nazir, 1929.

Alavi, Seema. "'Fugitive Mullahs and Outlawed Fanatics': Indian Muslims in Nineteenth Century Trans-Asiatic Imperial Rivalries." *Modern Asian Studies* 45, no. 6 (2011): 1337–82.

———. *Muslim Cosmopolitanism in the Age of Empire*. Cambridge, Mass.: Harvard University Press, 2015.

'Ali, Aruna Asaf. "Dihli se Landan." *Jahan-Numa (Allahabad)* 1, no. 5 (1947): 51–54.

'Ali, Haji Mansab. *Mah-i Maghrib, al-Ma'ruf bih, Ka'ba-Numa*. Meeruth: Muhibb-i Kishvar-i Hind, 1871.

'Ali Khan, Hamid. *Masir-i Hamidi: Ya'ni, Roznamcha-i Siyahat*. Vol. 1. Agra: Mufid-i 'Am, 1896.

'Ali Khan, Muhammad Mustafa. *Sair o Siyahat-i Hindustan*. Lucknow: Naval Kishore, 1906.

Aminchand. *Report on the Revised Land Revenue Settlement*. Lahore: Victoria Press, 1875.

———. *Safarnama*. 2nd ed. Lahore: Koh-i Nur, 1859.

Amrith, Sunil. *Crossing the Bay of Bengal: The Furies of Nature and the Fortunes of Migrants*. Cambridge, Mass.: Harvard University Press, 2013.

Amstutz, Andrew. "A New Shahrazad: The Travel Writings of Mahmooda Rizvia between India and Iraq during World War II." *Comparative Studies of South Asia, Africa and the Middle East* 40, no. 2 (2020): 372–86.

Anand Ram "Mukhlis." *Safarnama-i Bangarh*. Lahore: Fiction House, 2004.

Anderson, Benedict. *Imagined Communities*. London: Verso, 2006.

Anonymous [R. Temple]. "Village Schools and Peasant Proprietors in the N. W. Provinces." *Calcutta Review* 14, no. 27 (1850): 138–208.

Archambault, Hannah Lord. "Becoming Mughal in the Nineteenth Century: The Case of the Bhopal Princely State." *South Asia: Journal of South Asian Studies* 36, no. 4 (2013): 479–95.

———. "Geographies of Influence: Two Afghan Military Households in 17th and 18th Century South India." PhD diss., University of California, Berkeley, 2018.

Arnold, David. *Science, Technology, and Medicine in Colonial India*. Cambridge: Cambridge University Press, 2000.

Arondekar, Anjali. *For the Record: On Sexuality and the Colonial Archive in India*. Durham: Duke University Press, 2009.

Asad, Talal. "Two European Images of Non-European Rule." *Economy and Society* 2, no. 3 (1973): 263–77.

Asani, Ali. "Through the Lens of Mirza of Delhi: The Debbas Album of Early-Twentieth-Century Photographs of Pilgrimage Sites in Mecca and Medina." *Muqarnas* 15 (1998): 178–99.

Asif, Manan Ahmed. *The Loss of Hindustan: The Invention of India*. Cambridge, Mass.: Harvard University Press, 2020.

Auer, Blain. "Persian Historiography in India." In *Persian Prose Outside Iran: The Indian Subcontinent, Anatolia and Central Asia After Timur*, edited by John Perry, 94–139. London: I. B. Tauris, 2015.

Aydin, Cemil. "Imperial Paradoxes: A Caliphate for Subaltern Muslims." *ReOrient* 1, no. 2 (2016): 171–91.

———. *The Idea of the Muslim World: A Global Intellectual History*. Cambridge: Harvard University Press, 2019.

Azad, Muhammad Husain. *Sair-i Iran*. Lahore: Karimi Press, 1922.

———. *Unnisviñ Sadi meñ Vast Eshiya ki Siyahat*. Edited by Agha Muhammad Ashraf. Karachi: Hamdard Academy, 1959.

Babu Shiv Prasad. *Chhota Jam-i Jahan-Numa*. Lucknow: Naval Kishore, 1862.

Babur. *The Baburnama: Memoirs of Babur, Prince and Emperor.* Translated by W.M. Thackston. New York: Modern Library, 2002.

Baij Nath. *Englaind aind Indya.* Lucknow: Munshi Gulab Singh, 1899.

Bailey, Thomas Grahame. *A History of Urdu Literature.* Lahore: al-Biruni, 1977.

Banarasidas. *Ardhakathanak: A Half Story.* Translated by Rohini Chowdhury. New Delhi: Penguin Books, 2009.

Bard, Amy Carol. "Desolate Victory: Shīʿī Women and the Marsiyah Texts of Lucknow." PhD diss., Columbia University, 2002.

Barlas, Mirza Muhammad Kazim. *Lisan al-Jaza'ir.* Muradabad: Ahsan al-Matabiʿ, n.d.

———. *Sair-i Darya ki Pahli Mauj: Sair-i Rangun.* Barabanki: Maqbul al-Matabiʿ, 1892.

———. *Sair-i Darya: Pahli Mauj Jazira-i Lanka ke Halat Meñ.* Muradabad: Ahsan al-Matabiʿ, 1897.

Barlas Sahiba. "Safar-i Japan." *Tahzib al-Nivan* 36, no. 21 (1933): 281–84.

Bayly, C.A. *Empire and Information: Intelligence Gathering and Social Communication in India, 1780–1870.* Cambridge: Cambridge University Press, 1996.

Bayly, Susan. *Saints, Goddesses and Kings: Muslims and Christians in South Asian Society, 1700–1900.* Cambridge: Cambridge University Press, 1989.

Beg, Mirza Hamid. *Urdu Afsane ki Rivayat, 1903–2009: Urdu Afsane ki Tarikh maʿ Intikhab.* Islamabad: Dost Publications, 2010.

Begum Hasrat Mohani. *Begam Hasrat Mohani aur un ke Khutut o Safarnama.* Edited by Nafis Ahmad Siddiqi. Delhi: Maulana Hasrat Mohani Foundation, 2015.

Begum Sarbuland Jang. *Dunya ʿAurat ki Nazar meñ: Mashriq o Maghrib ka ek Safarnama.* Delhi: Barqi Press, n.d.

Behl, Aditya, and Simon Weightman. "Introduction." In *Madhumālāti: An Indian Sufi Romance,* by Mañjhana, xi–xlvi. translated by Aditya Behl. Oxford: Oxford University Press, 2000.

Bellamy, Carla. "Alternative Kingdoms: Shrines and Sovereignty in Jaora." *Comparative Studies of South Asia, Africa and the Middle East* 40, no. 3 (2020): 444–53.

Beverley, Eric. *Hyderabad, British India, and the World: Muslim Networks and Minor Sovereignty, c. 1850–1950.* Cambridge: Cambridge University Press, 2015.

Bhattacharji, Shobhana. "Indian Travel Writing." In *The Routledge Companion to Travel Writing,* edited by Carl Thompson, 125–38. London: Routledge, 2016.

Bidwell, Robin. *British Documents on Foreign Affairs: Reports and Papers from the Foreign Office.* Vol. 12. B. Frederick, Md.: University Publications of America, 1986.

Birla, Ritu. *Stages of Capital: Law, Culture, and Market Governance in Late Colonial India.* Durham: Duke University Press, 2009.

Bismil, Muhammad Fazl Husain. *Siyahat-i Habib.* Muradabad: n.p., 1907.

Bisvas, Ramnath. *Andhakarer Afrika.* Kolkata: Parjatak Prakashan Bhavan, 1945.

Borm, Jan. "Defining Travel: On the Travel Book, Travel Writing and Terminology." In *Perspectives on Travel Writing,* edited by Glenn Hooper and Timothy Youngs, 12–26. Aldershot: Ashgate, 2004.

Bose, Sugata. *A Hundred Horizons: The Indian Ocean in the Age of Global Empire.* Cambridge, Mass.: Harvard University Press, 2006.

Bose, Sugata, and Ayesha Jalal. *Modern South Asia: History, Culture, Political Economy.* London: Routledge, 2011.

Boyk, David. "Bound for Home: Books and Community in a Bihari Qasba." *South Asia: Journal of South Asian Studies* 43, no. 3 (2020): 493–504.

———. "Collaborative Wit: Provincial Publics in Colonial North India." *Comparative Studies of South Asia, Africa and the Middle East* 38, no. 1 (May 2018): 89–106.

———. "Provincial Urbanity: Intellectual Society and Patna, 1890–1930." PhD diss., University of California, Berkeley, 2015.

Boyk, David, Andrew Amstutz, and C. Ryan Perkins. "Unpacking the Library." *South Asia: Journal of South Asian Studies* 43, no. 3 (May 2020): 446–54.

Braginsky, Vladimir, and Anna Suvorova. "A New Wave of Indian Inspiration: Translations from Urdu in Malay Traditional Literature and Theatre." *Indonesia and the Malay World* 36, no. 104 (2008): 115–53.

Brass, Paul R. "The Partition of India and Retributive Genocide in the Punjab, 1946–47: Means, Methods, and Purposes." *Journal of Genocide Research* 5, no. 1 (2003): 71–101.

Brittlebank, Kate. *Tipu Sultan's Search for Legitimacy: Islam and Kingship in a Hindu Domain.* New York: Oxford University Press, 1997.

Buckland, Charles Edward. *Dictionary of Indian Biography.* London: S. Sonnenschein, 1906.

Burton, Antoinette. *At the Heart of the Empire: Indians and the Colonial Encounter in Late-Victorian Britain.* Berkeley: University of California Press, 1998.

———. *Dwelling in the Archive: Women Writing House, Home, and History in Late Colonial India.* New York: Oxford University Press, 2003.

———. "Introduction: Archive Fever, Archive Stories." In *Archive Stories: Facts, Fictions, and the Writing of History*, edited by Antoinette Burton, 1–24. Durham: Duke University Press, 2005.

———. "Making a Spectacle of Empire: Indian Travellers in Fin-de-Siècle London." *History Workshop Journal* 42, no. 1 (1996): 126–46.

Burway, Mukund Wamanrao. *Life of His Highness Maharaja Tukoji Rao Holdar II, G.C.S.I, Ruler of Indore (1835–1886).* Indore: Holkar State Printing Press, 1925.

Can, Lâle. *Spiritual Subjects: Central Asian Pilgrims and the Ottoman Hajj at the End of Empire.* Stanford: Stanford University Press, 2020.

Carpenter, Mary. *The Last Days in England of the Rajah Rammohun Roy.* London: Trübner & Co, 1866.

Carroll, Lucy. "The Seavoyage Controversy and the Kayasthas of North India, 1901–1909." *Modern Asian Studies* 13, no. 2 (1979): 265–99.

Casale, Giancarlo. *The Ottoman Age of Exploration.* Oxford: Oxford University Press, 2010.

Chakrabarty, Dipesh. *Provincializing Europe: Postcolonial Thought and Historical Difference*. Princeton, N.J.: Princeton University Press, 2000.

Chandra, Nandini. "The Pedagogic Imperative of Travel Writing in the Hindi World: Children's Periodicals (1920–1950)." *South Asia: Journal of South Asian Studies* 30, no. 2 (2007): 293–325.

Chatterjee, Kumkum. "Discovering India: Travel, History and Identity in Late Nineteenth- and Early Twentieth-Century India." In *Invoking the Past: The Uses of History in South Asia*, edited by Daud Ali, 192–227. New Delhi: Oxford University Press, 1999.

Chatterjee, Kumkum, and Clement Hawes. *Europe Observed: Multiple Gazes in Early Modern Encounters*. Lewisburg: Bucknell University Press, 2008.

Chatterjee, Partha. "Introduction: History in the Vernacular." In *History in the Vernacular*, edited by Raziuddin Aquil and Partha Chatterjee, 1–24. Ranikhet: Permanent Black, 2008.

———. *The Nation and Its Fragments: Colonial and Postcolonial Histories*. Princeton: Princeton University Press, 1993.

Chhabra, Vir Vinod. "Meri Bhi Yadeñ." Preface to *Zard Pattoñ ki Bahar: Meri Bhi Yadeñ*, by Ram La'l, 3–4. Lucknow: NotNul Publishing, 2013.

Chaudhuri, Supriya. "Indian Travel Writing." In *The Cambridge History of Travel Writing*, edited by Nandini Das and Tim Youngs, 159–74. Cambridge: Cambridge University Press, 2019.

Choudhury, Rishad. "The Hajj from India in an Age of Imperial Transitions, 1707–1820." Cornell University, 2015.

Chughta'i, 'Ismat. *Bari Sharam ki Bat*. Lahore: Rohtas Books, 1992.

Chughtai, Ismat. "Dilli ki Sair." In *Angaaray*, edited by Sajjad Zahir, translated by Snehal Shingavi, 107–10. New Delhi: Penguin Books India, 2014.

Codell, Julie, and James Ryan, eds. *Power and Resistance: The Delhi Coronation Durbars 1877, 1903, 1911*. Ahmedabad: Mapin, 2012.

Cohn, Bernard. *Colonialism and Its Forms of Knowledge: The British in India*. Princeton: Princeton University Press, 1996.

Commission on Education. *Abstract and Analysis of the Report of the Indian Education Commission*. London: Hamilton, Adams & Co., 1884.

Cust, Robert Needham. *Linguistic and Oriental Essays Written from the Year 1861 to 1895*. London: Luzac & Co., 1895.

Dalmia, Vasudha. *The Nationalization of Hindu Traditions: Bhāratendu Hariśchandra and Nineteenth-Century Banaras*. Delhi: Oxford University Press, 1997.

Danapuri, Shah Muhammad. *Sair-i Dihli*. Agra: Matba'-i Riyaz-i Hind, 1894.

Daryabadi, 'Abd al-Majid. *Dha'i Hafte Pakistan meñ, ya, Mubarak Safar*. Lucknow: Maulana 'Abd al-Majid Daryabadi Academy, 1981.

Das Gupta, Ashin, and M.N. Pearson. *India and the Indian Ocean 1500–1800*. New Delhi: Oxford University Press, 1999.

Datla, Kavita. *The Language of Secular Islam: Urdu Nationalism and Colonial India.* Honolulu: University of Hawai'i Press, 2013.

Deloche, Jean. *La Circulation en Inde avant la Révolution des Transports.* Paris: Ecole Française d'Extrême-Orient, 1980.

Desai, Gaurav. *Commerce with the Universe: Africa, India, and the Afrasian Imagination.* New York: Columbia University Press, 2013.

Deshpande, Prachi. *Creative Pasts: Historical Memory and Identity in Western India, 1700–1960.* New York: Columbia University Press, 2007.

Digby, Simon. "Bāyazīd Beg Turkmān's Pilgrimage to Makka and Return to Gujarat: A Sixteenth Century Narrative." *Iran* 42 (2004): 159–77.

———. "Some Asian Wanderers in Seventeenth Century India: An Examination of Sources in Persian." *Studies in History* 9, no. 2 (1993): 247–64.

Dirks, Nicholas. *Autobiography of an Archive: A Scholar's Passage to India.* New York: Columbia University Press, 2015.

Dodson, Michael. "Translating Science, Translating Empire: The Power of Language in Colonial North India." *Comparative Studies in Society and History* 47, no. 4 (2005): 809–35.

Dubrow, Jennifer. *Cosmopolitan Dreams: The Making of Modern Urdu Literary Culture in Colonial South Asia.* Honolulu: University of Hawai'i Press, 2018.

Eagleton, Terry. *The English Novel: An Introduction.* Malden, Mass.: Blackwell, 2005.

East India Company. *Correspondence Relating to the Education Despatch of 19 July 1854.* London: H. M. Stationary Office, 1859.

Eaton, Richard. *A Social History of the Deccan, 1300–1761: Eight Indian Lives.* Cambridge: Cambridge University Press, 2008.

Eck, Diana. *India: A Sacred Geography.* New York: Harmony Books, 2012.

Ernst, Carl, and Bruce Lawrence. *Sufi Martyrs of Love: Chishti Sufism in South Asia and Beyond.* New York: Palgrave Macmillan, 2002.

Fabian, Johannes. "Time, Narration, and the Exploration of Central Africa." *Narrative* 9, no. 1 (2001): 3–20.

Farooqi, Mehr Afshan. "Changing Literary Patterns in Eighteenth Century North India: Quranic Translations and the Development of Urdu Prose." In *Before the Divide: Hindi and Urdu Literary Culture*, edited by Francesca Orsini, 222–48. New Delhi: Orient BlackSwan, 2010.

Faruqi, Shamsur Rahman. *Early Urdu Literary Culture and History.* New Delhi: Oxford University Press, 2001.

Fatima Begum. "Fatima Begum." In *Three Centuries of Travel Writing by Muslim Women*, edited by Siobhan Lambert Hurley, Daniel Majchrowicz, and Sunil Sharma, translated by David Boyk, 158–67. Boomington: Indiana University Press, 2022.

———. *Hajj-i Baitullah o Ziyarat-i Diyar-i Habib*. Lahore: Kutub Khana Paisa Akhbar, 1959.

Fisher, Michael. *Counterflows to Colonialism: Indian Travellers and Settlers in Britain, 1600–1857*. Delhi: Permanent Black, 2004.

———. "From India to England and Back: Early Indian Travel Narratives for Indian Readers." *Huntington Library Quarterly* 70, no. 1 (2007): 153–72.

———. *Indirect Rule in India: Residents and the Residency System, 1764–1858*. Delhi: Oxford University Press, 1991.

———. *The First Indian Author in English: Dean Mahomed (1759–1851) in India, Ireland, and England*. Delhi: Oxford University Press, 1996.

Fowler, Alastair. *Kinds of Literature: An Introduction to the Theory of Genres and Modes*. Cambridge, Mass.: Harvard University Press, 1982.

Framji, Dosaboy. *Gret Britain Khate ni Musafiri*. Bombay: Ashkara Chapkhana, 1861.

Frere, Henry Bartle. *The Speeches and Addresses of Sir Henry Bartle Edward Frere*. Bombay: Ganpat Krishnaji's Press, 1870.

Fuerst, Morgenstein. "Locating Religion in South Asia: Islamicate Definitions and Categories." *Comparative Islamic Studies* 10, no. 2 (March 24, 2017): 217–41.

Fussell, Paul. *Abroad: British Literary Traveling between the Wars*. Oxford: Oxford University Press, 1982.

Fyzee-Rahamin, Atiya Begum. *Atiya's Journeys: A Muslim Woman from Colonial Bombay to Edwardian Britain*. Edited by Siobhan Lambert-Hurley and Sunil Sharma. New Delhi: Oxford University Press, 2010.

Ganga Prasad. *Rasta Jatriyan*. Agra: Indu Prakash, 1893.

Geider, T. "Early Swahili Travelogues." *Matatu: Journal for African Culture and Society* 9 (1992): 27–65.

Gelvin, James, and Nile Green. "Introduction: Global Muslims in the Age of Steam and Print." In *Global Muslims in the Age of Steam and Print*, edited by James Gelvin and Nile Green, 1–22. Berkeley: University of California Press, 2014.

General Report on Public Instruction in the Lower Provinces of the Bengal Presidency for 1856–7. Calcutta: Calcutta Gazette Office, 1857.

General Report on Public Instruction in the North Western Provinces of the Bengal Presidency for 1833–1843. Agra: Agra Ukhbar Press, 1843.

General Report on Public Instruction in the North Western Provinces of the Bengal Presidency for 1843-1844. Agra: Agra Ukhbar Press, n.y.

General Report on Public Instruction in the North Western Provinces of the Bengal Presidency for 1845–1846. Agra: Agra Ukhbar Press, 1847.

General Report on Public Instruction in the North Western Provinces of the Bengal Presidency for 1846–1847. Agra: Agra Ukhbar Press, 1848.

General Report on Public Instruction in the North Western Provinces of the Bengal Presidency for 1852–53. Agra: Secundra Orphan Press, 1853.

Ghalib, Asadullah. *Ghalib ke Khutut*. Lucknow: Anvar Book Dipot, n.d.

Ghalib Lakhnavi, and 'Abdullah Husain Bilgrami. *The Adventures of Amir Hamza: Lord of the Auspicious Planetary Conjunction.* Translated by Musharraf Farooqi. New York: Modern Library, 2008.

Ghosh, Anindita. *Power in Print: Popular Publishing and the Politics of Language and Culture in a Colonial Society, 1778–1905.* New Delhi: Oxford University Press, 2006.

Ghosh, Durba. *Sex and the Family in Colonial India: The Making of Empire.* Cambridge: Cambridge University Press, 2006.

Ghulam 'Abd al-Qadir Nazir. *Bahar-i A'zam-Jahi.* Edited by Muhammad Yusuf Kukan. Madras: Kutubkhana Dauli, 1961.

Ghulam al-Hasnain, Khwaja. "Shazrat." *Al-Va'iz* 1, no. 3 (1921): 1–2.

Gommans, J. *Mughal Warfare: Indian Frontiers and Highroads to Empire, 1500–1700.* New York: Routledge, 2002.

Goswami, Manu. *Producing India: From Colonial Economy to National Space.* Chicago: University of Chicago Press, 2004.

Green, Nile. "Africa in Indian Ink: Urdu Articulations of Indian Settlement in East Africa." *The Journal of African History* 53, no. 2 (2012): 131–50.

———. "Anti-Colonial Japanophilia and the Constraints of an Islamic Japanology: Information and Affect in the Indian Encounter with Japan." *South Asian History and Culture* 4, no. 3 (2013): 291–313.

———. *Bombay Islam: The Religious Economy of the West Indian Ocean, 1840–1915.* New York: Cambridge University Press, 2011.

———. "Forgotten Futures: Indian Muslims in the Trans-Islamic Turn to Japan." *The Journal of Asian Studies* 72, no. 3 (2013): 611–31.

———. "The Trans-Border Traffic of Afghan Modernism: Afghanistan and the Indian 'Urdusphere.'" *Comparative Studies in Society and History* 53, no. 3 (2011): 479–508.

———. "The Waves of Heterotopia: Toward a Vernacular Intellectual History of the Indian Ocean." *The American Historical Review* 123, no. 3 (2018): 846–74.

———. "Urdu as an African Language." *Islamic Africa* 3, no. 2 (2012): 173–99.

Grewal, Inderpal. *Home and Harem: Nation, Gender, Empire, and the Cultures of Travel.* Durham: Duke University Press, 1996.

Guha, Ramachandra. *Gandhi before India.* New York: Alfred A. Knopf, 2014.

Guha, Sumit. "Speaking Historically: The Changing Voices of Historical Narration in Western India, 1400–1900." *The American Historical Review* 109, no. 4 (2004): 1084–1103.

Gupta, Charu. "Masculine Vernacular Histories of Travel in Colonial India: The Writings of Satyadev 'Parivrajak.'" *South Asia: Journal of South Asian Studies* 43, no. 5 (2020): 836–59.

———. *Sexuality, Obscenity, Community: Women, Muslims, and the Hindu Public in Colonial India.* New York: Palgrave, 2002.

Gupta, Charu, Laura Brueck, Hans Harder, and Shobna Nijhawan. "Literary Sentiments in the Vernacular: Gender and Genre in Modern South Asia." *South Asia: Journal of South Asian Studies* 43, no. 5 (2020): 803–16.

Guy Who Travels, "This Is How PAKISTANI People Treat an INDIAN Tourist! - Kartarpur Corridor," YouTube video, 19:23, December 27, 2021, https://youtube/9z1uvDSiUQ0. Accessed November 5, 2022.

Hasan, Mushirul, ed. *India Partitioned: The Other Face of Freedom*. New Delhi: Lotus Collection, 1995.

Hashmi, Qutub al-Nisa. *Tin Musafir*. Hyderabad: Sagar Book Dipot, 1966.

Hathaway, Michael J. *Environmental Winds: Making the Global in Southwest China*. Berkeley: University of California Press, 2013.

Hermansen, Marcia. "Common Themes, Uncommon Contexts: The Sufi Movements of Hazrat Inayat Khan (1882–1927) and Khwaja Hasan Nizami (1878–1955)." In *A Pearl in Wine: Essays on the Life, Music and Sufism of Hazrat Inayat Khan*, edited by Zia Inayat-Khan, 323–53. New Lebanon: Omega Publications, 2001.

Ho, Engseng. *The Graves of Tarim: Genealogy and Mobility across the Indian Ocean*. Berkeley: University of California Press, 2006.

Hodgson, Marshall G.S. *The Venture of Islam: Conscience and History in a World Civilization, Volume One, The Classical Age of Islam*. Vol. 1. Chicago: University of Chicago Press, 1974.

Hughes, Julie. *Animal Kingdoms: Hunting, the Environment, and Power in the Indian Princely States*. Cambridge, Mass.: Harvard University Press, 2013.

Husain, Intizar. *Basti*. Translated by Frances Pritchett. New York: New York Review of Books, 2013.

———. "Pesh Lafz." In *Dekha Hindustan*, by Hasan Rizvi, 9–14. Lahore: Maktaba-i 'Aliya, 1987.

———. *Zamin Aur, Falak Aur*. Lahore: Sang-e-Meel Publications, 1984.

Husain, Muhammad. "1907 ka Japan." Edited by Sayyid Altaf 'Ali Barelvi. *Adabi Dunya*, February 1947.

Husain, Muhammad Muhi al-Din. *Safarnama-i Haramain Sharifain*. Madras: Matba'-i Hidayat, 1906.

Hyder, Syed Akbar. *Reliving Karbala: Martyrdom in South Asian Memory*. New York: Oxford University Press, 2006.

Ibn-i Insha. *Avara-gard ki Da'iri*. Karachi: Pak Publishers, 1971.

Imam, Mir Jaffar, and K.C. Kanda. *Mirza Ghalib and the Mirs of Gujarat*. New Delhi: Rupa & Co., 2003.

Ingram, Brannon. *Revival from Below: The Deoband Movement and Global Islam*. Oakland: University of California Press, 2018.

Iqbalunnisa Hussain. "Iqbalunnisa Hussain." In *Three Centuries of Travel Writing by Muslim Women*, edited by Siobhan Lambert Hurley, Daniel Majchrowicz, and Sunil Sharma, 333–43. Boomington: Indiana University Press, 2022.

Iyer, Muthusami. "The Twenty-Fifth Convocation of the University of Madras, 1882." In *Convocation Addresses of the Universities of Bombay and Madras*, edited by K. Subba Rau, 155–68. Madras: Lawrence Asylum Press, 1892.

Jabavu, Davidson. *In India and East Africa: A Travelogue in IsiXhosa and English*. Johannesburg: Wits University Press, 2020.

Jahanara Begum. "Jahanara Begum." In *Three Centuries of Travel Writing by Muslim Women*, edited by Siobhan Lambert-Hurley, Daniel Majchrowicz, and Sunil Sharma, translated by Sunil Sharma, 385–93. Boomington: Indiana University Press, 2022.

Jalal, Ayesha. *Self and Sovereignty: Individual and Community in South Asian Islam since 1850*. London: Routlege, 2000.

Jasanoff, Maya. *Edge of Empire: Lives, Culture, and Conquest in the East, 1750–1850*. New York: Alfred A. Knopf, 2005.

Jhanjhorvi, Vajahat Husain. *Safarnama-i Bamba'i*. Lahore: Naval Kishore, 1910.

Jones, Justin. "The Local Experiences of Reformist Islam in a 'Muslim' Town in Colonial India: The Case of Amroha." *Modern Asian Studies* 43, no. 4 (2009): 871–908.

Jones, Rebecca. *At the Crossroads: Nigerian Travel Writing and Literary Culture in Yoruba and English*. Woodbridge: James Currey, 2019.

———. "Journeys to the Hinterland: Twentieth-Century Nigerian Travel Writing and Local Heterogeneity in Lagos and Beyond." *Postcolonial Text* 9, no. 4 (2014): 1–19.

Joshi, Sanjay. *Fractured Modernity: The Making of a Middle Class in Colonial North India*. New Delhi: Oxford University Press, 2001.

Kali Rai and Tulsi Ram. *Sair-i Punjab*. Patiala: Naval Kishore, 1872.

Kambalposh, Yusuf Khan. *Tarikh-i Yusufi*. Edited by Muhammad Ikram Chughta'i. Lahore: Sang-e-Meel Publications, 2004.

Kane, Eileen. *Russian Hajj: Empire and the Pilgrimage to Mecca*. Ithaca: Cornell University Press, 2015.

Kantor, Roanne. *South Asian Writers, Latin American Literature, and the Rise of Global English*. Cambridge: Cambridge University Press, 2022.

Karimullah Khan. "Sair-i Karimi." Rampur, 1826. Qalami Farsi 29. Saulat Library.

Kashifi, Husain Va'iz. *Anvar-i Suhaili*. Edited by Edward Backhouse Eastwick. Hertford: S. Austin, 1851.

Keen, Caroline. *Princely India and the British: Political Development and the Operation of Empire*. London: I. B. Tauris, 2012.

Kerr, Ian, ed. *27 Down: New Departures in Indian Railway Studies*. New Delhi: Orient Longman, 2007.

Khalidi, Omar. "A Guide to Arabic, Persian, Turkish, and Urdu Manuscript Libraries in India." *MELA Notes*, no. 84 (2011): 1–85.

Khan, 'Abd al-Rahman. *Sharh-i Safarnama-jat-i Shah-i Iran*. Muradabad: n.p., 1888.

Khan, Dargah Quli. *Muraqqa'-i Dihli*. Delhi: Shu'ba-i Urdu-i Delhi University, 1982.

Khan, Dildar Husain. *Dala'il al-Zafar fi Tazkirat al-Safar*. Lucknow: n.p., 1893.

Khan, Ghaus Muhammad. *Sair al-Muhtasham*. Ja'ora: Matba'-i Sarkar-i Gulshanabad, 1852.

Khan, Ghulam Haidar. *Sair-i Maqbul*. Kanpur: Naval Kishore, 1898.

Khan, Hamidullah. *Safarnama-i Qustuntuniya*. Hyderabad: Qasim Press, 1912.

Khan, Khudadad. *Pa Payada Safar-i Hajj*. Aligarh: Aligarh Barqi Press, 1935.

Khan, Mubarriz al-Daula. *Sairistan*. Multan: Matba' Riyaz-i Nur, 1854.

Khan, Muhammad 'Umar 'Ali. *Qand-i Maghribi*. Kanpur: Matba'-i Nizami, 1897.

———. *Zad-i Safar o Vasilat al-Zafar*. Delhi: Nusrat al-Matabi', 1876.

Khan, Muhammad Ya'qub. *Tarikh-i Badi'*. Qasur: Matba'-i Qadiri, 1879.

Khan, Muhammad Yusuf. *Tarikh-i Yusufi: Darbar-i Ja'ora*. Agra: Riyaz-i Hind, 1895.

Khan, Pasha Muhammad. "Marvellous Histories: Reading the *Shāhnāmah* in India." *Indian Economic and Social History Review* 49, no. 4 (2012): 527–56.

———. *The Broken Spell: Indian Storytelling and the Romance Genre in Persian and Urdu*. Detroit: Wayne State University Press, 2019.

———. "The Broken Spell: The Romance Genre in Late Mughal India." Columbia University, 2013.

———. "The Lament for Delhi." In *Nationalism in the Vernacular: Hindi, Urdu, and the Literature of Indian Freedom*, edited by Shobna Nijhawan, 88–92. Ranikhet: Permanent Black, 2010.

Khan, Razak. "The Case of Falling Walls: Politics of Demolition and Preservation in Rampur." *Economic and Political Weekly* 49, no. 20 (2014): 25–28.

Khan, Sami'ullah. *Musafiran-i Landan*. Edited by Asghar 'Abbas. Aligarh: Educational Book House, 2012.

———. *Safarnama-i Maulvi Muhammad Sami'ullah Khan*. Amroha: 'Umdat al-Matabi', 1880.

Khan, Sayyid Ahmad. *Musafiran-i Landan*. Edited by Muhammad Isma'il Panipati. Lahore: Majlis-i Taraqqi-i Adab, 1961.

Khan, Yasmin. *The Great Partition: The Making of India and Pakistan*. New Haven: Yale University Press, 2007.

Khatlani, Sameer Arshad. *The Other Side of the Divide: A Journey into the Heart of Pakistan*. Gurgaon: Ebury Press, 2020.

Khazeni, Arash. *The City and the Wilderness: Indo-Persian Encounters in Southeast Asia*. Berkeley: University of California Press, 2020.

———. "Through an Ocean of Sand: Pastoralism and the Equestrian Culture of the Eurasian Steppe." In *Water on Sand: Environmental Histories of the Middle East and North Africa*, edited by Alan Mikhail, 133–58. New York: Oxford University Press, 2013.

Khera, Dipti. "Picturing India's 'Land of Kings' Between the Mughal and British Empires: Topographical Imaginings of Udaipur and Its Environs." Columbia University, 2013.

Khwaja, Jamal. "Family Background: Professor Jamal Khwaja." Accessed April 17, 2022. http://www.jamalkhwaja.com/jamalbooksite/AuthorFamilyBackground.html.

Kia, Mana. "Adab as Literary Form and Social Conduct: Reading the Gulistan in Late Mughal India." In *No Tapping around Philology: A Festschrift in Honor of Wheeler McIntosh Thackston Jr.'s 70th Birthday*, edited by Alireza Korangy and Daniel J. Sheffield, 281–308. Wiesbaden: Harrassowitz Verlag, 2014.

King, Christopher Rolland. *One Language, Two Scripts: The Hindi Movement in Nineteenth Century North India*. Bombay: Oxford University Press, 1994.

Kinlock, Charles Walter. *Vaqa'i'-i Kaip*. Translated by Brij Bhukanlal. Lucknow: Naval Kishore, 1853.

Kirk, Gwendolyn. "The Books in the Bunker: Global Flows of Meaning and Matter in Academic Assemblages." *South Asia: Journal of South Asian Studies* 43, no. 3 (2020): 537–53.

Kling, Blair. *Partner in Empire: Dwarkanath Tagore and the Age of Enterprise in Eastern India*. Berkeley: University of California Press, 1976.

Kolff, Dirk. H.A. *Naukar, Rajput, and Sepoy: The Ethnohistory of the Military Labour Market in Hindustan, 1450-1850*. Cambridge: Cambridge University Press, 1990.

Kumar, Santosh. *Lahaurnama*. Lahore: Book Home, 2004.

———. *Lahore Nama*. New Delhi: Vibha, 2002.

La'l, Ram. *Zard Patton ki Bahar: Safarnama-i Pakistan*. Lucknow: Uttar Pradesh Urdu Academy, 1982.

Lally, Jagjeet. *India and the Silk Roads: The History of a Trading World*. New York: Oxford University Press, 2021.

Lambert-Hurley, Siobhan. *Elusive Lives: Gender, Autobiography, and the Self in Muslim South Asia*. Stanford: Stanford University Press, 2018.

———. "Fostering Sisterhood: Muslim Women and the All-India Ladies' Association." *Journal of Women's History* 16, no. 2 (2004): 40–65.

Lambert-Hurley, Siobhan, Daniel Majchrowicz, and Sunil Sharma, eds. *Three Centuries of Travel Writing by Muslim Women*. Bloomington: Indiana University Press, 2022.

Lanzillo, Amanda. "Translating the Scribe: Lithographic Print and Vernacularization in Colonial India, 1857–1915." *Comparative Critical Studies* 16, no. 2–3 (2019): 281–300.

Leed, Eric. *The Mind of the Traveler: From Gilgamesh to Global Tourism*. New York: Basic Books, 1991.

Lelyveld, David. "Jute Hain Japani Kapre Inglistani: Sayyid Ross Masood's Passage to Japan." In *Urdu and Indo-Persian Thought, Poetics, and Belles Lettres*, edited by Alireza Korangy, 217–28. Leiden: Brill, 2017.

Levi, Scott, and Muzaffar Alam, eds. *India and Central Asia: Commerce and Culture, 1500–1800*. New Delhi: Oxford University Press, 2007.

Low, Michael. *Imperial Mecca: Ottoman Arabia and the Indian Ocean Hajj*. New York: Columbia University Press, 2020.

Macaulay, Thomas Babington. *Miscellaneous Works of Lord Macaulay*. Vol. 1. New York: Harper & Bros., 1880.

MacCannell, Dean. *The Tourist: A New Theory of the Leisure Class*. Berkeley: University of California Press, 2013.

Madni, Nazir al-Din. *Miyan Dad Khan Sayyah aur un ka Kalam*. Hyderabad: I'jaz Printing Press, 1957.

Maimuna Sultan. "Maimuna Sultan." In *Three Centuries of Travel Writing by Muslim Women*, edited by Siobhan Lambert-Hurley, translated by Daniel Majchrowicz, 303–13. Boomington: Indiana University Press, 2022.

———. *Siyahat-i Sultani*. Karachi: Oxford University Press, 2008.

Majchrowicz, Daniel. "Archive Review: Twenty Libraries in Delhi You've Never Visited." *Sagar: A South Asia Research Journal*, October 2013.

———. "Begum Hasrat Mohani's Journey to Iraq." In *Worlds of Knowledge in Women's Travel Writing*, edited by James Uden, 140–67. Boston: Ilex Foundation, 2022.

———. "Malika Begum's Mehfil: Retrieving the Lost Legacy of Women's Travel Writing in Urdu." *South Asia: Journal of South Asian Studies* 43, no. 5 (2020).

———. "'Can't Touch This': Early Indian Muslim Responses to the Saudi Conquest of the Hijaz." *Journal of Urdu Studies*, forthcoming.

Majeed, Javed. *Autobiography, Travel and Postnational Identity: Gandhi, Nehru and Iqbal*. New York: Palgrave Macmillan, 2007.

———. "Geographies of Subjectivity, Pan-Islam and Muslim Separatism: Muhammad Iqbal and Selfhood." *Modern Intellectual History* 4, no. 1 (2007): 145–61.

Malcolm, John. *Halat-i Iran*. Translated by Amjad 'Ali Ashhari. Lahore: Karkhana-i Paisa Akhbar, 1906.

———. *Sketches of Persia*. London: Murray, 1827.

Malcolm X. *The Autobiography of Malcolm X*. New York: Ballantine Books, 1984.

Malhotra, Anshu, and Siobhan Lambert-Hurley. "Gender, Performance, and Autobiography in South Asia." In *Speaking of the Self: Gender, Performance, and Autobiography in South Asia*, 1–30. Durham: Duke University Press, 2015.

———. *Speaking of the Self: Gender, Performance, and Autobiography in South Asia*. Durham: Duke University Press, 2015.

Mandhwani, Aakriti. "The Hindi Library and the Making of an Archive: The Hindi Sahitya Sammelan from 1911 to 1973." *South Asia: Journal of South Asian Studies* 43, no. 3 (2020): 522–36.

Mangalagiri, Adhira. "Ellipses of Cultural Diplomacy: The 1957 Chinese Literary Sphere in Hindi." *Journal of World Literature* 4, no. 4 (2019): 508–29.

Mani, Venkat. *Recoding World Literature: Libraries, Print Culture, and Germany's Pact with Books.* New York: Fordham University Press, 2017.

Manjapra, Kris. "Introduction." In *Cosmopolitan Thought Zones: South Asia and the Global Circulation of Ideas,* edited by Sugata Bose and Kris Manjapra, 1–21. New York: Palgrave Macmillan, 2010.

Manzur ʿAli. *Safarnama-i Manzur ʿAli.* Kanpur: Matbaʿ-i Ahmadi, 1894.

Markovits, Claude, Jacques Pouchepadass, and Sanjay Subrahmanyam. *Society and Circulation: Mobile People and Itinerant Cultures in South Asia, 1750–1950.* Delhi: Permanent Black, 2003.

Masood, Syed Ross. *Some Impressions of Japan: A Lecture Delivered to the Teachers' Association, Hyderabad-Deccan, on the 24th of June, 1926.* Hyderabad: Government Central Press, 1926.

———. *Travels in Japan: Diary of an Exploring Mission.* Karachi: Ross Masood Education and Culture Society of Pakistan, 1968.

Massy, Charles Francis. *Chiefs and Families of Note in the Dehli, Jalandhar, Peshawar and Derajat Divisions of the Panjab.* Allahabad: Pioneer Press, 1890.

Masʿud, Nayyar. *Muntakhab Mazamin.* Karachi: City Press, 2009.

Mathur, Tapsi. "How Professionals Became Natives: Geography and Trans-Frontier Exploration in Colonial India." PhD diss., University of Michigan, 2018.

McDonnell, Mary Byrne. "Patterns of Muslim Pilgrimage from Malaysia, 1885–1985." In *Muslim Travellers: Pilgrimage, Migration, and the Religious Imagination,* edited by Dale F. Eickelman and James P. Piscatori, 205–34. Berkeley: University of California Press, 1990.

Metcalf, Barbara. *Islamic Revival in British India: Deoband, 1860–1900.* Princeton: Princeton University Press, 1982.

———. "The Pilgrimage Remembered: South Asian Accounts of the Hajj." In *Muslim Travellers: Pilgrimage, Migration, and the Religious Imagination,* edited by Dale F. Eickelman and James P. Piscatori, 85–107. Berkeley: University of California Press, 1990.

———. "What Happened in Mecca: Mumtaz Mufti's *Labbaik.*" In *The Culture of Autobiography: Constructions of Self-Representation,* edited by Robert Folkenflik, 149–67. Stanford: Stanford University Press, 1993.

Mills, Sara. *Discourses of Difference: An Analysis of Women's Travel Writing and Colonialism.* London: Routledge, 1991.

Minault, Gail. "Master Ramchandra of Delhi College: Teacher, Journalist and Cultural Intermediary." *Annual of Urdu Studies* 18 (2003): 95–104.

———. *Secluded Scholars: Women's Education and Muslim Social Reform in Colonial India.* Delhi: Oxford University Press, 1998.

———. *The Khilafat Movement: Religious Symbolism and Political Mobilization in India*. New York: Columbia University Press, 1982.

Mir, Farina. *The Social Space of Language: Vernacular Culture in British Colonial Punjab*. Berkeley: University of California Press, 2010.

Mir, Vali Muhammad. *Safarnama-i Undulus*. Lucknow: Nami Press, 1927.

Mirza, Sughra Humayun. *Safarnama-i Yurap*. Vol. 2. Hyderabad: A'zam Steam Press, 1926.

———. "Siyahat-i Nanda'ir." *Zeb al-Nisa* 1, no. 5 (September 1934): 1–8.

Mishra, Saurabh. *Pilgrimage, Politics, and Pestilence: The Haj from the Indian Subcontinent, 1860––1920*. New Delhi: Oxford University Press, 2011.

Mitchell, Lisa. *Language, Emotion, and Politics in South India: The Making of a Mother Tongue*. Bloomington: Indiana University Press, 2009.

Mongia, Radhika. *Indian Migration and Empire: A Colonial Genealogy of the Modern State*. Durham: Duke University Press, 2018.

Mufti, Aamir. *Enlightenment in the Colony: The Jewish Question and the Crisis of Postcolonial Culture*. Princeton: Princeton University Press, 2007.

Mufti, Mumtaz. *Hind Yatra*. Lahore: Izhar Sons, 1982.

Muhammadi Begum. "Diary," 1934. Property of Zehra Masud.

Mu'in, 'Abida. "Bila Zarurat Safar." *'Ismat* 95, no. 1 (1955): 27–28.

Mukasa, Ham. *Uganda's Katikiro in England*. Translated by Ernest Millar. London: Hutchinson, 1904.

Mukhopadhyay, Aparajita. *Imperial Technology and "Native" Agency: A Social History of Railways in Colonial India, 1850–1920*. London: Routledge, 2018.

———. "Wheels of Change? Impact of Railways on Colonial North Indian Society, 1855–1920." PhD diss., SOAS, 2013.

Mukhopadhyay, Bhaskar. "Writing Home, Writing Travel: The Poetics and Politics of Dwelling in Bengali Modernity." *Comparative Studies in Society and History* 44, no. 2 (2002): 293–318.

Mulji, Karsanadas. *Sairistan-i England*. Delhi: Matba'-i Hasani, 1870.

Nadvi, Sayyid Sulaiman. "Dibacha." In *Safar-i Hijaz*, by 'Abd al-Majid Daryabadi 1–6., 'Azamgarh: Ma'arif Press, 1931.

Naim, C.M. "Disappearing Treasures: Public Libraries and Urdu Printed Books." *Annual of Urdu Studies*, no. 26 (2011): 53–63.

———. "Interrogating 'The East,' 'Culture,' and 'Loss' in Abdul Halim Sharar's *Guzashta Lakhna'u*." In *Indo-Muslim Cultures in Transition*, edited by Alka Patel and Karen Leonard, 189–204. Leiden: Brill, 2012.

———. "Prize-Winning Adab: A Study of Five Urdu Books Written in Response to the Allahabad Government Gazette Notification." In *Moral Conduct and Authority: The Place of Adab in South Asian Islam*, edited by Barbara Metcalf, 290–314. Berkeley: University of California Press, 1984.

Nair, Savita. "Moving Life Histories: Gujarat, East Africa, and the Indian Diaspora, 1880–2000." PhD diss., University of Pennsylvania, 2001.

Nenzi, Laura Nenz Detto. *Excursions in Identity: Travel and the Intersection of Place, Gender, and Status in Edo Japan*. Honolulu: University of Hawai'i Press, 2008.

Nerlekar, Anjali, and Francesca Orsini. "Introduction: Postcolonial Archives." *South Asia: Journal of South Asian Studies* 45, no. 2 (2022): 211–19.

Ní Loingsigh, Aedín. "African Travel Writing." In *The Routledge Companion to Travel Writing*, edited by Carl Thompson, 185–95. New Delhi: Routledge, 2016.

———. *Postcolonial Eyes: Intercontinental Travel in Francophone African Literature*. Liverpool: Liverpool University Press, 2009.

Niyazi, Kausar. *Naqsh-i Rahguzar*. Delhi: New Bisma Kitab Ghar, 2007.

Nizamat Jang. "Muqaddama." In *Lady Evelyn Cobbald ka Safarnama-i Haramain*, by Lady Evelyn Cobbald, alif–be. Translated by Mohsin bin Shabbir. Mughalpura: A'zam Steam Press, 1939.

Nizami, Farhan. *Atlas Project: The Social and Intellectual History of Muslims in South Asia*. New York: Oxford University Press, forthcoming.

Nizami, Khwaja Hasan. *Safarnama-i Pakistan*. Delhi: Printing Works, 1952.

Novetzke, Christian. *Religion and Public Memory: A Cultural History of Saint Namdev in India*. New York: Columbia University Press, 2008.

Nu'mani, Shibli. *Safarnama-i Rum o Misr o Sham*. Delhi: Qaumi Press, 1901.

———. *Turkey, Egypt, and Syria: A Travelogue*. Translated by Gregory Maxwell Bruce. Syracuse: Syracuse University Press, 2020.

———. "Dibacha." In *Sayyid Ahmad Khan ka Safarnama-i Punjab*, by Sayyid Iqbal 'Ali, i. Aligarh: Aligarh Institute Press, 1884.

Nur Begum. *Mazahir al-Nur, al-Ma'ruf bih, Safarnama-i Nur Bara'e Hajj o Ziyarat-i Huzur*. 3rd ed. Lahore: Rahmani Press, 1952.

———. "Nur Begum." In *Three Centuries of Muslim Women Travelers*, translated by Daniel Majchrowicz, 137–47. Boomington: Indiana University Press, 2022.

Ochonu, Moses. *Emirs in London: Subaltern Travel and Nigeria's Modernity*. Bloomington: Indiana University Press, 2022.

Oesterheld, Christina. "From a Slave Garden into Cyberspace: Mirza Athar Baig's Novels *Ghulam Bagh* and *Sifr Se Ek Tak*." In *Urdu and Indo-Persian Thought, Poetics, and Belles Lettres*, edited by Alireza Korangy, 229–49. Leiden: Brill, 2017.

Orsini, Francesca. "Between *Qasbas* and Cities: Language Shifts and Literary Continuities in North India in the Long Eighteenth Century." *Comparative Studies of South Asia, Africa and the Middle East* 39, no. 1 (2019): 68–81.

———. "Detective Novels: A Commercial Genre in Nineteenth-Century North India." In *India's Literary History. Essays on the Nineteenth Century*, edited by Stuart Blackburn and Vasudha Dalmia, 435–82. Ranikhet: Permanent Black, 2004.

———. "Present Absence: Book Circulation, Indian Vernaculars and World Literature in the Nineteenth Century." *Interventions* 22, no. 3 (2020): 310–28.

———. *Print and Pleasure: Popular Literature and Entertaining Fictions in Colonial North India*. Ranikhet: Permanent Black, 2009.

———. *The Hindi Public Sphere 1920–1940: Language and Literature in the Age of Nationalism*. New Delhi: Oxford University Press, 2002.

Pandey, Gyanendra. "Can a Muslim Be an Indian?" *Comparative Studies in Society and History* 41, no. 4 (1999): 608–29.

———. "Partition and the Politics of History." In *The Nation, the State, and Indian Identity*, edited by Madhusree Dutta, Agnes Flavia, and Neera Adarkar, 1–26. Calcutta: Samya, 1996.

Pandit Kanhaiyalal. *Sair-i Kashmir*. Lakhna'u: Naval Kishore, 1861.

Pandit Rataneshvar. *Patramalika*. Agra: Agra School Book Society, 1841.

Park, Mungo. *Safarnama Mungo Park Sahib ka Bayan meñ Mulk Habsh Ke*. Agra: Agra School Book Society, 1842.

———. *Safarnama Mungo Park Sahib ka Bayan meñ Mulk Habsh Ke*. Calcutta: Calcutta School Book Society, 1853.

———. *Travels in the Interior Districts of Africa*. London: W. Bulmer and Co., 1799.

Parsons, Neil. *King Khama, Emperor Joe, and the Great White Queen: Victorian Britain through African Eyes*. Chicago: University of Chicago Press, 1998.

Pearson, M.N. *Pilgrimage to Mecca: The Indian Experience, 1600–1800*. Princeton: Markus Wiener, 1996.

Penner, Peter. *Robert Needham Cust, 1821–1909: A Personal Biography*. Lewiston: The Edwin Mellen Press, 1987.

Perkins, Ryan. "From South Asian Print to the Digital Archive: The Quest for Access and Sustainability." *South Asia: Journal of South Asian Studies* 43, no. 3 (2020): 554–70.

———. "From the *Mehfil* to the Printed Word: Public Debate and Discourse in Late Colonial India." *Indian Economic and Social History Review* 50, no. 1 (2013): 47–76.

———. "London, Lucknow and the Global Indian City, c. 1857–1920." *Journal of the Royal Asiatic Society* 27, no. 4 (2017): 611–26.

———. "Partitioning History: The Creation of an *Islami Pablik* in Late Colonial India, c. 1880–1920." University of Pennsylvania, Philadelphia, 2011.

Pernau, Margrit. *Ashraf into Middle Classes: Muslims in Nineteenth-Century Delhi*. New Delhi: Oxford University Press, 2013.

———. *Emotions and Modernity in Colonial India: From Balance to Fervor*. New Delhi: Oxford University Press, 2019.

———. "Entangled Translations: The History of Delhi College." In *The Delhi College: Traditional Elites, the Colonial State, and Education before 1857*, 1–32. New Delhi: Oxford University Press, 2006.

———. "From Morality to Psychology: Emotion Concepts in Urdu, 1870–1920." *Contributions to the History of Concepts* 11, no. 1 (2016): 38–57.

———. "The *Delhi Urdu Akhbar*: Between Persian *Akhbarat* and English Newspapers." *Annual of Urdu Studies* 18, no. 1 (2003): 105–31.

———. "The Virtuous Individual and Social Reform: Debates among North Indian Urdu Speakers." In *Civilizing Emotions*, edited by Margrit Pernau and Helge Jordheim, 168–86. Oxford: Oxford University Press, 2015.

Pernau, Margrit, and Yunus Jaffery, eds. *Information and the Public Sphere: Persian Newsletters from Mughal Delhi*. New Delhi: Oxford University Press, 2009.

Platts, John. *A Dictionary of Urdu, Classical Hindi, and English*. London: Crosby Lockwood and Son, 1899.

Pollock, Sheldon. "Cosmopolitan and Vernacular in History." *Public Culture* 12, no. 3 (2000): 591–625.

———. "Introduction." In *Forms of Knowledge in Early Modern Asia*, edited by Sheldon Pollock, 1–16. Durham: Duke University Press, 2011.

———. *The Language of the Gods in the World of Men: Sanskrit, Culture, and Power in Premodern India*. Berkeley: University of California Press, 2006.

Porter, W.A. "The Sixteenth Convocation of the University of Madras, 1873." In *Convocation Addresses of the Universities of Bombay and Madras*, edited by K. Subba Rau. Madras: Lawrence Asylum Press, 1892.

Prasad, Ritika. "Tracking Modernity: The Experience of Railways in Colonial India, 1853–1947." PhD diss., University of California, Los Angeles, 2009.

Pratt, Mary Louise. *Imperial Eyes: Travel Writing and Transculturation*. London New York: Routledge, 2008.

Pritchett, Frances W. *Nets of Awareness: Urdu Poetry and Its Critics*. Berkeley: University of California Press, 1994.

———. "Story Notes (Toba Tek Singh)." Accessed June 1, 2022. http://www.columbia.edu/itc/mealac/pritchett/00urdu/tobateksingh/storynotes.html.

Punjab District Gazetteer: Rawalpindi District. Vol. 28A. Lahore: Civil and Military Press, 1907.

Pyare Laʻl. *Dunya ki Sair*. Aligarh: Vidya Sagar Press, 1897.

Qaisari Begum *Kitab-i Zindagi*. Edited by Zehra Masrur Ahmad. Karachi: Fazli Sons, 2003.

Qasimi, ʻAta al-Haqq. *Dilli Dur Ast*. Lahore: Nastaʻliq Matbuʻat, 2009.

Qasmi, Ali Usman, and Megan Eaton Robb, eds. *Muslims against the Muslim League: Critiques of the Idea of Pakistan*. Cambridge: Cambridge University Press, 2017.

Raban, J. *For Love and Money: Writing, Reading, Travelling, 1968–1987*. London: Picador, 1988.

Rahman, M. Raisur. *Locale, Everyday Islam, and Modernity: Qasbah Towns and Muslim Life in Colonial India*. New Delhi: Oxford University Press, 2015.

———. "*Qaṣbas* as Place: A Sense of Belonging and Nostalgia in Colonial India." *Journal of the Economic and Social History of the Orient* 58, no. 5 (2015): 668–92.

Raj, Kapil. *Relocating Modern Science: Circulation and the Construction of Knowledge in South Asia and Europe, 1650–1900*. New York: Palgrave Macmillan, 2007.

Ramabai Sarasvati. *Pandita Ramabai's America*. Edited by R.E. Frykenberg. Grand Rapids, Mich.: Roundhouse, 2003.

Ramaswamy, Sumathi. *Terrestrial Lessons: The Conquest of the World as Globe*. Chicago: University of Chicago Press, 2018.

Ramusack, Barbara. *The Indian Princes and Their States*. Cambridge: Cambridge University Press, 2004.

Ranade, Rekha. *Sir Bartle Frere and His Times: A Study of His Bombay Years, 1862–1867*. New Delhi: Mittal Publications, 1990.

Rao, Velcheru Narayana. *Text and Tradition in South India*. Syracuse: SUNY Press, 2018.

Rastegar, Kamran. *Literary Modernity between Middle East and Europe: Textual Transactions in 19th Century Arabic, English and Persian Literatures*. London: Routledge, 2010.

Rathi, Karim 'Ali. *Bagh-i Nau Bahar*. [Indore]: Matbaʿ-i Maharaja Holkar Bahadur, 1851.

Raza, Safdar Amjad. "Sara'iki Safarname ki Rivayat." *Journal of Research (Urdu)*, no. 32 (2017): 259–66.

Raziq al-Khairi. "Do Hafte Mashriqi Pakistan Meñ." *'Ismat* 107, no. 2 (1961): 116–20.

Reese, Scott. *Imperial Muslims: Islam, Community and Authority in the Indian Ocean, 1839–1937*. Edinburgh: Edinburgh University Press, 2017.

Reid, Kirsty, and Fiona Paisley. "Introduction." In *Sources and Methods in Histories of Colonialism: Approaching the Imperial Archive*, edited by Kirsty Reid and Fiona Paisley, 1–10. London: Routledge, 2017.

Report of the General Committee of Public Instruction of the Presidency of Fort William in Bengal for the Year 1836. Calcutta: Bengal Military Orphan Press, 1836.

Report on the State of Popular Education in the North Western Provinces for 1858–59, Report Number 59. Benares, 1859.

Ricci, Ronit. *Islam Translated: Literature, Conversion, and the Arabic Cosmopolis of South and Southeast Asia*. Chicago: University of Chicago Press, 2011.

Robb, Megan Eaton. "Gendered Nationalism and Material Texts: An Urdu Women's Periodical in 1960s Pakistan." *South Asia: Journal of South Asian Studies* 45, no. 2 (2022): 285–302.

———. *Print and the Urdu Public: Muslims, Newspapers, and Urban Life in Colonial India*. New York: Oxford University Press, 2020.

Robinson, Francis. *Separatism among Indian Muslims: The Politics of the United Provinces' Muslims, 1860–1923*. London: Cambridge University Press, 1974.

———. "Technology and Religious Change: Islam and the Impact of Print." *Modern Asian Studies* 27, no. 1 (1993): 229–51.

Rockwell, Daisy. "The Myth of the Lone Ranger." *The Caravan*, May 31, 2013. Accessed November 1, 2022. https://caravanmagazine.in/reviews-essays/myth-lone-ranger.

Rumi, Raza. *Delhi by Heart: Impressions of a Pakistani Traveller*. Delhi: Harper Collins, 2013.

Ruswa, Muhammad Hadi. *Umra'o Jan "Ada."* Lahore: Majlis-i Taraqqi-i Adab, 1988.

Sabzvari, Dr 'Ali Shah. *Khaufnak Dunya: Hissa-i Avval, Afriqa 1899–1901*. Allahabad: Barakat-i Akbari Press, 1935.

Sadid, Anvar. *Urdu Adab men Safarnama*. New Delhi: M. R. Publications, 2012.

Sair-i Afriqa, al-Mashhur, Nazzara-i Afriqa. Lahore: J.S. Sant Singh and Sons, n.d.

Saksena, Munshi Shiv Narayan. *England Yatra*. Jaipur: Jail Press, 1902.

Sarkar, Tanika. *Words to Win: The Making of Amar Jiban*. New Delhi: Zubaan, 2014.

Sayyah, Miyan Dad Khan. *Sair-i Sayyah*. Lucknow: Naval Kishore, 1872.

Sayyid 'Ali Akhtar. "Somaliland se Khat." *'Ismat*, September 1946.

Schaflechner, Jürgen, and Christoph Bergmann, eds. *Ritual Journeys in South Asia: Constellations and Contestations of Mobility and Space*. New York, N.Y.: Routledge, 2020.

Schimmel, Annemarie. *Islam in the Indian Subcontinent*. Leiden: E.J. Brill, 1980.

Scott, J. Barton. "Translated Liberties: Karsandas Mulji's *Travels in England* and the Anthropology of the Victorian Self." *Modern Intellectual History* 16, no. 3 (2017): 803–33.

Scott, J. Barton, and Brannon D. Ingram. "What Is a Public? Notes from South Asia." *South Asia: Journal of South Asian Studies* 38, no. 3 (2015): 357–70.

Segura-Garcia, Teresa. "Picturing Indian Kingship: The Photographic Practices of Maharaja Sayaji Rao III of Baroda." In *Visual Histories of South Asia*, edited by Annamaria Motrescu-Mayes and Marcus Banks, 115–31. Delhi: Primus Books, 2018.

Selections from the Records of Government of the North-Western Provinces, Second Series. Vol. 3. Allahabad: Government Press, 1870.

Sen, Simonti. *Travels to Europe: Self and Other in Bengali Travel Narratives, 1870–1910*. New Delhi: Orient Longman, 2005.

Server-ul-Mulk, Nawab Bahadur. *My Life: Being the Autobiography of Nawab Server-Ul-Mulk Bahadur*. London: A.H. Stockwell, 1931.

Shackle, C., and Javed Majeed. *Hali's Musaddas: The Flow and Ebb of Islam*. Delhi: Oxford University Press, 1997.

Shankar, Babu Uma. *A'ina-i Sikandari*. Delhi: Matba'-i Muhibb-i Hind, 1887.

Shankar, Subramanian. *Flesh and Fish Blood: Postcolonialism, Translation, and the Vernacular*. Berkeley: University of California Press, 2012.

Shankarrao, Raghunathrao. *Twenty-One Weeks in Europe*. Poona: R.K. Deshpande, 1937.

Sharar, 'Abd al-Halim. *Jan-i 'Alam: Vajid 'Ali Shah ke Matya Burj ke Halat*. Lahore: Idarah-i Furogh-i Urdu, 1951.

Sharma, Sunil. "Delight and Disgust: Gendered Encounters in the Travelogues of the Fyzee Sisters." In *On the Wonders of Land and Sea*, edited by Roberta Micallef and Sunil Sharma, 114–31. Boston: Ilex Foundation, 2013.

———. *Mughal Arcadia: Persian Literature in an Indian Court*. Cambridge, Mass.: Harvard University Press, 2017.

———. "Speaking Without Language: 19th-Century British Women Travelers in Iran and India." In *Worlds of Knowledge in Women's Travel Writing*, edited by James Uden, 99–116. Boston: Ilex Foundation, 2021.

———. "The Chameleonic Identities of Mohan Lal Kashmiri and His Travels in Persianate Lands." In *Illusion and Disillusionment: Travel Writing in the Modern Age*, edited by Roberta Micallef, 80–97. Boston: Ilex Foundation, 2018.

———. "The City of Beauties in Indo-Persian Poetic Landscape." *Comparative Studies of South Asia, Africa and the Middle East* 24, no. 2 (2004): 73–81.

Shaw, Graham. "Calcutta: Birthplace of the Indian Lithographed Book." In *The History of the Book in South Asia*, edited by Francesca Orsini, 159–81. Farnham: Ashgate, 2013.

———. "Lithography v. Letter-Press in India Part I." *South Asia Library Notes and Queries* 29 (1993): 1–11.

———. "Lithography v. Letter-Press in India Part II." *South Asia Library Notes and Queries* 30 (May 1994): 1–10.

Sheriff, Abdul, and Engseng Ho, eds. *The Indian Ocean: Oceanic Connections and the Creation of New Societies*. London: Hurst & Company, 2014.

Shervaniya, Rahil. *Zad al-Sabil, ya, Rahlat al-Rahil*. Aligarh: Matba'-i Muslim University, 1929.

Shree, Geetanjali. *Tomb of Sand*. Translated by Daisy Rockwell. London: Tilted Axis Press, 2021.

Shri, Gitanjali. *Ret Samadhi*. Delhi: Rajkamal Prakashan, 2018.

Shulman, David Dean. *The King and the Clown in South Indian Myth and Poetry*. Princeton: Princeton University Press, 2014.

Siddiqi, 'Abd al-Rashid. *Pandit Ratan Nath Sarshar ke Tarajim: Ek Tanqidi Ja'iza*. Sultanpur: Dr. 'Abd al-Rashid Siddiqi, 1997.

Siddique, Soofia. "Worlds of Advice." *Journal of World Literature* 4, no. 2 (2019): 169–87.

Sikandar Begum. "Tarikh-i Safar-i Makka." Bhopal, 1867. Ref. number: PP MS 55, Durand, Box 2, file 12. SOAS.

Simpson, Edward. *Muslim Society and the Western Indian Ocean: The Seafarers of Kachchh*. London: Routledge, 2006.

Singh, Bhavani. *Safarnama Shri Badri Narayan-ji Maharaj Ka*. Muradabad: Bidya Bhushan Press, 1900.

Singh, Bhavani. *Travel Pictures: The Record of a European Tour*. London: Longmans, Green, and Co., 1912.

Singh, Raja Shiv Prasad. *Bhugol Hastamalika*. Allahabad: n. p., 1876.

Singha, Radhika. *The Coolie's Great War: Indian Labour in a Global Conflict, 1914–1921*. New York: Oxford University Press, 2020.

Sinha, Nitin. *Communication and Colonialism in Eastern India: Bihar, 1760s–1880s*. London: Anthem Press, 2012.

Slate, Nico. *Colored Cosmopolitanism: The Shared Struggle for Freedom in the United States and India*. Cambridge, Mass.: Harvard University Press, 2012.

Sohrabi, Naghmeh. *Taken for Wonder: Nineteenth-Century Travel Accounts from Iran to Europe*. Oxford: Oxford University Press, 2012.

Spurr, David. *The Rhetoric of Empire: Colonial Discourse in Journalism, Travel Writing, and Imperial Administration*. Durham: Duke University Press, 1993.

Sri Vadiraja. *Sri Vadiraja's Theerthaprabandha*. Edited by S K. Achar. Udupi: Srinivasa Publications, 1997.

Srivastava, Dharma Bhanu. *The Province of Agra: Its History and Administration*. New Delhi: Concept, 1979.

Stark, Ulrike. *An Empire of Books: The Naval Kishore Press and the Diffusion of the Printed Word in Colonial India*. Ranikhet: Permanent Black, 2007.

———. "Associational Culture and Civic Engagement in Colonial Lucknow: The Jalsah-e Tahzib." *Indian Economic and Social History Review* 48, no. 1 (2011): 1–33.

———. "Chapakhana." Chapakhana. Accessed May 14, 2022. https://chapakhana.rcc.uchicago.edu/.

Strauch, Ingo. *Foreign Sailors on Socotra: The Inscriptions and Drawings from the Cave Hoq*. Bremen: Hempen, 2012.

Subrahmanyam, Sanjay. *Three Ways to Be Alien: Travails and Encounters in the Early Modern World*. Waltham, Mass.: Brandeis University Press, 2011.

Sultan Jehan Begum. *Rauzat al-Rayahin*. Bhopal: Matba' Sultani, 1906.

Tabor, Nathan L.M. "A Local Apocalypse: District Fairs and Poetry Recitation in Rural India." *Journal of Urdu Studies* 1, no. 1 (January 2020): 67–89.

Tagliacozzo, Eric. *The Longest Journey: Southeast Asians and the Pilgrimage to Mecca*. Oxford: Oxford University Press, 2013.

Tagore, Rabindranath. *Letters from a Sojourner in Europe*. Kolkata: Visva-Bharati, 2008.

Tavakoli-Targhi, Mohamad. *Refashioning Iran: Orientalism, Occidentalism, and Historiography*. Basingstoke: Palgrave, 2001.

The Asiatic Journal and Monthly Register for British and Foreign India, China and Australasia, v. 38. London: Wm.H. Allen and Co., 1842.

The Asiatic Journal and Monthly Register for British India and Its Dependencies. London: Kingsbury, Parbury and Allen, 1823.

Thompson, Carl. *The Routledge Companion to Travel Writing*. New Delhi: Routledge, 2016.

Thum, Rian. *The Sacred Routes of Uyghur History*. Cambridge, Mass.: Harvard University Press, 2014.

Tommakkattanar, Paremmakkal. *The Varthamanappusthakam*. Rome: Institutum Orientalium Studiorum, 1971.

Touati, Houari. *Islam and Travel in the Middle Ages*. Chicago: University of Chicago Press, 2010.

Trnovec, Silvester. *The Conquest of the African Mind: History, Colonial Racism, and Education in Senegal and French West Africa, 1910–1945*. Bratislava: Ustav Orientalistiky Slovenska, 2019.

Troll, Christian. "A Note on an Early Topographical Work of Sayyid Aḥmad Khān: *Āṣār al-Ṣanādīd*." *Journal of the Royal Asiatic Society of Great Britain and Ireland* 104, no. 2 (1972): 135–46.

Trouillot, Michel-Rolph. *Silencing the Past: Power and the Production of History*. Boston: Beacon Press, 1995.

Ummat al-Ghani, Nur al-Nisa. *Safarnama-i Hijaz, Sham, o Misr (1909)*. Hyderabad: Wordmaster Publications, 1996.

Ummat al-Hafiz. "Madagascar ka Safar." *'Ismat* 67, no. 1 (1941): 29–30.

Vasishth, Padmini. "Padmini Vasishth, Interview." South Asian Oral History Project, 2005. Accessed November 1, 2022. https://digitalcollections.lib.washington.edu/digital/collection/saohc/id/12/.

Viswanathan, Gauri. *Masks of Conquest: Literary Study and British Rule in India*. New York: Columbia University Press, 1989.

Wagner, Kim A. *Thuggee: Banditry and the British in Early Nineteenth-Century India*. Basingstoke: Palgrave Macmillan, 2007.

Waheed, Sarah Fatima. *Hidden Histories of Pakistan: Censorship, Literature, and Secular Nationalism in Late Colonial India*. New York: Cambridge University Press, 2021.

Weaver-Hightower, Rebecca. *Empire Islands: Castaways, Cannibals, and Fantasies of Conquest*. Minneapolis: University of Minnesota Press, 2007.

Wheeler, Talboys. "Introduction." In *The Travels of a Hindoo to Various Parts of Bengal and Upper India*, by Bholanauth Chunder, xi–xxv. London: Trübner, 1869.

White, Owen. "Sanitation and Security: The Imperial Powers and the Nineteenth Century Hajj." In *The Rise and Fall of Modern Empires, Volume I*, 389–406. Routledge, 2017.

Williams, Richard. "Songs between Cities: Listening to Courtesans in Colonial North India." *Journal of the Royal Asiatic Society* 27, no. 4 (2017): 591–610.

Williams, Tyler W. "Sacred Sounds and Sacred Books: A History of Writing in Hindi." PhD diss., Columbia University, 2014.

Wilson, Horace Hayman. *The History of British India, from 1805–1835*. Vol. 2. London: Madden and Malcolm, 1846.

Wright, Andrea. *Between Dreams and Ghosts: Indian Migration and Middle Eastern Oil*. Stanford: Stanford University Press, 2021.

Yang, Anand. "Introduction." In *Thirteen Months in China: A Subaltern Indian and the Colonial World*, by Gadhadhar Singh, edited by Kamal Sheel and Ranjana Sheel, 1–32. New Delhi: Oxford University Press, 2017.

Zaidi, S. Akbar. *Making a Muslim: Reading Publics and Contested Identities in Nineteenth Century North India*. Cambridge: Cambridge University Press, 2021.

Zamindar, Vazira Fazila-Yacoobali. *The Long Partition and the Making of Modern South Asia: Refugees, Boundaries, Histories*. New York: Columbia University Press, 2007.

Zarif Lakhnavi. *Intikhab-i Kalam-i Zarif*. Lucknow: Uttar Pradesh Urdu Academy, 1998.

Ziad, Homayra. "The Return of Gog: Politics and Pan-Islamism in the Hajj Travelogue of Abd al-Majid Daryabadi." In *Global Muslims in the Age of Steam and Print*, edited by James L. Gelvin and Nile Green, 227–48. Berkeley: University of California Press, 2014.

Zuelow, Eric. *A History of Modern Tourism*. London: Palgrave Macmillan, 2016.

Index

CAMBRIDGE LIBRARY COLLECTION

Books of enduring scholarly value

Philosophy

This series contains both philosophical texts and critical essays about philosophy, concentrating especially on works originally published in the eighteenth and nineteenth centuries. It covers a broad range of topics including ethics, logic, metaphysics, aesthetics, utilitarianism, positivism, scientific method and political thought. It also includes biographies and accounts of the history of philosophy, as well as collections of papers by leading figures. In addition to this series, primary texts by ancient philosophers, and works with particular relevance to philosophy of science, politics or theology, may be found elsewhere in the Cambridge Library Collection.

Lectures and Essays

A fellow of Trinity College, Cambridge, and of the Royal Society, William Clifford (1845–79) made his reputation in applied mathematics, but his interests ranged far more widely, encompassing ethics, evolution, metaphysics and philosophy of mind. This posthumously collected two-volume work, first published in 1879, bears witness to the dexterity and eclecticism of this Victorian thinker, whose commitment to the most abstract principles of mathematics and the most concrete details of human experience resulted in vivid and often unexpected arguments. Volume 1 includes a detailed biographical introduction by Clifford's colleague, Frederick Pollock, who situates his close friend's interests in Darwin and Spinoza within a larger, life-long devotion to the principles of scientific enquiry and experiment. This volume also features two important essays, 'On Some of the Conditions of Mental Development', his first public lecture delivered at the Royal Institute in London, and 'The Philosophy of the Pure Sciences'.